MEDIA PORTRAYALS OF R
AND THE SECULAR SAC

Ashgate AHRC/ESRC
Religion and Society Series

Series Editors:

Linda Woodhead, University of Lancaster, UK
Rebecca Catto, University of Lancaster, UK

This book series emanates from the largest research programme on religion in Europe today – the AHRC/ESRC Religion and Society Programme which has invested in over seventy-five research projects. Thirty-two separate disciplines are represented looking at religion across the world, many with a contemporary and some with an historical focus. This international, multi-disciplinary and interdisciplinary book series will include monographs, paperback textbooks and edited research collections drawn from this leading research programme.

Other titles in the series:

Ageing, Ritual and Social Change
Comparing the Secular and Religious in Eastern and Western Europe
Edited by Peter Coleman, Daniela Koleva and Joanna Bornat

Understanding Muslim Chaplaincy
Sophie Gilliat-Ray, Stephen Pattison and Mansur Ali

Discourses on Religious Diversity
Explorations in an Urban Ecology
Martin D. Stringer

Social Identities Between the Sacred and the Secular
Edited by Abby Day, Giselle Vincett and Christopher R. Cotter

Religion in Consumer Society
Brands, Consumers and Markets
Edited by François Gauthier and Tuomas Martikainen

Contesting Secularism
Comparative Perspectives
Edited by Anders Berg-Sørensen

Media Portrayals of Religion and the Secular Sacred

Representation and Change

KIM KNOTT
Lancaster University, UK

ELIZABETH POOLE
Keele University, UK

TEEMU TAIRA
University of Turku, Finland

ASHGATE

To Bob Towler

Media Portrayals of Religion and the Secular Sacred

Representation and Change

Is it true that Christianity is being marginalized by the secular media, at the expense of Islam? Are the mass media Islamophobic? Is atheism on the rise in media coverage?

Media Portrayals of Religion and the Secular Sacred explores such questions and argues that television and newspapers remain key sources of popular information about religion. They are particularly significant at a time when religious participation in Europe is declining yet the public visibility and influence of religions seems to be increasing. Based on analysis of mainstream media, the book is set in the context of wider debates about the sociology of religion and media representation. The authors draw on research conducted in the 1980s and 2008–10 to examine British media coverage and representation of religion and contemporary secular values, and to consider what has changed in the last 25 years.

Exploring the portrayal of Christianity and public life, Islam and religious diversity, atheism and secularism, and popular beliefs and practices, several media events are also examined in detail: the Papal visit to the UK in 2010 and the ban of the controversial Dutch MP, Geert Wilders, in 2009. Religion is shown to be deeply embedded in the language and images of the press and television, and present in all types of coverage from news and documentaries to entertainment, sports reporting and advertising. A final chapter engages with global debates about religion and media.

Published by
Ashgate Publishing Limited
Wey Court East
Union Road
Farnham
Surrey, GU9 7PT
England

Ashgate Publishing Company
110 Cherry Street
Suite 3-1
Burlington, VT 05401-3818
USA

www.ashgate.com

British Library Cataloguing in Publication Data
A catalogue record for this book is available from the British Library

The Library of Congress has cataloged the printed edition as follows:
Knott, Kim.
  Media portrayals of religion and the secular sacred : representation and change / by Kim Knott, Elizabeth Poole, and Teemu Taira.
     pages cm. -- (Ashgate AHRC/ESRC religion and society series)
  Includes bibliographical references and index.
  ISBN 978-1-4094-4805-1 (hbk) -- ISBN 978-1-4094-4806-8 (pbk) -- ISBN 978-1-4094-4807-5 (ebook) -- ISBN 978-1-4724-0633-0 (epub) 1. Mass media in religion--Great Britain. 2. Mass media--Religious aspects. I. Title.
  BL980.G7K56 2013
  305.60941--dc23
                                                                2013004621

ISBN 9781409448051 (hbk)
ISBN 9781409448068 (pbk)
ISBN 9781409448075 (ebk – PDF)
ISBN 9781472406330 (ebk – e PUB)

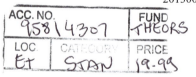

MIX
Paper from responsible sources
FSC   FSC® C013985
www.fsc.org

Printed in the United Kingdom by Henry Ling Limited,
at the Dorset Press, Dorchester, DT1 1HD

Contents

List of Figures   ix
List of Tables   xi
Notes on Contributors   xiii
Acknowledgements   xv

Introduction   1

1   Media, Religion and Society: Terrain and Debates   15

2   Changing Media Portrayals of Religion and the Secular Sacred   39

3   Media Representations of Christianity in Public Life   57

4   The Reporting of Islam and Other Religious Traditions   79

5   Media Representations of Atheism and Secularism   101

6   Popular Belief and Ritual Practice, and their Media Representations   119

7   The Case of Geert Wilders, Multiculturalism and Identity   139

8   Reclaiming Religion in Secular Public Life:
    The Media on the Papal Visit   155

    Conclusion: Religion, Media and Society Revisited   173

    Appendix 1: Main Categories and Subcategories used in Coding
    References to Religion and the Secular Sacred in 2008–2009   191

    Appendix 2: Percentages of Newspaper References to Main
    Categories of Conventional Religion, Common Religion and
    the Secular Sacred, 1982 and 2008   197

    Appendix 3: Percentages of Television References to Main
    Categories of Conventional Religion, Common Religion and
    the Secular Sacred, 1982 and 2009   201

Bibliography *205*
Index *227*

List of Figures

2.1	References by type, 2008–2009 and 1982	41
2.2	Newspaper references by type, 2008	46
2.3	Percentages of religious references in different newspaper genres, 2008 (all papers)	47
2.4	Television references by type, 2009	50
2.5	References by television genre, 2009	52
3.1	References to Christianity 1982 and 2008–2009	61
6.1	Media references to popular belief and practice, 1982 and 2008–2009	125

List of Tables

2.1   Literal and metaphorical references, 1982 and 2008–2009   55

4.1   Media references to religions other than Christianity
       (1982, 2008–2009)   80
4.2   References to Islam in the newspapers in 2008: Sub-categories   81

5.1   Incidence of articles referring to atheism, secularism,
       religion and faith on *The Guardian* website, 1999–2009   103

6.1   Change in belief or practice of aspects of popular religion,
       1980s to 2000s   123

7.1   Quantitative analysis of newspaper articles: Location and type   142

8.1   Newspaper coverage of the Papal visit in September 2010   157

Notes on Contributors

Kim Knott is Professor of Religious and Secular Studies at Lancaster University and a Global Uncertainties Leadership Fellow. She has worked extensively on religions in Britain, with a focus on diversity, identity, community, media and locality. Her recent publications include *The Location of Religion: A Spatial Analysis*, and *Diasporas: Concepts, Intersections, Identities* (edited with Seán McLoughlin), and the website *Moving People, Changing Places*.

Elizabeth Poole is Senior Lecturer and Programme Director of Media, Communications and Culture at Keele University. She works on representations of race, Islam and the media, news, new media and audiences, and has recently completed research on 'Muslims in the European Mediascape' with Siobhan Holohan for the Institute of Strategic Dialogue. She is author of *Reporting Islam: Media Representations of British Muslims* and co-editor (with John Richardson) of *Muslims and the News Media*.

Teemu Taira is Researcher in Comparative Religion at the University of Turku, Finland. His recent research has focused on religion in the media, atheism and the category of 'religion'. He is the author of two monographs, editor of five volumes and author of more than 40 scholarly articles in English and Finnish.

Acknowledgements

Media Portrayals of Religion and the Secular Sacred is the result of a collaborative study carried out between 2008 and 2010 as part of 'Religion and Society', a programme of research funded by the Arts and Humanities Research Council and the Economic and Social Research Council. Conducted by Kim Knott and Teemu Taira at the University of Leeds and Elizabeth Poole at Staffordshire University, it replicated research undertaken in the early 1980s at Leeds by Kim Knott and Robert Towler, funded by the Christendom Trust and the Independent Broadcasting Authority. We acknowledge with gratitude the financial support that made the research possible, and in particular the inspiration, friendship, assistance and efficiency of the 'Religion and Society' team: Linda Woodhead, Rebecca Catto and Peta Ainsworth. Our thanks must also go to other programme researchers: to those at British Religion in Numbers and colleagues at Loughborough University who worked on '*Fitna*, the Video Battle' (Liesbet van Zoonen, Sabina Mihelj and Farida Vis) with whom we discussed the Geert Wilders case.

Our Advisory Board gave us enormous encouragement and appropriate critical support, and participated in two formative discussions, on *The One Show* and newspaper coverage of the Wilders case. Warm appreciation to Stewart Hoover, Jolyon Mitchell, Gordon Lynch, Bob Towler, John Richardson, Marie Gillespie, Michael Wakelin, and latterly, Annika Mutanen, to whom we extend our gratitude for sharing findings from her research on faith in British and Finnish journalism. In particular, thanks to Jolyon for collegial co-authoring of 'The Changing Faces of Media and Religion', to Michael for research on religion on radio, and to Marie and her team for organizing the 'Mediating Religion' conference in 2010 in which we showcased our findings. On that occasion, we were grateful to Martin Beckford of *The Telegraph* and Simon Barrow of *Ekklesia*, and again to Michael, for their contributions, and – also in that year – to Andrew Brown of *The Guardian* for accepting an invitation to speak in Leeds. Thanks to Jackie Gregory for turning our research into news stories. Friends working in religion and media also helped us with suggestions and questions: Mia Lövheim and colleagues at Uppsala, the NoRel team, Knut Lundby, Birgit Meyer, Peter Horsfield, and especially Lori Beaman and co-researchers in the 'Religion and Diversity Project' in Canada (with whom Kim is conducting the next phase of this research).

Thanks to departmental colleagues for their support and patience at Leeds and Staffordshire, and latterly at Lancaster, Keele and Turku, to our religion and media students, to Sam Jordan (for data collection) and Anita Murdoch (for preliminary discourse analysis on popular rituals and for setting out the bibliography).

We send love to family and friends who have sacrificed time they would have spent with us so that we could work on the book. Thanks for your emotional support and encouragement: from Kim to John, Anita, Ma, Claud and Marcus; from Liz to Richard, the boys and her parents Pam and Gordon, and from Teemu to significant others.

Introduction

In this book we consider what can be learnt about contemporary society and public debate by focusing on how the media portray religious and secular issues, institutions, people, practices and beliefs. Using material collected and analysed from mainstream British media in the 1980s and 2000s we examine how religious traditions and debates, popular spirituality and the unexplained, and atheist and secularist ideologies and campaigns are represented, and what their portrayals show about changes in society, religion and the media.

We ask whether media coverage supports assumptions about secularization and the declining significance of religion, whether it suggests that society is being re-sacralized or just that religion is now more visible. Just how much religion is there on TV and in the newspapers, what kinds of themes and issues are represented, how are they received by the public, and why – in an online age – do these 'old media' remain important for public knowledge of religion? In what ways has this changed in the last quarter of a century, from a time when there were few media sources, to one in which they are ubiquitous and available in different formats?

We are also interested in what this changing treatment of religion suggests about the media's own priorities, purposes and values. Given that those who work in the media don't always 'get religion' and, according to some, are less likely to be religious than the population as a whole, is their portrayal of religious people, issues and events biased?[1] Is Christianity persecuted or marginalized? Are the media Islamophobic?

But stories and even passing references about religion open up broader social questions too. When and why do religion, atheism and secularism get covered in the news, or in other types of output, such as sport or entertainment? And how does such coverage feed into contemporary issues, such as integration, global terrorism and the financial crisis, or into ethical debates on sexuality or assisted suicide? What social, moral and political concerns get refracted through stories about religion in the media, and what can we learn about the nature and priorities of society and the changing place of religion within it?

It is contemporary religion, media and society in Britain that is most clearly illuminated in this account, but our discussion takes us beyond this time and place. In the next two chapters we set the current picture in historical and sociological context, in particular comparing it to the 1980s when the British population was less diverse, Christianity more prominent, the internet in its infancy and the media far less influenced by global processes. We acknowledge the major

---

[1]   Marshall, Gilbert and Ahmanson (eds) 2009; Davie 2000, p. 104; Holmes 2010, p. 1.

developments that have occurred since then to change the picture: the impact of migration on national populations, transnational connections and the religious and media practices of diasporic communities; and the rapid development of new information technologies and media globalization leading to acceleration in the speed of communication, contagion and repeated recycling of news and media events. These developments link our research into the global circulation of representations of religion, media practices, and public debates about priorities, values, ethics and ideologies. Furthermore, our methodology need not be limited to the immediate research context but is capable of translation to others. Our methods of data collection and analysis, and our use of media portrayals of religion to refract broader social, media and religious issues have a wider remit with potential for comparison with other national contexts and studies.

In order to illustrate the capacity of religion to shape the reporting and framing of international news stories, we begin by looking back to the autumn of 2008, to the peak of the global financial crisis.

Religion and the Moral Narration of the 'Credit Crunch'

Autumn 2008. The world was embroiled in the worst financial crisis since the 1930s with defaults on sub-prime loans and banks ceasing to trade with one another. Central banks pumped cash into economies to improve liquidity. Stock markets were in free-fall, banks and other lenders were failing and being bailed out, and countries were borrowing from the International Monetary Fund. In November and December, despite attempts to shore up financial institutions and stimulate markets, the UK, Eurozone and US all slipped into recession. The news media assailed its consumers with tales of doom and gloom, dire warnings, brinks, bailouts, injections and rescues. Levels of public anxiety were raised by the continuous updating of economic news online and the graphic and visual representations of falling stock markets, runs on banks, declining growth, the shift to recession, and the impact on unemployment, housing and high streets.

How were the 'credit crunch', its roots and principal protagonists to be exposed and narrated, and what myths and metaphors would do justice to its scale and nature? Seen in retrospect, religion proved to be a vital resource for journalists and commentators reporting the crisis. Taken together, news coverage, commentaries and editorial reflection in Britain generated a broad moral narrative of where society went wrong and who was responsible, of the importance of casting out false gods and reassessing our values, and the need for faith and inspired prophecy.[2] The country had 'worshipped at the temple of money',[3] and the media sought out moral interpreters – particularly religious leaders but also economic soothsayers, and political and literary visionaries – who could interpret the crisis. The Christian

---

[2]   For a discussion of comparable issues, see Mitchell 2012, pp. 7–30.
[3]   *Mail Online* 2009.

liturgical calendar of Advent and Christmas provided a temporal framework for straight-talking, moral reflection and the call for charity, patience, trust and new beginnings.[4] Biblical figures, stories and language as well as theological concepts were drawn on to narrate, explain and give colour to the account of financial rise and fall.

Belief and faith became central tenets for explaining how we got into this mess as well as what was needed to get us out of it. In his analysis of our beguilement and betrayal by 'false gods, idols, silver and gold', a Catholic commentator in *The Times* summarized the crisis as 'belief in the money we do not actually have … exposed as faith without foundation'.[5] In its need to identify those responsible, primarily banks and their 'culture of greed and immorality', the media cast bankers in the Biblical and Shakespearean mould of money-lenders; they quoted the Archbishop of York, on 'asset strippers and bank robbers' and noted the rise of a new 'demonology'.[6] With all their 'talk of trust, belief, faith' in neo-liberal capitalism, economists too were criticized, for relying on an 'orthodoxy built on superstition', a 'corrupt mythology [which] lies in tatters'.[7] But the problem was seen to go deeper than debt, capital and a broken banking sector, with its foundations in our moral as well as financial 'bankruptcy'. Drawing on Biblical passages and literary fables, the novelist, Ben Okri, saw the failure of false oracles and economic meltdown as symptoms of a wider cultural impoverishment brought on by a reliance on the Enlightenment values of individualism and scientific rationality and their fulfilment in greed, selfishness and the silencing of our 'sages, guides, bards, holy fools, seers'.[8] Only a fundamental re-examination of our values, 'a new vision to live by' and a cultural renewal would help us to discover new and more sustaining myths to live by: 'we must transform ourselves or perish', he wrote.[9]

The discussion of faith and morality extended to economic and political interlocutors as well as religious and cultural ones, and was not restricted to the causes and perpetrators of the crisis, but included the future of the economy, financial institutions and the role of government and even religious bodies. Such issues were not to be exempt from moral interrogation and renewal. Religious metaphors were drawn on to argue that moral questions about uncertainty and the limits to growth had been silenced by the 'false belief that market economics is a purely technical business'.[10] One political economist noted that, it had become impossible in financial circles to question the West's worship of false gods; 'theological language' no longer had any credence. Another saw the financial

---

4   For example, Pitcher 2008; Savill 2008; Moore 2008.

5   Strange 2008.

6   Kamm 2008; Pettifor 2008.

7   Bunting 2008.

8   Okri 2008.

9   Ibid.

10   Skidelsky 2008.

crisis as a profoundly spiritual one: 'the crisis of a society that idolizes money above love, community, wellbeing and the sustainability of our planet', one in which 'faith organizations ... have effectively colluded'.[11] No less than religious commentators, political economists called for moral questions to be faced.

Whether attentive to the spiritual and cultural bankruptcy of civilization, the failure of false gods and prophets and a corrupt mythology, binge banking, instant gratification or the immorality of bust and boom, commentators in national daily newspapers in the UK drew on moral tropes and narratives in their interpretation of the financial crisis. Furthermore, we find this at local level too where the moral issues of debt, selfishness and the need for charity were personalized by a Bishop speaking to his flock through the medium of the local newspaper. His plea for people 'not to be greedy and to save for the future' was reinforced by the editor: 'we should take these home truths on board ... we must accept responsibility for our own actions ... tighten our belts and start saving in earnest'.[12]

Getting out of the crisis, no less than diagnosing its causes, required a moral agenda and religious language, and religious leaders were quoted as stressing the need for small, local gestures, a reassertion of the basic values of care, patience and foresight, and the importance of building communities based on trust. Those writing explicitly about the economy perpetuated religious metaphors by pleading, for example, for 'an act of faith' by the government to stop the flight of cash, and for belief in the market: 'we don't need money: we need belief'.[13] Although such commentators were not explicitly motivated by religious interests, and their references were to faith and belief in the banking system and market processes not to God or the Church, their choice of language indicates a certain moral continuity between religious and financial cultures and communities. Such references were no mere play on words, but rather sincere pleas for the enactment of faith and belief, together with the rescinding of false gods and an ethical reassessment.

What work did religion do in these media accounts of the financial crisis, its causes, consequences and proposed solutions? Why was it thought necessary to call on religious and other prophetic voices, to explore moral avenues, to draw on mythology, fables and Biblical stories, and make extensive use of religious language?

Religions provide valuable material and personnel for dealing with crises. They offer myths and rituals, moral teachings and norms, as well as those who do the work of preaching, teaching, counselling, and theology. Even in modern secular societies where religions are often presented as a matter of mere tradition or false consciousness, a minority interest or cultic practice, they may be an important last resort in the absence of a ready and obvious supply of other moral arbiters, soothsayers and storytellers. In addition, the Judeo-Christian roots of Western

---

[11]   Pettifor 2008.

[12]   Baldwin 2008; *Yorkshire Evening Post* 2008b.

[13]   Kaletsky 2008; Barnes 2008a. But see Bunting's critique, 'Faith. Belief. Trust', Bunting 2008.

secular culture have by no means been cut, and the language and narratives of this tradition are embedded within contemporary culture, and may be drawn on – literally or metaphorically – to set the tone, act as a foil, and add weight or colour to a media account. Precisely because religious language and subject matter serves such purposes, it is invaluable in media discourse. So, when we encounter references to religion in an article, programme, advert, comment, blog or tweet, it is not only what that journalist, programme maker, editor or commentator is saying *about religion* and how they are choosing to portray it, but what such references indicate *beyond their religious content*. What might such references indicate about the plight of society or reveal about public priorities or the media's own values? Are they drawn on in some types of reports and stories and not others, perhaps called on in particular in the narration of crises, controversies, ethical debates, major media events, and political issues such as multiculturalism and integration, equality and diversity, and identity and representation?

Although our analysis will provide evidence that such topics and issues are indeed refracted through the lens of religion, we will see others too in which religious tropes play a part. Stories about sport, adverts for cars and domestic products, stand-up comedy and soaps, cultural supplements and travel guides all at times feature religion. What does the use of religion in such accounts tell us about these wider topics and issues, and what kind of a narrative device is it?

Before we consider these issues in more depth, some explanation of our research is needed, of why we looked principally at newspapers and television, what time-periods we focused on, and what questions we asked. This is followed by an introduction to the methods we used and a discussion of 'religion' and the 'secular sacred'.

Researching Media Portrayals of Religion in Britain

As researchers, we came to this research with different experiences and interests in studying religion and media. Elizabeth Poole had worked within media and communication studies on representations of Islam, British Muslims and multicultural issues. With a background in religious and cultural studies, Teemu Taira had analysed the writings of unemployed people before focusing on discourse on religion and public life in Finland's principal daily paper, *Helsingin Sanomat*. Kim Knott's first academic post in the sociology of religion was as researcher on a project in the early 1980s on 'Media portrayals of religion and their reception'. It is in this study that the book has its inception. When the opportunity arose to apply for funding to undertake a second study on this subject and to compare the results, we joined forces to combine our skills and interests in a new project on religion in the British media.

As part of a wider programme of publicly-funded research on 'Religion and Society', the project examined the extent and nature of media portrayals of religion and secular beliefs and values (what we called the 'secular sacred').[14] The focus was chiefly on traditional media, on newspapers and terrestrial television, so that we could replicate the research process and methods used in the earlier study, and compare findings between the two. Despite the growing significance of new social media, such as Facebook and Twitter – as well as innovative approaches to citizen journalism and access to religion online – mainstream news and entertainment media (in analogue and digital formats) continued to be the principal medium for public exposure to information and debates about religion. Many readers preferred their newspapers in hard copy, though others chose to read the online versions.[15] In 2011 television was still the most trusted UK media outlet (followed by radio, websites, then newspapers), with blogs and social media lagging behind for the general public in both the UK and US.[16]

The first project had been carried out in 1982–1983 at a time when religion was assumed by sociologists to be increasingly irrelevant to society, clergy saw congregations decline, the 'death of God' was debated, and the media often treated religion as a minority interest and matter of tradition.[17] Despite this, the project revealed that the media portrayal of religion in Britain was extensive and wide-ranging, covering the conventional religiosity of the major Christian denominations, international religious affairs, but also folk beliefs and practices.[18] It made clear that, despite all the talk of decline and insignificance, references to religion – both literal and metaphorical – continued to be deeply embedded in everyday language and popular culture. The findings supported David Martin's thesis, of the continued presence in the English imagination of 'subterranean theologies' that had, in general, escaped the rationalization of modernity.[19] Evident also was the rising power of the media, television in particular, often described as a secular rival to religion; journalists and programme makers were referred to as the new priesthood.[20] Religious critics suggested that there was 'a natural

---

[14]   'Media portrayals of religion and the secular sacred; A longitudinal study of British newspaper and television representations and their reception' (AH/F009097/1), funded by the Arts and Humanities Research Council and Economic and Social Research Council in the UK as part of the 'Religion and Society Programme', 2008–2010. It was conducted by Kim Knott (University of Leeds) and Elizabeth Poole (Staffordshire University); Teemu Taira (University of Leeds/University of Turku) was the researcher.

[15]   Ipsos MediaCT 2011.

[16]   Thompson 2011.

[17]   'Media portrayals of religion and their reception' was conducted at the University of Leeds in 1982–83 and funded by the Christendom Trust, with further support from the Independent Broadcasting Authority. It was directed by Robert Towler, with research conducted by Kim Knott. On irrelevance, decline and the 'death of God' from the 1960s to the 1980s: Cupitt 1980; Martin 1969; Robinson 1963; Wilson 1966; Wilson 1982.

[18]   Knott 1984a.

[19]   Martin 1969, p. 107.

[20]   Goethals 1982.

disaffinity' between religion and the media, the latter rating its own success, in terms of audience and reader ratings, at the expense of its moral, religious or educational content.[21] The project agreed that there was a tendency to simplify and stereotype religious ideas and to feature those stories and issues with strong headlines and entertainment value, but no more so than for other political, social or cultural issues.

Unlike race in the media, which had been the subject of sustained academic interest from the 1970s onwards, by the late 2000s very few studies had been published on media and religion in the UK: just two collections of essays, and several studies of religious broadcasting and more recent ones on the representation of Islam (all of which will be discussed in more detail in the next chapter). Our project in the 1980s remained the only major empirical description and analysis of religion in the British media until 2008, when the opportunity arose to see how the picture had changed some 25 years on.[22]

Research conducted on the twenty-first century British media, we thought, might reveal very different issues, priorities and assumptions to the earlier study, about diverse faith communities and interfaith encounter, the resurgence of religion in public life, the relationship of Islam to the global 'war on terror', the intersection of religion, ethnicity, gender and race in the formation of British identities, spirituality outside the church, and the impact of New Age ideas and alternative rituals and therapies. Furthermore, in addition to the continued portrayal of a variety of conventional and common religious themes (see our definitions in the next section), we imagined that a new study would highlight prevailing secular ideals and values.

It is well known that the media construct, as well as reflect, private and public life and the place of religion within it: they are the producers as well as products of society.[23] In the early 1980s, when Britain was held to be in the grip of secularization, the media reflected and contributed to the retreat of religion from the public domain.[24] In the early years of the twenty-first century, when issues, events and controversies involving religion have never been far from the top of the media agenda, how far did they contribute to the renewed visibility of religion and even to a 'resacralization' of society?[25] To what extent did late-modern ideologies and processes of multiculturalism, political and economic globalization, the standardization of news production and new media developments, as well as the continuing presence of secular liberalism, Orientalism and nationalism contribute to current media representations of religion and the secular sacred? We saw it as vital to be attentive to the impact of such new developments whilst replicating the earlier study to ensure valid comparisons could be made and changes identified.

---

[21] Longley 1983.

[22] Knott 1982; Knott 1983; Knott 1984b.

[23] Hoover 2006, p. 8.

[24] Knott 1982, pp. 60–75; Independent Broadcasting Authority 1983.

[25] Micklethwait and Wooldridge 2009; Ward and Hoelzl (eds) 2008.

But it was not all a story of change, as later chapters will show. There were important continuities to consider. In the late 2000s, the Church of England remained the established Church and continued to play a significant role in public life. The Pope was still in the news – though a different Pope (John Paul II died in 2005, and as Benedict XVI Cardinal Ratzinger became head of the Roman Catholic Church). Britain was again at war, though with troops in Iraq and Afghanistan rather than the Falklands. And ethical issues and debates about religion and science remained on the public agenda. Furthermore, people had retained their sense that there's more to life than meets the eye, and continued to refer to lady luck and the hand of destiny. Capturing and comparing the media's portrayal of such continuities would be as important as pursuing the changes. With these thoughts in mind, our second project was designed to answer the following questions:

1. How are religion and secular beliefs and values portrayed and represented in contemporary newspapers and on terrestrial television? What key themes emerge, and how are they treated?
2. What does the portrayal of these themes reveal about religion, media and society and their inter-relationship?
3. How are media portrayals of religion received and experienced by their audiences in light of their own religious and/or secular interests?
4. How do findings from research in 2008–2010 compare to those from the 1982–1983 study, and how can any changes be interpreted historically and sociologically?

These questions underpin the discussions in this book, but do not determine its structure. The first two questions will be explored throughout; the third, in chapters 3–7, where the focus will be on contemporary media representations of religion but their reception will also be considered. Comparisons between the earlier and later studies will be made in particular in chapters 2 and 8, and, together with the second question, will be discussed in the final chapter.

Methods and Definitions

Anyone studying religion in the media has to set limits to the sources and times on which they will focus, to identify what exactly they are looking for and work out an analytical strategy. Which media will be consulted and over what period? What do we mean by 'religion' and 'secular' beliefs and values, and how will they be identified and recorded (will we count brief references or only examine whole articles or programmes, for example)? Once data have been collected, how will they then be analysed?

In answering these questions for our research in 2008–2010, we were constrained somewhat by how they had been answered in the earlier study. Being able to compare portrayals across the two periods depended on us adopting a similar research process and methods, although there was room for considerable elaboration and development in the light of newly emerging religious issues, and in the analysis of themes and case studies. In 1982 our choice of what media sources to select was relatively limited compared to the possibilities open to researchers today. Radio was popular and important for coverage of religious worship and the discussion of religious issues, but we decided against it as newspapers and television had become the traditional fare for media researchers the latter being increasingly favoured for analysis of popular culture.[26] If we were to engage research on religion with wider interests in news reporting and entertainment, these were the important sources to focus on.

Until Channel 4 was launched in November 1982 and satellite and cable channels became available in the late 1980s and 1990s, there were just three television channels. There was a greater choice of newspapers, but several of today's titles had not yet been introduced: all were available exclusively in paper format and typeset manually. We chose three popular daily newspapers (*The Sun*, *The Times*, the *Yorkshire Evening Post*) for data collection over two months, February and March 1982, and three television channels (BBC1, BBC2 and ITV) recorded over a seven-day period in April of the same year. We undertook both quantitative and qualitative content analysis, counting all references to a wide range of keywords associated with religion (according to our definitions below), and then analysing selected key themes in depth.[27]

The three newspapers we selected in 1982, and then analysed again over a two month period in October and November 2008, were different from one another. *The Times* was a quality 'broadsheet' read by a broadly middle-class, establishment and conservative readership, selected for its commitment to covering religious issues; *The Sun* was the most popular daily paper, a 'tabloid', broadly right-wing in its views and associated in the 1980s with a working-class readership. In 1982, as in 2008, both were owned by Rupert Murdoch, though each retained its own identity, editorial policy and characteristic readership.[28] Both had a national circulation and were printed in London. The third paper, the *Yorkshire Evening Post*, was local with its head office and main circulation in the city of Leeds in the North of England. By 2008, all three papers were available digitally as well as in hard copy. In both studies, whilst our quantitative analysis was restricted to these three, we examined a wider range of newspapers (and, in 2008, online as well as paper formats) in our case studies.

When it came to television channels, in 1982 we opted to collect data for one week from all three channels: BBC1, BBC2 and ITV (by the time of the second

---

[26]   Curran (ed.) 1978; Glasgow University Media Group 1976; Glasgow University Media Group 1980; Fiske and Hartley 1978; Tunstall 1983; Silverstone 1981.

[27]   Knott 1984a; Knott 1982. In the early 1980s, the large-scale corpus analysis of online news archives was not a possibility.

[28]   Rupert Murdoch bought *The Sun* in 1969 and *The Times* in February 1981. For further discussion, see Chapter 1.

project this had become ITV1). The BBC was Britain's public service television provider, BBC1 being the principal channel identified with wide coverage of news, drama, entertainment, sport and religion, and BBC2 associated with more alternative fare, including documentaries, films and non-fictional series. ITV was a commercial television station, offering nationwide material spliced with regional news, weather and programmes, and – of course – advertisements.[29] We adopted the same research strategy in February 2009 as we had in April 1982, viewing all television from 7.00 am to midnight, though in the 1980s breakfast television had not been introduced and daily broadcasting began later and ended earlier.[30]

What were we looking for when we read the papers and watched the television output? If we look back first of all to the 1980s, there was considerable sociological discussion about how best to define religion.[31] Robert Towler, who had directed that first project, differentiated the field by distinguishing between 'conventional religion' and 'common religion'.[32]

> On the one hand then this meant studying institutionalized religion, the religion associated with the Pope and the Archbishop of Canterbury, the parishes, other world faiths, and the new religious movements: "conventional religion". On the other hand it involved a consideration of religious beliefs and practices not associated with the Church, that is superstition, fate, luck, the paranormal, astrology and spiritualism: "common religion". Although such things may seem to some degree unlikely aspects of a definition of religion, they are nonetheless important because they share with the churches a common concern for the "supernatural".[33]

This distinction informed how we recorded and analysed our data. We developed what media researchers call a 'coding frame', that is a list of categories and subcategories (keywords), to help us describe and differentiate the references to religion generated by our reading and viewing. For example, 'Roman Catholicism' was one of the Conventional Religion categories, and 'Fortune-Telling Techniques' one that related to Common Religion. These were further divided into multiple sub-categories (e.g. Second Vatican Council, the Pope; Clairvoyance, Tarot). These

---

[29]   In 1982, the relevant regional face of ITV was Yorkshire Television (YTV).

[30]   In 1982, television recording was undertaken by the Media Unit at the University of Leeds using video technology; in 2009, it was carried out by the British Universities Film and Video Council using blu-ray. In each case they recorded all three channels continuously and simultaneously (excluding children's and educational programmes).

[31]   Yinger 1970; Towler 1974.

[32]   Towler 1974; 1983; Toon 1981.

[33]   Knott 1984a, p. 3.

were used to record all references – occurrences of words or relevant images – to conventional and common religion found in the newspapers and on television.[34]

However, observation of the changing social and cultural milieu as well as our own research interests led us to develop and extend our categories in the second project. It was important for comparative purposes to retain the distinction between conventional and common religion, but we included what we referred to as the 'secular sacred'. By this we meant those beliefs, values, practices, places, symbols and objects that are formally speaking 'non-religious' but are nevertheless prioritized by people, deemed to be inviolable and non-negotiable, and often referred to as 'sacred'.[35] By the end of the second project we were operating with 49 categories, with 410 subcategories in total.[36] We had, for example, divided the 1982 category of 'World Religions' into new categories such as 'Islam', 'Buddhism' and 'Hinduism' with their own sub-categories, and we had coded for references to the 'secular sacred' (e.g. main category: Sacred; sub-categories: Market, Life, Football, Music).

The newspaper and television data we collected was analysed quantitatively, using content analysis, and then in depth, using discourse analysis. Further discussion of our approach appears in Chapter 2 – where we examine how much religion there was in newspapers and on television in 1982–1983 and 2008–2009, what kind of subjects were covered and how the various media sources differed in their portrayals – and in the following four chapters in which we turn our attention to media representations. Throughout, we consider how media preoccupations and portrayals of religion and the secular sacred have changed in the last quarter of a century.

In both projects we also looked at the media treatment of major events involving religion, focusing on coverage from a wide variety of news media in hard and digital copy. In 1982 it was the pastoral visit to Britain of Pope John Paul II. Fortuitously, we were able to follow this up and compare it with the state visit of Pope Benedict XVI 28 years later. Key themes in the media portrayal of these visits were the health of Christianity in Britain, and ecumenical and interfaith relations. The visit of another public figure provided the media with an opportunity to rehearse different anxieties: freedom of speech, religion and liberal secularism, double standards and the preferential treatment of Muslims, and the ever-popular theme of the folly of government ministers. In February 2009 we scoured the media, not only daily papers, but online news sites and blogs, for reports and commentary on the failed attempt by Dutch politician, Geert Wilders, to enter the UK in order to participate in a discussion about his controversial and inflammatory Islamophobic film, *Fitna*.

---

[34]   For further information on what constitutes a 'reference' and how they were coded, see Chapter 2.

[35]   Knott 2010, pp. 115–33; Knott 2013a.

[36]   See Appendix 1 for the list of categories and sub-categories from the 2008–2010 project.

We were also able to gather public views on the Geert Wilders case, the representation of Islam, liberal values and political correctness, and general media treatment of religion in a short reception study. Using focus groups, we piloted topics and questions with a group of students, and followed this with meetings in London and Birmingham: two with self-identified non-religious people, and two with people from different religious backgrounds.[37] Involving audiences in the study, albeit briefly, enabled us to discover how far they participated in media discourses, as well as revealing their capacity for critical judgement. Insights were also gleaned by comparing the responses of religious and non-religious people.

Book Outline

Over the course of the following chapters a gradual picture will unfold of the media portrayal of religion and the secular sacred, of what representations were favoured, and what these show about media and broader public interests and priorities.

In Chapter 1, we set media portrayals of religion and the secular in historical, social and global context before outlining some key theories and areas of debate of relevance to the issues that will arise in later chapters (e.g. secularization and re-sacralization, mediation and mediatization, multiculturalism and integration, Islamophobia and changing place of Christianity, the rise of New Atheism and the crisis of liberal secularism). We indicate those areas and issues that will be illuminated by our analysis of changing media portrayals and to which we will return in the final chapter.

In Chapter 2, we consider data arising from our quantitative analysis of newspaper and television references to religion and the secular sacred in 2008–2009, and compare this to findings from the early 1980s to see what has changed.

Over the next four chapters we consider contemporary media representations of religion and what they tell us about the changing place of religion, media priorities and values, and social preoccupations and concerns. In Chapter 3 the focus is on the representation of Christianity in public life and, in Chapter 4, on Islam and other minority religions. In Chapter 5, our attention shifts to the increasingly important issue of the media representation of atheism and secularism, and in Chapter 6 we examine popular religion, in particular references to religious practice, the paranormal, luck and superstition.

In the following chapters we consider key media events and what they reveal about multiculturalism and identity (Chapter 7, on the Wilders case), and Christianity in a multi-faith Britain (Chapter 8 on the Papal visits of 1982 and 2010). These cases provide an opportunity to see how competing discourses about

---

[37]   Pilot focus group carried out by Elizabeth Poole at Staffordshire University, Stoke-on-Trent; other groups organized, recorded and analysed by Carol McCloskey on behalf of The Focus Group.

religion and the secular sacred are presented and argued, and – in the second case – to observe how they have changed.

In the final chapter, we consider what such representations and discourses tell us about media priorities and values, and wider social issues and concerns. We review what our research has shown about media portrayals of 'conventional religion', 'common religion' and the 'secular sacred', and reflect on the significance of mainstream media for information and education about religion. In light of our findings and analysis, we assess the various claims made by scholars and public commentators about religion, media and society and their interrelationship.

Chapter 1

Media, Religion and Society:
Terrain and Debates

In April 2008, Mark Thompson, then Director-General of the BBC, gave a lecture to a Catholic audience on 'Faith and the Media' in which he looked back over his career in television and forward to the future of religious broadcasting.[1] On joining the BBC in 1979, he had become part of the team working on the religious documentary, *Everyman*.[2] He had enjoyed its creativity and energy, but 'at the same time I couldn't help noticing that one thing that *Everyman* didn't seem to do very often was actually to make programmes about religion'.[3] Apart from a handful made each year on conventional religious subjects 'most editions of *Everyman* were only "religious" in the broadest possible sense', dealing with 'science and spirituality', 'New Age cults' or religion as a way into social and political issues.[4] Furthermore, religion was 'marginal at best' in mainstream drama, documentaries, comedy and news.[5]

Thompson accounted for this by referring to the acceptance in media circles of post-Enlightenment assumptions that rationalism would lead to the long-term decline of organized religion, and that religion as a collective force would give way to individualized belief and practice.[6] This was how the media thought about religion in the eighties and it helped to explain the nature of its coverage. But this 'easy consensus' had later been undermined, he suggested, by global and local events (in Tehran and Bradford, for example), by troubling questions about tolerance, rights and freedom, the renewed centrality of religion to political and ethical issues, the churches' own internal struggles, and indeed by the failure of the prediction of religion's wholesale decline. He concluded his lecture by talking about the 'remarkable creative revival and a new spirit of experimentation in religious programming', and his hope for the future of religion in the delivery of public service broadcasting.[7]

---

[1]   Thompson 2008.

[2]   *Everyman* (1977–2005), like programmes dedicated to Christian worship and hymn-singing, was delivered by the BBC's Religious Broadcasting Department.

[3]   Thompson, p. 2.

[4]   Ibid., p. 3.

[5]   Ibid.

[6]   On secularization as the media's default position, see Woolley 2012, pp. 61–75.

[7]   Ibid., p. 7.

Thompson's description of an increasingly positive climate for religion in the media by 2008 and an increase in its coverage may have been greeted with raised eyebrows by some in his predominantly Catholic audience. For them, as for many religious critics of the media, a more plausible narrative might have been one of an ever-declining number of hours dedicated to religious broadcasting, a failure to cover religion and faith issues in peak-time schedules, and of bias against Christianity in a context of raised secularist and atheist voices.[8]

Thompson's twin points of reference – the early 1980s and late 2000s – accord with the periods of our research. His account will be tested in the following chapters when we examine and compare the extent and nature of coverage of religion in television and newspaper output in those periods, and look at how it has changed. Later in this chapter, however, we will see that the opposing perspectives he mentions – of a halt to secularization and a revitalization of religious broadcasting, and the counter thesis of unremitting religious decline and media neglect – reflect broader debates about the changing nature of religion and its public visibility. They also reveal the diversity of views about media attitudes and knowledge of religion, and the effect they have on its treatment on TV and in the press.

The purpose of this chapter is to establish the social, historical and theoretical context for the analysis that follows. We consider the state of religion, the media and society in Britain and their changing relationships over the last thirty years, and examine previous empirical and theoretical studies for what they tell us (or neglect to tell us) about the place of religion in public life and how it has been portrayed in the media. In the final section we introduce a series of propositions about the nexus of the media/religion/society that emerge from our discussion. These statements will be considered in the discussions that follow and, in the concluding chapter, we will assess their salience.

The Changing Religious and Secular Context

By the time we began our research in 2008 the news was that religion was back on the agenda. 'Almost everywhere you look, from the suburbs of Dallas to the slums of São Paulo to the back streets of Bradford, you can see religion returning to public life', wrote Micklethwait and Wooldridge as they introduced their argument about the global rise of faith, its compatibility with modernity, and how we might learn to live with it.[9] Irrespective of the apparent universality of this state of affairs, however, they recognized that different continents, nations and communities approached it from differing starting points, noting in particular the 'European way', of the loss of religion, and the 'American way', of religion

---

[8]   For example, Holmes 2000; Holmes 2010; Wilson 2010; Woolley, p. 66. For public discord concerning religious broadcasting, see Viney 1999, pp. 4–28; Noonan 2008, pp. 92–4.

[9]   Micklethwait and Wooldridge 2009, p. 12.

ingrained in the national consciousness.[10] We will discuss theoretical perspectives on secularization, re-sacralization and the public visibility of religion later in the chapter, but first we must establish some basic information about religion and its public face in the last thirty years. For this study, of course, the key information concerns Britain. However, as this chapter will show, even though the facts and figures about Britain may suggest a certain narrative about religious change and the place of religion in society, how that information is interpreted and represented in the media or elsewhere is not straightforward; neither is it isolated from global events and processes.

The most reliable religious statistics at the time of our research in 2008–2010 were from the population census of 2001 when a question on religious identity was included for the first time.[11] The results surprised people because they showed that the vast majority continued to see themselves as religious (77.1 per cent), the largest group identifying as Christian (over 41 million or 71.8 per cent).[12] About two-thirds of these were Anglican, most of the rest Catholic, Presbyterian and Methodist, and other Christian denominations accounting for just a tenth of the Christian total. Muslims formed the second largest group (2.8 per cent, 1.6 million), with small percentages of Hindus (1 per cent), Sikhs (0.6 per cent), Jews (0.5 per cent) and Buddhists (0.3 per cent). The category 'Any other religion' (0.3 per cent) included different neo-Pagan groups (Wiccans, Druids and Asatrus), Jains, Bahá'ís and Zoroastrians. Although the figures had changed a decade later – in England and Wales, Christians down to 59.3 per cent, Jews remaining at 0.5 per cent, with Muslims up to 4.8, Hindus to 1.5, Sikhs to 0.8, Buddhists to 0.4, and other religions to 0.4 per cent respectively – it was clear that a substantial, though decreasing, majority of people continued to identify as religious (67.7 per cent).[13]

Figures for religious identity don't tell the full story, however. Another source of information showed that only about 7 per cent of people in England regularly attended Christian churches.[14] With so little formal engagement, why did so many identify as Christian in the population census? Interviews with people on why they ticked the 'Christian' box revealed a multitude of reasons including family background, class, history, values, ethnicity and national identity.[15]

Even though the majority of people identified with Christianity or another religious tradition in 2001, 15 per cent said they had no religion; the remainder,

---

[10]   Ibid., 'Part One: Two Roads to Modernity'.

[11]   Percentages presented are for Great Britain not the UK (they exclude Northern Ireland). They are from Dobbs, Green and Zealey (eds) 2006. Statistics were combined for England/Wales and Scotland, though different religious questions had been asked. See also Weller 2008.

[12]   Dobbs et al. (eds) 2006, p. 21.

[13]   Office of National Statistics 2011.

[14]   From *UK Christian Handbook: Religious Trends 6, 2006/7* in Woodhead, 'Introduction', in Woodhead and Catto (eds) 2012a, p. 5.

[15]   Day 2011.

7.8 per cent, gave no response ('religion not stated').[16] In 2001, then, there were at least 8.5 million 'non-religious' people in England, Wales and Scotland, and possibly as many as 13 million (by 2011, as many as 18 million). These are significant numbers when compared to the total number of religious people who were non-Christian (slightly over 3 million in 2001, rising to 4.7 million by 2011). Other surveys and polls have given rather different percentages for non-religion. According to the European Values Survey for 2001, for example, 5 per cent of people claimed to be 'a convinced atheist', while over 53 per cent stated they were 'not a religious person'.[17]

The close relationship between religious and ethnic profile was important.[18] Most people who identified as Asian were affiliated to a religious tradition.[19] Three religious traditions accounted for nearly 90 per cent of all Asians: 40 per cent were Hindu or Sikh, and half were Muslim. Despite this, the overwhelming majority of Muslims (nearly 9 out of 10) were from other ethnic groups, from Africa, the Middle East, South East Asia, and Central and Eastern Europe. Turning to Buddhists, most were 'White' and only some 10 per cent classified as Asian.

To what extent had the profile of religion in Britain changed from the 1980s to the 2000s? Comparison is difficult because there are no equivalent figures from the 1981 population census (people were not asked about their religion then).[20] Data from another source, the British Social Attitudes survey, showed that, excluding those from ethnic minorities, religious affiliation (belonging to a religion) declined from 68.4 per cent in 1983 to 54.5 per cent in 2008.[21] Nevertheless, despite the evident decline in affiliation, most people continued to identify with a religion.

Comparing numbers from particular religious groups is difficult too. The most reliable measures for Christians are not those for informal identity or belonging, but for formal church membership and church attendance. Both have declined

---

[16]   The 'no religion' category included nearly 400,000 people who explicitly self-identified as 'Jedi', but who were coded as non-religious. By 2011, in England and Wales, the respective figures were 25.1 per cent (no religion), and 7.2 per cent (religion not stated): Office of National Statistics 2011.

[17]   Weller 2008, pp. 50–51. These numbers do not tell us about the lived significance of religion. When asked about this in the 2001 European Values Survey, more than 60 per cent of British respondents considered religion to be unimportant in their lives: 29.7 per cent stated that religion was 'not at all' important, 33 per cent, 'not important'. Religion was 'very important' only for 12.6 per cent. See also Woodhead 2012a, 'Introduction', p. 6.

[18]   Weller 2008, pp. 13–23.

[19]   In Britain, the 'Asian' population is made up predominantly of those belonging to families of South Asian heritage (originating from India, Pakistan, Bangladesh and Sri Lanka), though it includes smaller numbers from East and South East Asia.

[20]   Field 2009a, pp. 7–8.

[21]   British Religion in Numbers, 'Religious Affiliation and Monthly Church Attendance, 1983–2008'.

steadily since the Second World War.[22] Taking just one measure – churchgoing in England – those attending on Sundays halved in number between 1979 (11.7 per cent) and 2005 (6.3 per cent).[23] Set against this pattern of decline, however, according to new case studies, 'there has been substantial church growth in Britain since 1980. That growth is focused in London and amongst black, Asian and minority ethnic communities and amongst new churches'.[24]

Statistics for religions other than Christianity in the early 1980s had to be estimated. The most reliable sources at the time suggested there were about 350,000 Jews, between 500,000 and one million Muslims, 300,000 Hindus, a similar number of Sikhs, and smaller numbers of Buddhists, Jains and Zoroastrians.[25] The numbers of Muslims and Hindus had clearly grown since the 1980s, but the size of the other religious groups has not changed significantly.

And what about the 'nones', those people who do not identify with a religion, including those who are agnostic or atheist, how had their numbers changed since the 1980s? In the absence of relevant census statistics from 1981, we must again turn to other sources. Analysing data from the British Household Panel Survey and the British Attitudes Survey, Voas and Crockett concluded that people at the end of the twentieth century were less religious than a decade earlier, and that each generation is less religious than the last.[26] Furthermore, Gallup and Lindsay reported that more people stated 'no religion' in 1999 (39 per cent) than twenty years previously (24 per cent).[27]

In addition to religious identity, the presence of diverse religious communities is embedded in the landscape. Between the 1980s and 2004, the number of mosques rose from 193 to 708, and Sikh gurdwaras from 90 to 190.[28] Over the same period the number of Christian places of worship declined by 815, though there were still more than 44,000 churches in the UK in 2004. Despite the trend towards increasing diversity, Christianity continued to dominate the landscape.

Statistics on the religious population and landscape of the UK showed that Britain is simultaneously Christian, secular and religiously diverse.[29] Mainstream Christian denominations and new Christian expressions dominated as they did in the early 1980s. However, broad changes flagged up by the statistics – increased

---

[22]   Except Roman Catholics whose numbers grew until the 1960s before declining. British Religion in Numbers, 'Churches and Churchgoers: Patterns of Church Growth in Britain 1700-1970'. For detailed analysis of figures for church association, see Guest, Olson and Wolffe 2012, pp. 61–5.

[23]   Woodhead 2012a, 'Introduction', p. 5.

[24]   Goodhew 2012.

[25]   Knott 1988; British Religion in Numbers, 'Estimates of the Hindu, Muslim and Sikh Populations of England and Wales 1961–2001'.

[26]   Voas and Crockett 2005, pp. 11–28.

[27]   Gallup and Lindsay in Woodhead 2012a, 'Introduction', p. 8.

[28]   Weller 2008, pp. 32–42, 63.

[29]   Ibid., p. 9.

numbers of Muslims and Hindus, and the larger number of non-religious people – are also having an impact on the changing nature of religion in public life. Diversity, along with atheism, secularism and secularization raise questions about the decline of Christianity and the normative role of Christian cultural heritage. We will show later how these issues – both continuities and changes – are visible in the media. It will become clear, however, that it is not simply the number of adherents or places of worship that forms the basis for media decisions about how much coverage to give to different communities, traditions and issues, though the public visibility of religious and non-religious groups and individuals no doubt creates pressure for coverage and recognition.

The Changing Media Context

The media environment in Britain has also changed with an increase in the number of sources, and the fragmentation and diversification of the global media sphere.[30] With the emergence of 24-hour news, 'rolling news' services and online journalism, the media world never rests. Furthermore, there has been a rise of new media 'publics' with distinctive needs and demands. These changes have their roots in both technological innovation and the identity politics of different cultural, ethnic and religious groups.[31]

The Status and Role of Traditional Media

Despite such changes, people have continued to access the so-called 'old media', to read newspapers and watch the main terrestrial television channels.[32] Public surveys and polls have repeatedly shown the importance of broadcast media and newspapers for knowledge about what goes on in the world, the country and in Britain's towns and cities. Furthermore, despite major public inquiries that were highly critical of media processes, decisions and management, people have continued in general to trust them. In 2005, a year on from the Hutton Inquiry, a YouGov poll showed that the BBC continued by some margin to be the most trusted source of news, with Sky News, ITN (ITV and Channel 4 news) and a number of daily papers also mentioned (including both *The Times* and *The Sun*,

---

[30]   One consequence is that the research data collected during the 2008–2010 project represented a smaller proportion of what was available across the media than material collected in the early 1980s. As we were not aiming for a comparable representative sample, this was not thought to be a problem.

[31]   McNair 2005.

[32]   The problematic nature of the concepts of 'old' and 'new' media is discussed in Lievrouw and Livingstone (eds) 2002 and Lister, Dovey, Giddings, Grant and Kelly 2003.

though the former was deemed the more trustworthy of the two).[33] After the phone-hacking scandal in Britain in 2011, the newspaper industry saw public trust decline, but television, closely followed by radio, continued to be a trusted source, with websites also polling well.[34] Blogs and social media – including Facebook and Twitter – despite large numbers of users, were not thought to be trustworthy.[35]

In the face of media diversification, traditional sources evidently continued to be respected. Television, in particular, was still valued for offering multiple perspectives and opportunities for debate, for challenging the government and raising awareness of important issues.[36] It was television, followed some way behind by newspapers, that was deemed to be the most important source for national, local and international news.[37] Nevertheless, around 80 per cent of people in Britain still claimed to read at least one daily newspaper: despite falling circulation, nearly 12 million copies were bought daily.[38] News websites were consulted increasingly for international coverage, but radio fared better for local news.

For people who already have religious commitments or interests, new interactive media are vital for engaging with others on religious topics, for downloading and consuming sermons, lectures and music, and even for worship online.[39] Furthermore, the traditional media may well be of secondary importance for them, valued as a means of receiving information and forming opinion but less as an extension of religious practice. However, for those people who do not follow religious issues closely, mainstream newspapers and television remain vital sources for the public understanding of religion.[40] Furthermore, keeping different types of readers in mind, layered reporting is on the increase. General information is provided in a newspaper, with reference made to more detailed explanation online in the newspaper's blogs, which then contain links to yet more specific sources. This allows consumers either to skim read on the surface of an issue or to dive deeply into the details, the back story, and a variety of opinions. Ruth Gledhill, the religion correspondent of *The Times*, has been cited as an inspired

---

[33]   YouGov 2005. The inquiry by Lord Hutton into the death of the weapons expert, David Kelly, criticized the BBC for its role in reporting events leading up to his death.

[34]   Thompson 2011. In this period the *News of the World* – one of Rupert Murdoch's News International papers – was closed after the disclosure of journalistic and editorial malpractice. Trust in the BBC was damaged by failures in its coverage of sex abuse cases in 2012.

[35]   Ibid. A similar pattern was reported in both the UK and US.

[36]   YouGov 2007.

[37]   Ibid., p. 10.

[38]   McNair 2005, p. 21; Temple 2008, p. 93.

[39]   Brasher 2004; Bunt 2009; Campbell 2010; Dawson and Cowan (eds) 2004.

[40]   In focus groups we ran in 2010, despite an interest in current religious affairs, few religious or non-religious participants followed any specifically religious media source. McCloskey 2010.

example of this approach.[41] In this respect, traditional and new media are more allies than enemies.

Evidently, television and newspapers – along with radio, which was not the focus of this study – remain of central importance, for information and debate about news in general, and for public discourse on religion and its place in contemporary culture and society.[42] In a period when, in general, fewer and fewer people in Britain participate actively in religion and each generation seems to be less religious than the last, what are the means by which people come to know about religion, by which they become religiously literate? For a minority, the answer remains religious institutions and those family members who are sufficiently well informed to provide religious socialization for their children and grandchildren. For the majority, however, schools and the media have become key resources.[43] But the agenda for religious literacy – Elaine Graham identifies the three paradigms of information, formation and the cultivation of skills of civic responsibility – is complicated by the medium of delivery. In the case of the media, information and debate about religion, as well as formation and cultivation, are themselves 'mediatized'; they are shaped by the medium.[44] Media portrayals do not simply reflect the religious world; along with other agents of religious literacy – such as education and the arts – they construct it. Such portrayals are a means by which media users, readers and audiences can access public discourses about religion in contemporary culture and society, discourses formed in large part by the media themselves.

Television and the Press

The transformation of the media sphere is well illustrated by what has happened in recent decades to television. New competition arose with changes to the structure of broadcasting. The BBC and independent television (ITV) were the only providers in the early 1980s, but the mid 1980s saw the beginning of a debate about their 'comfortable duopoly'.[45] Although subsequent deregulation led to the rise of competitor providers, including SKY, the duopoly continued to dominate, with cable and satellite television as supplements rather than true competitors.[46] In addition to the shift from three terrestrial channels to a multi-channel environment

---

[41]   Rusbridger 2010; Beckett 2012, pp. 102–4.

[42]   Because we replicated selection decisions made in the first research project, radio was not included in 2008–2009, despite its continued importance for religious broadcasting. For religion on radio, see Wakelin 2011; Mitchell 1999; Noonan 2008.

[43]   Elaine Graham discusses both in 'Religious Literacy and Public Service Broadcasting: Introducing a Research Agenda', Graham 2012, pp. 228–43; see also essays by Woolley and Landau in Mitchell and Gower 2012.

[44]   Graham 2012, pp. 231–5. Mediatization is discussed later in the chapter.

[45]   Crisell 1999, pp. 61–73.

[46]   Ibid., p. 65; Crisell 2002, pp. 227–30; McNair 2005, pp. 90–91.

(five terrestrial channels, with over 400 channels available in the UK), restricted airtime gave way to 24-hour television, and an increase also in the airtime on BBC1, BBC2 and ITV1.[47]

As the major commercial terrestrial channel, ITV continued to compete with the BBC. Despite the relative audience share of each falling with the rise of multi-channel television, the terrestrial channels did not lose their dominance.[48] For a minority of viewers, however, there was a preference for channels which appealed to ethnic, religious or other special interests.

Turning now to the world of print media, increasing plurality was the promise of new print technology and more inexpensive printing costs in the 1980s. Over the years that followed, there were many new as well as existing titles, few of which survived. Two 1980s favourites, *The Times* and *The Sun*, remained popular in the twenty-first century, together accounting for more than 30 per cent of daily circulation, despite a general decline within the newspaper industry.[49] In addition to its online version, the daily paper circulation of *The Times* in 2009 was 571,783 (down on the 2000 figure of over 700,000), making it the seventh largest national daily after five popular tabloids and *The Daily Telegraph*.[50] Although there were accusations of 'dumbing down' under the ownership of Rupert Murdoch – from the world's greatest newspaper to a scandal-sheet – *The Times* continued to maintain its public reputation as a quality paper.[51] Although traditionally conservative in its values and readership, it supported New Labour until the general election of 2010.[52] Much of its religion coverage in the late 2000s was provided by its well-known religion correspondent, Ruth Gledhill, who saw her job as 'bridg[ing] between the secular and the religious'.[53]

The Sun remained the most popular tabloid in Britain in 2009, its daily circulation being over 3 million (down from more than 3.5 million in 2000). Its total readership – as opposed to circulation – was estimated at 8 million daily, and it was named the eighth most popular newspaper in the world, despite its reputation as sensationalist. Its conservative bias was evident in its implied readership – predominantly white, xenophobic, Christian – and strengthened by

---

[47]   BBC breakfast television, which increased broadcasting hours, began in 1983. ITV began breakfast TV in the same year, and Channel 4 followed suit in 1992.

[48]   BBC1 and ITV1 have traditionally rivalled one another in the race to be the most popular channel. According to figures for May 2010, BBC1 was the most popular channel, having 20.6 per cent of the audience share. ITV1 had 16 per cent, BBC2, 6.7 per cent, Channel 4, 6.2 per cent and Channel 5, 4.7 per cent. The remaining 44.7 per cent went to other channels. BARB, May 2010.

[49]   McNair 2005, pp. 15–16.

[50]   Data on circulations were from www.nmauk.co.uk/nma, accessed 26 November 2009 (now http://www.newsworks.org.uk/Facts-Figures). See Kuhn 2007, p. 3.

[51]   Temple 2008, p. 178.

[52]   Kuhn 2007, pp. 214, 219.

[53]   From an audio interview with Ruth Gledhill, in Gower 2009.

recurrent references to 'us' or 'we' in editorials and columns, thus assuming an identity of interest between paper and reader. Nevertheless, the actual readership was known to be more diverse than the editorial policy would suggest.[54]

Even though the fragmentation and diversification of the media sphere led to different 'publics' and increased competition, the 1980s and 1990s were decades of increased concentration of ownership, with the expansion of Rupert Murdoch's News International perhaps the clearest example.[55] In the same period, however, the nature of ownership itself changed: by the late 2000s, most newspapers were owned by corporations whose primary purpose was not so much political propaganda – the favoured approach of patriarchs – but profit, making space for 'a flexible range of ideological activities so long as they produce the right reward'.[56] The political orientations of Murdoch's two papers, *The Times* and *The Sun* – both part of this study – broadly upheld this view. When News International began to support Tony Blair and the New Labour government in the mid 1990s, *The Sun* followed little by little, but *The Times* remained pro-Conservative or ambivalent. In the run up to the General Election in 1995 Murdoch stated that, for *The Times*, he would back the editor's choice; but for *The Sun*, he would contribute to editorial decision-making.[57] However, before the 2010 General Election both papers voiced their support for the Conservatives. An ambiguous picture of the relationship between ownership and editorial stance emerges from this, but one in which political intervention seems to be strategic and less important than profit.

The local newspaper that was included in our study, the *Yorkshire Evening Post*, was based in northern England but owned by one of the UK's largest regional newspaper publishers – Johnston Press – responsible for over three hundred local papers in the UK in the late 2000s.[58] Like other papers it witnessed a decline in circulation, selling approximately 50,000 copies daily in 2009, a decrease of 12 per cent on the previous year.[59] A major challenge came from free papers which emerged from the mid 1990s.[60] Nevertheless, there continued to be some demand for local and regional newspapers, which were noted for both their trustworthiness and their unique focus on locality.[61] The *Yorkshire Evening Post*'s mission was to provide news and information on what was going on in the area. Several pages were dedicated to national issues, but even then a local angle was often sought. A final threat for local papers was that their orientation around the idea of 'community'

---

54   Temple 2008, pp. 191–2; Allan 2004, p. 147.
55   McNair 2005, pp. 56, 156.
56   Davies 2009, pp. 16–17.
57   Kuhn 2007, p. 38; McNair 2005, pp. 86–87, 159–60.
58   Johnston Press, www.johnstonspress.co.uk, 2010.
59   Luft 2009.
60   McNair 2005, pp. 17, 207–8, 216.
61   Temple 2008, pp. 94–8.

left them exposed at a time when communities were said to be breaking down in the face of multicultural and global pressures.[62]

Research on Religion in the Media

This discussion about television and the press shows that *how* we are informed and entertained about what happens in our own backyard, our country and the wider world is never static. Moreover, media changes occur in a dynamic social context in which the nature and place of religion is also changing. Religious individuals and organizations have generally been among the earliest adopters of new media, and have adapted them to their own needs, in accordance with their traditions, teachings and values.[63] And media producers have always found material in religious stories, events, controversies and celebrities that can be reproduced and shaped to excite readers, listeners, viewers and, increasingly, interlocutors.

Religion in the British Media: History and Analysis

On the whole, the history of the religion/media relationship in Britain remains to be told. We have nothing to rival the lively story told by Mark Silk for religion in the American press.[64] He illustrates an ambiguous relationship which began with eighteenth-century journalists giving offense, found them maintaining the religious consensus from the mid nineteenth to the late twentieth century, and returning to more critical stances with the 'new prominence of religion in the news' from the 1980s.[65] He found that, though religious people thought otherwise, 'the news media, far from promoting a secularist agenda of their own, approach religion with values and presuppositions that the American public widely shares'.[66]

What we have for Britain is partial, revealed in a study of the religious press, in general media histories, and in accounts of the rise of particular media sources.[67] Newspapers were the principal source of news on all subjects from the seventeenth to the mid-twentieth century, the nineteenth century seeing 'the establishment of the periodical press as the preeminent medium of communication on all subjects, secular and religious'.[68] At that time, there were some 4,000 religious periodicals which took Christian communication from the pulpit to another level by circulating sermons, essays and information about church affairs.[69] With the

---

[62] Ibid., pp. 98, 110.
[63] Campbell 2010.
[64] Silk 1998.
[65] Ibid., p. 36.
[66] Ibid., p. 141.
[67] Altholz 1989; Seymour-Ure 1996; Boyce, Curran and Wingate 1978; Crisell.
[68] Boyce et al. 1978; Altholz 1989, p. 1.
[69] Altholz 1989, p. 2.

formation of the British Broadcasting Company in 1922, first radio, then television became the principal public service medium for news and entertainment, with the Sunday 'closed period' (often referred to as the 'God-slot') secured and protected, though declining in length and status, from the earliest days of the BBC until the deregulation of broadcasting in the 1990s.[70]

Knott and Mitchell's discussion of the relationship of religion and the media post 1945 introduced the changing faces of media audiences, protagonists, content, and production in respect of religion, and examined the impact of social and religious change in Britain on the media's various portrayals of religion.[71] The increasing range of religions covered in newspaper articles and TV programmes, and the variety of religious faces shown in media images reflected growing religious diversity. But, as they concluded, questions continue to be asked about media bias, the representation of religions, particularly Islam, and the media's role in the so-called marginalization of Christianity. These questions were aired in 2012 in Mitchell and Gower's edited book, *Religion and the News*, where the normative question of what religious reporting should be like was debated, and improvements suggested.[72] Religious representatives presented their expectations and criticisms (religion is 'more spinned against than spinning') and called for greater religious literacy among British media professionals; the professionals answered back, arguing that religion was treated no differently to other issues, explaining the impact of changes in the funding of journalism, and calling for more active and informed engagement by religious bodies themselves ('Don't get mad, get media. Stop complaining and do something about your coverage').[73]

Lynch et al noted that there were reasons to be cheerful about research on the media, culture and religion: the burgeoning scholarly literature 'reflects a growing awareness ... that it is increasingly difficult to think about religious phenomena in contemporary society without thinking about how these are implicated with various forms of media and cultural practice'.[74] What was striking, though, was the selective focus of this literature, which reflected the ever moving cutting-edge of technology and new theoretical interests, but often neglected other important issues. As technological change affected globalization and informed the introduction of new media formats, so the narrative on the mediation of social and cultural institutions, issues and priorities shifted accordingly, with increasing interest in how religious people use digital media.[75] Furthermore, the focus turned

---

[70]   Wolfe 1984; Noonan 2008; Wakelin 2011; Viney 1999.

[71]   Knott and Mitchell 2012, pp. 243–64.

[72]   Mitchell and Gower (eds) 2012.

[73]   Ibid.; Hill 2012; Landau 2012; for religious critics see, for example, Woolley 2012, Hussain 2012 and Singh 2012; for media defence, see Gledhill 2012, Beckett 2012 and Brown 2012.

[74]   Lynch, Mitchell and Strhan 2012, p. 1. This positive message was endorsed in the US, despite despondency ten years earlier: Stout and Buddenham 2008, p. 227.

[75]   Brasher 2004; Bunt 2009; Campbell 2010; Dawson and Cowan 2004; Wagner 2012.

from the treatment of the media and religion as separate spheres – from studies of religion *in* the media and the effect of the media *on* religion – to approaches which construe them as intertwined: 'They occupy the same spaces, serve many of the same purposes, and invigorate the same practices in late modernity'.[76] The focus shifted from media texts to audiences, users and participants in these intertwined cultural fields, to the media's role in religious identity, and to questions about ethics and literacy.[77]

However, despite the revitalization of theoretical discussions and normative debates about the relationship of religion and the media, several substantive questions remain, the answers to which depend on empirical research: Has media coverage of religion declined and, if so, is this evidence of secularization? Does the British media, like its American counterpart, 'approach religion with values and presuppositions that the ... public widely shares' or instead pursue a secularist agenda?[78] In his longitudinal study of religion in British newspapers, Gill found that, whilst there was evidence of a decrease in coverage from 1969 to 1990, there was very little media hostility towards religion: both decline and indifference being potential indicators of secularization.[79] In the second period, 1990 to 2011, the trend was reversed, both media coverage and hostility increasing. He asked whether the latter could be explained by a rise in 'polemical secularism' and New Atheism.[80] But secularist and atheist hostility was directed at religion in general, whereas press hostility focused predominantly on Islam and Muslims, and hardly at all on Christianity. Neither secularization nor polemical secularism could convincingly account for the changing extent and nature of religion reporting, an issue to which we will return later.

Gill's work is an exception. In recent decades scholars have in large part ignored the empirical study of media coverage and representation of religions. This is less apparent in the US than in the UK and Europe. In the former, a tradition of quantitative and qualitative research on religion in the media has been supported by the on-going work of dedicated research centres and organizations.[81] However, in the UK, in the decades following our research on media portrayals of religion

---

[76]   Hoover 2006, p. 9.

[77]   Ibid.; Mitchell and Marriage (eds) 2003; Stout and Buddenham 2008; Lynch, Mitchell and Strhan 2012.

[78]   Silk 1998, p. 141.

[79]   Gill 2012, pp. 45–60.

[80]   Ibid., p. 57.

[81]   The Center for Media, Religion and Culture at the University of Colorado at Boulder (see Hoover 1998; the Center for the Study of Religion in Public Life at Trinity College (see Silk 1998); the Pew Research Center's annual review of religion in the news (Pew Forum 2012); and Media Matters for America, a web-based not-for-profit progressive research and information center (see Media Matters for America 2007). One European exception is NOREL ('The role of religion in the public sphere. A comparative study of the five Nordic countries'), one strand of which is on the role of religion in newspapers.

in the early 1980s, religion and the media largely disappeared as a subject for empirical study, with two principal exceptions: Islam, and religion and television.

Islam in the British Media

In the 1980s and 1990s, it was race and ethnicity, not religion, which were favoured subjects in media studies.[82] From 1997, however, with the publication of the Runnymede Trust's report, *Islamophobia: A Challenge for Us All*, the subject of the representation of Islam in the media began to be given serious attention, though often under the rubric of race and racism. Poole's *Reporting Islam: Media Representations of British Muslims* (2002) was the first major study, followed by Richardson's book on the racism and rhetoric of the press, *(Mis)Representing Islam*, and Poole and Richardson's edited collection in 2006.[83] Channel 4 commissioned further research on media representations of Islam in 2008 (Moore, Mason and Lewis), and further books on the subject followed.[84]

This body of work found the media wanting when it came to the representation of Islam. The 'othering' and 'demonization' of Muslims, and their over-association with extremism, fundamentalism and terrorism were found to be key discourses, with the problem of integration another favoured theme.[85] Muslim women were stereotyped as veiled, and Muslim men as hate preachers and radicalized Islamists, with Islam in general being represented as violent and oppressive. Some variations in reporting were found between different media sources, but the picture across all sources was broadly negative.

Religion and Television

Turning now to empirical studies of religion and television, the chronology is reversed, much of the research being published before 2001 (just as interest in the representation of Islam began to increase).[86] This decline relates to our earlier point that quantitative research on religion in the media has depended on public funding or the support of interested research organizations. The scale of media research in the US, as well as sustained public interest in religion, enabled several academic and non-academic bodies to keep this type of research going; in the UK,

---

[82]   For a review, see Cottle 1992, pp. 3–57.

[83]   Poole 2002; Richardson 2004; Poole and Richardson (eds) 2006.

[84]   Moore, Mason and Lewis 2008; Morey and Yaqin 2011; Petley and Richardson (eds) 2011; Elgamri 2011; Flood, Hutchings, Miazhevich and Nickels 2012; Baker, Gabrielatos and McEnery 2012.

[85]   The issues uncovered in academic research were highlighted in policy circles by the lobbying organization, Engage, founded in 2008 'to help empower and encourage British Muslims within local communities to be more actively involved in British media and politics', http://www.iengage.org.uk/.

[86]   But see Noonan 2008.

however, this role was maintained by a single organization, the body responsible for independent broadcasting regulation.[87] Independent research on television and religion began in 1964 with a survey commissioned by ABC Television (undertaken by Gallup); another soon followed, by the Independent Television Authority (ITA) in 1970.[88] In both, respondents were asked questions on religion in general, and others about religious programmes on television, their popularity, role and potential for helping people with problems.

The importance of responding to the religious and broader spiritual interests and needs of television audiences, the role of religious broadcasting, the significance of the whole television schedule (rather than religious programmes alone) for portraying relevant human issues, and the power of television were all recognized in this report, and they remained some of the key issues in research conducted by ITA's successor, the Independent Broadcasting Authority (IBA), in the 1980s and 1990s.[89] The most useful overview and summary of this body of research was provided by Viney in 1999.[90] Focusing on religious broadcasting by the BBC as well as independent television, she charted changes in broadcasting policy, audiences and programming, weighed up the evidence for claims about the decline of religious broadcasting and noted the challenges to come, particularly of digital television.

The importance of television for religion, its representation, its delivery to large audiences (non-religious as well as religious), and its role in education, information, and ethical and theological debate – as well as its rivalry with religion – was discussed in academic as well as policy literature. An edited collection from 1993 reflected the field at the time, containing essays on televangelism, soap operas and adverts as sources of ethics and community, popular religion and religious music on TV, Islamic and theological perspectives on the news, and the religious effects of television.[91] Although ostensibly a book on *Religion and the Media*, it was overwhelmingly a book about religion and *television*.

> TV has assumed an iconic role in modern society ... TV has become the common touchstone of what is real and what we should value ... Given the fact

---

[87]   First known as the Independent Television Authority, then the Independent Broadcasting Authority, and – from 1991 to 2003 – the Independent Television Commission, this body regulated various aspects of television and radio provision (excluding the BBC). In 2003, the Office of Communications (OfCom) took over many of its roles, but not its research brief.

[88]   ABC Television, *Television and Religion* (London, 1964); Independent Television Authority (ITA), *Religion in Britain and Northern Ireland* (London, 1970).

[89]   The Independent Broadcasting Authority supported additional research on religion and television in 1983: Knott 1984a; Knott 1983. Later studies included Svennevig 1988, and Gunter and Viney 1994.

[90]   Viney 1999; see also Noonan 2008.

[91]   Arthur (ed.) 1993.

that for millions of people TV rather than religion now provides the symbols which offer answers to fundamental questions … one is bound to wonder if media mythologies will eventually eclipse more traditional religious outlooks.[92]

This reflected a commonly-articulated fear, of television *as* religion, of television professionals as the new priesthood. As Grace Davie wrote at the century's end: 'In dominating the agendas of so much of modern society, are they (the media) a form of religion in themselves?'[93]

This anxiety offers a fitting way to situate the research undertaken for this book. If new forms of digital and social media were the principal source of excitement and concern when we began our second research project in 2008, back in the early 1980s it was very definitely television that challenged religious commentators and scholars of religion. They were not only anxious about the quasi-religious role and power of television, but about what happened when the Gospel or other religious messages were communicated through it.[94] In the 1970s, the moral critic, Malcolm Muggeridge, stated of television: 'Even if you put the truth into it, it comes out a deception', and a decade later *The Times*'s religious correspondent, Clifford Longley, declared there to be a 'natural disaffinity' between religion and the media.[95] The pervasiveness of this view was witnessed twenty years later by Grace Davie who questioned whether the 'nature of the message alters with the manner of transmission'.[96] One preacher may be able to reach a far larger audience through the mass media than he or could ever reach face-to-face in a church sermon, but the 'amplification' of the message would come at the expense of its 'distortion'.[97]

As these two cases of Islamophobia and religion on television show, the twin fears of misrepresentation and distortion have continued to haunt the relationship between religious communities and the media. However, although the analogy of religion and metaphors of church and priesthood are no longer applied to television, its importance for the communication of information and images of religion has not declined. Religious organizations remain concerned about how they are portrayed on television – as well as in the press.[98] Their views find expression, along with those of journalists, in *Religion in the News*, in which mutual frustrations are aired and they 'offer their views on how to create a more engaged relationship'.[99] And

---

[92]   Ibid., pp. 3–4. See also Goethals 1982; Silverstone 1981.

[93]   Davie 2000, p. 100.

[94]   Knott 1984a, pp. 60–66.

[95]   Muggeridge in Green 1982, p. 177; Longley 1983, p. 34.

[96]   Davie 2000, p. 113. This builds on McLuhan's idea – 'the medium is the message' – that inherent in any message is the medium that purveyed it: see McLuhan 1964.

[97]   Ibid., pp. 112–13.

[98]   See earlier (footnote 8). See also Mitchell and Gower 2012; The Media Trust in association with the Inter Faith Network for the UK and Respect 2004.

[99]   Mitchell and Gower 2012, p. 2.

television – like other mainstream news sources such as newspapers and radio – remains crucial for public knowledge and debate about religion.

Despite several decades of research on both Islam in the press and the relationship of religion and television, the empirical study of the representation of religion in general in the mainstream British media – so necessary for the contextualization of these issues – remains under-researched.[100] This book – and the two projects that lie behind it – aims to fill that gap and to make connections with similar studies and debates beyond the UK.

Interpreting the Changing Relationship of Religion, the Media and Society

Summarizing the secularization of Britain in 2009, Simon Barrow, co-Director of the beliefs and values think-tank, Ekklesia, wrote:

> A dispassionate look at accumulated research over the past few years would indicate that institutional religion is on the decline, that strong belief commitment has devolved into less established forms, that the "spiritual but not religious" constituency has grown, that a majority are vague and uncommitted in their beliefs, and that a secular mindset has grown without a significant increase in affiliation to explicitly non-religious groups.[101]

A rather different interpretation was offered by Alex Klaushofer in 2006 on the 'rise of religion' in Britain at the time of New Labour.

> In terms of the mainstream liberal-left discourse which currently dominates discussion about how we run our society, the orthodoxies of a secular state have become incontestable truths. However, on the ground, things have moved on. Whether due to the burgeoning confidence of the country's devout immigrant groups, the global importance of Islam, or to some less easily definable "Age of Aquarius" zeitgeist, Britain is becoming re-spiritualised – and government, albeit rather clumsily, is responding to that.[102]

Although one narrative was cast in terms of fall and the other of rise, in other ways they were not wholly opposed. Both mentioned the 'spiritual' and recognized the significance of a 'secular mindset', but Barrow suggested the religion glass was being depleted whilst Klaushofer wrote that it was being replenished.

Klaushofer echoed the spirit with which we opened the chapter, of Mark Thompson's optimism about the challenge to secularization and dawn of a more

---

[100]   A similar assessment was made by Ruth Deller, Deller 2007, p. 11.

[101]   Simon Barrow quoted in Ekklesia, 'Mixed Picture Emerges on British Attitudes to Religion in Public Life' (2009).

[102]   Klaushofer 2006.

positive and creative approach to religion in public service broadcasting. A survey conducted by the BBC in 2009 revealed that two-thirds of those questioned agreed that 'religion has an important role to play in public life' (though a similar proportion believed that religion was more divisive than race).[103] Evidence of the readiness to discuss these issues in the media and online was not hard to find: 'What role should religion play in the public sphere?'; 'Is Islam good for London?'; 'UK: Christian or secular?' These were just a few of the topics debated in Britain in the late 2000s.[104]

As we saw earlier, the statistical evidence revealed a country that was Christian, secular *and* religiously diverse. These three aspects had not developed independently, but were firmly intertwined. It is not possible or indeed appropriate to separate them in an attempt to theorize religious change or its media portrayal. Rather, we need to understand them as interrelated and co-produced. In this final section, we will look briefly at some of the theories of contemporary religious change and consider how they relate to public discourse and the media in particular.

Secularization or the Return of the Sacred?

The idea of secularization, that process whereby social differentiation and rationalization lead to the decline of religion in modernity, has been the dominant paradigm for narrating the contemporary fate of religion. With its roots in classical sociology, it formed the meta-narrative of the sociology of religion from the 1960s to the 1980s. At the time of our first study, it was the dominant discourse about religion in both churches and the media, as well as the academy.[105] Criticisms of the thesis in its various forms have grown since then, but it remains impossible to discuss the relationship of religion and modern society without reference to it.[106] The secularization paradigm has included many different theories and arguments, and these have been matched by others on the 'return of the sacred', of religion's vitality and resurgence.[107] 'Return' can mean: (a) an increase in activities and practices, beliefs and membership; (b) the heightened meaning of religion for individual and collective identities; and (c) the increased presence of religion in the public sphere, in the state, institutions or wider civil society. Although these three types are sometimes treated separately, in empirical analysis they often overlap.

The idea that religions will flourish in a free market situation, because they answer people's varied needs and demands, is promoted in theories of rational choice. Although this provides an arena for discussing the possibility of religious resurgence and continuing vitality, it has been easier to apply in the US than the

---

[103]   Ekklesia, 'Mixed Picture Emerges'.

[104]   Debates organized 2007–2009 by Ekklesia, the *London Evening Standard*, and the think-tank, Theos.

[105]   Knott 1984a, pp. 69–74; Towler 1974; Wilson 1982; Martin 1978.

[106]   See Woodhead 2012a, 'Introduction', for a recent summary.

[107]   Ibid; this notion was first introduced by Daniel Bell in Bell 1978, pp. 187–208.

UK and elsewhere in Europe where statistics confirm the continuing decline of religious beliefs, attendance and affiliation, as well as an increase in non-religious identification. These measures have been offered in recent years in support of secularization, though with a narrower remit than in early articulations of the thesis.[108] Even with the claim of 'desecularization', the original thesis has not been wholly abandoned, with Peter Berger referring to the 'interplay of secularizing and counter-secularizing forces'.[109] It is not surprising then that some scholars have suggested that Europe is an 'exceptional case', because elsewhere religions seem to have remained both vital and compatible with modernization.[110] These observations have resulted in the development of new terms, such as 'Eurosecularity', and the proposition of multiple modernities with different relations to religiosity rather than a single secularizing form.[111] But, even in Europe, secularization is not the only explanatory candidate. There have been suggestions put forward that traditional religiosity is giving way to spirituality and that the location of religiosity is changing from institutions to popular culture.[112] While there are visible signs of such developments, at the moment none of these theses succeeds in fully overturning the conception of a secularizing Europe.[113]

'Fundamentalism' and the maximizing of religious identities, and their consequences for political order, have been used as evidence for the return of religion thesis.[114] This has been argued mainly for Islam, the rise of which has itself been connected to increased migration and mobility. Expressions such as the 'Islamization of Europe' have been used in popular parlance, but they have more to do with fears for the future combined with Islamophobia than with current statistics. More generally, some scholars have suggested that religion is becoming more important with the decline of the hegemony of enlightenment reason.[115]

Religion: Public Visibility and Discourse

Empirically-informed theoretical debates on the increase or decrease in religion are important: they offer information and a framework for understanding broader

---

[108] For early articulations, see Wilson 1966; Wilson 1982; Martin 1978. More recent elaborations are by Bruce 1996; Bruce 2002; Bruce 2011; Voas and Bruce 2007, pp. 43–61.

[109] Berger 1999, pp. 6–7.

[110] Davie 2002; Berger, Davie and Fokas 2008.

[111] Berger et al. 2008.

[112] Heelas and Woodhead 2005, on the spiritual revolution; Carrette and King 2005, on capitalist spiritualities; Lynch 2007, on progressive spirituality; and Partridge, 2004–2005, on the impact of spirituality on popular culture; Noonan 2011, pp. 727–46.

[113] Only Heelas and Woodhead offer numerical analysis and prediction of the growth of spirituality, but the evidence is ambiguous. See criticisms in Voas and Bruce 2007; Warner 2010.

[114] Kepel 1994; Tibi 1998.

[115] For example, Derrida 1998, pp. 1–78.

changes. However, they cannot – and are not designed to – answer all the questions that arise for scholars in the current socio-religious context. From the perspective of this study, theorizing focused on the rise or decline of *discourse* on religion is arguably more relevant than that related to religion as a social force, though the two may be interrelated. In practice, the idea of the resurgence or return of religion is a signal that religion has become a visible public issue. Even Micklethwait and Wooldridge, who proclaim boldly that God is back, that the global rise of faith is changing the world, and the US will provide the future model for religion in European countries, are more modest when they admit that the 'most important development is not quantitative but qualitative: the fact that religion is playing a much more important role in public and intellectual life'.[116] That governments are happy to let religious organizations take care of social issues that were once public responsibilities is just one example. Religious groups are becoming more visible agents at the level of civil society, as well as in relation to global politics.[117]

Evidence for the return of religion suggests that something is happening to privatization – the idea that in modernity religion will become an ever more private matter. While it is still easy to find support for the distinction between private religion and the public sphere of secular politics, perhaps the strongest argument for a return of religion has been presented by José Casanova, who introduced the term 'deprivatization'.[118] Casanova argued that, although the secularization thesis includes the idea of institutional differentiation and the decline of religious beliefs, it does not necessarily require privatization. Rather, religion seems to be 'de-privatized', Christian and non-Christian religious charities becoming rational, 'society-oriented' – as opposed to 'state-oriented' – conversation partners in the public sphere. The strict separation between private religion and the secular public sphere was the ideal of an earlier form of modernization, but this very ideal has been challenged and has turned out to be 'a historical option'.[119] As de Vries notes, however, Casanova was surprisingly silent about the media in his assessment of de-privatization.[120] More recently, Ward and Hoelzl have argued not for a return but for a new visibility and new awareness of religion.[121] This is a more modest claim than insisting on the resurgence of religion, or on some kind of reversal of secularization. They have also hinted that what appears new or more visible may not be exactly the same religion or faith as that which used to be hidden or private. Although neither Ward and Hoelzl nor their contributing authors focused on the media, it is obvious that there could be no new visibility or awareness without it.

In 2001 Jacques Derrida posed the question, 'What would the said "return of the religious" have to do with media?', and commented elsewhere that 'digital

---

116 Micklethwait and Wooldridge 2009, p. 27.

117 Herbert 2003.

118 Casanova 1994.

119 Ibid., p. 215. But see public attitudes to religion as a private matter (Chapter 6).

120 de Vries 2001, pp. 16–18.

121 Ward and Hoelzl (eds) 2008. See also Herbert 2011, pp. 626–48.

culture, Jet and TV' are three things 'without which there could be no religious manifestation today'.[122] He emphasized the constitutive nature of the media and technology in the 'return' of religion to the current agenda. Our task in this study is not to establish whether religion is in fact declining or returning, but rather to underline the importance of the media and discourse on religion in general both in themselves and as a component in current processes of change.

Of the supporters of a continuing process of secularization Callum Brown, in particular, has focused on 'discursive religion' rather than affiliation or beliefs, not in the context of the media but in the narration of everyday lives.[123] He has argued for two main phases in secularization in which the first saw the decline of organized Christianity, and the second, accelerating in the 1960s, 'the death of culture which formerly conferred Christian identity upon the British people as a whole'.[124] The links between Britain, Christianity and people's self-narratives have weakened. As we shall see in Chapter 3, Brown's account resonates well with current British media anxieties about the crisis of the Christian nation and the marginalization of Christianity. What makes the two-phase theory of secularization complicated in this context, though, is that some newspapers – along with Christian leaders and organizations – are fighting back in an attempt to change the (predicted) end of this narrative of the 'death of Christian culture'. We suggest that the scholarly debate would benefit from a closer investigation of competing contemporary discourses in support of Christianity, atheism/secularism and religious diversity. If there is any credence to the idea of the return of religion or its new visibility, it is not limited to Christianity only but is conjoined with the new visibility of non-religion as well as religion in all its plurality.

Religion, Mediation and Mediatization

Nowadays different traditions, religious or otherwise, must justify themselves in public discourse; they must mark out and express themselves in the public space.[125] As Giddens has argued, the idea of the 'post-traditional' does not mean the end of traditions as such – in fact, there may even be a redundancy of them in post-traditional society – but rather the end of traditions *as tradition*.[126] Previously, tradition was something taken for granted, something that was not in need of discursive justification. Operating now in a post-traditional setting entails two things for religion. First, traditions must be justified in public discourse and, second, they change from tradition in this taken for granted sense to 'traditions as cultural heritage' and 'traditions as cultural diversity'.[127] The need to justify

---

[122]   Derrida 2001, p. 61; Derrida 1998, p. 20.
[123]   Brown 2009.
[124]   Ibid., p. 193.
[125]   Knott 2005; Knott 2010, pp. 115–33.
[126]   Giddens 1994, pp. 56–109.
[127]   Ibid.

a single religious tradition or to live with competing non-privileged others does not mean that tradition-based discourses have vanished, but rather that they have to be voiced and debated publicly. The media is not the only setting where such justifications are defended and struggles fought out, but it is difficult to overestimate its importance for mediating traditions. Activities in places of worship and membership of religious groups are no longer sufficient for maintaining identities and transmitting religious cultures and traditions. Religions must get their message across. They must participate and represent themselves in the public sphere; hence the importance of the media.

But this process of mediation is not without its consequences for either religion or the media. Religion must conform to – and is thereby shaped by – the 'logics' of the media.[128] The media, in turn, find themselves to be the gatekeepers of public religious literacy and ethical debate, and exposed – as we saw earlier – to criticisms of misrepresentation, distortion and bias.[129] They may even find their technologies high-jacked for religious purposes.[130] As Stolow, Meyer and others have noted, religion 'can only be manifested through some process of mediation', and this extends to contemporary media forms no less than traditional texts, rituals and images.[131] This notion of 'religions *as* media' may seem to overturn the fear voiced in the 1980s about the media as the new religion.[132] Both institutions, in fact, 'draw on a very general form of symbolic power to represent the world', making analogies and comparisons between them inevitable.[133]

Despite their potential relevance for debates about secularization and the return of the sacred, the relationship between religion and the media has been overlooked by sociologists of religion.[134] The development of mediatization theory and its subsequent embellishments and criticisms has been a response to this absence, providing 'a perspective that relates to other processes of modernization such as individualization, societal differentiation and globalization'.[135] A key protagonist, Stig Hjarvard, is inclined towards a 'media *as* religion' perspective, asserting that 'as a cultural and social environment, the media have taken over many of the cultural and social functions of the institutional religions and provide spiritual guidance, moral orientation, ritual passages and a sense of community and belonging'.[136] On the one hand, the media acquire some previously religious functions which are thereby secularized; on the other, they 'produce and circulate various banal religious representations [which] become the backdrop for the

---

128 Hjarvard 2011, pp. 119–35; Lövheim and Lynch 2011, pp. 111–17.
129 Lövheim and Lynch 2011; Graham 2012; Lynch, Mitchell and Strhan 2012 .
130 Campbell 2010.
131 Stolow 2005, p. 125; Meyer and Moors (eds) 2006.
132 Stolow 2005.
133 Couldry 2012, p. 151; Meyer and Moors (eds) 2006.
134 Lövheim and Lynch 2011, p. 114.
135 Ibid.; for earlier studies see Hjarvard 2008, pp. 9–26; Lundby (ed.) 2009.
136 Hjarvard 2008, p. 119.

modern individual's knowledge about religious issues and may ... encourage the subjectivized spiritual imagination'.[137] Critics have suggested, however, that mediatization theory neglects religious agency and applies better to some contexts than others, in particular, contemporary 'Northern and Western, de-Christianized societies'.[138]

Religious mediation and mediatization offer additional ways to think about interactions between religion, the media and society: (1) the media are a key part of the process whereby religion becomes more publicly visible; (2) the media may indeed become a primary source of information about religion; (3) media portrayals of religion have not been untouched by social change and may indeed have become secularized or banal; and (4) contemporary social transformations have changed the power relationship between religion and the media, and may account for the latter's quasi-religious role.

Testing Claims about Religion, Media and Society

A number of contending ideas have emerged in the first two chapters about the changing empirical and theoretical relationships between religion, the media and society. They are presented here as paired propositions, and will be tested in the remainder of the book and discussed in the concluding chapter.[139]

Religion in the Media: Secularization or Return?

1. As society has become more secularized, media coverage of religion has declined and been marginalized.
2. 'Religion never really went away, so that talk of its "re-emergence" or "return" ... is misleading', and the same is true of religion in the media.[140]

The Secularity or Religiosity of Media Professionals
and the Reporting of Religion

1. The media's reporting of religion is unfair and inaccurate because of the secularity of media professionals who have no interest in religion or are biased against it.
2. The media and media professionals are animated by the religious values that are embedded in the national culture.

---

[137]   Ibid., p. 132.

[138]   For criticisms see Lynch 2011, pp. 203–10 (p. 203); Couldry 2012, pp. 151–5; Hjarvard and Lövheim (eds) 2012.

[139]   For the sake of brevity, some of these propositions conflate several assertions.

[140]   Woodhead 2012a, 'Introduction', p. 7.

Religion in the Media: Minority or Majority Interest?

1. Religion is 'positioned, represented and constructed as a minority interest' by the media.[141]
2. Religion is treated as a major public concern as people rely on the media for information and education about religion.

The Status of Religion in the Shaping of Media Narratives

1. Because of their commercial interests and priorities, the media are only interested in bad news and controversy about religion.
2. Religion is important to the media because it provides language and subject matter that are essential for the construction of media narratives.

Religions and the Media: Disempowerment or Agency?

1. 'Contemporary religion is increasingly mediated through secular, autonomous media institutions, and is shaped according to the logics of those media'.[142]
2. Religious individuals and organizations are active agents in the use and appropriation of the media, and are influential in setting media agendas.

Religion as Media; the Media as Religion

1. Religions 'can only be manifested through some process of mediation' and are themselves media.[143]
2. The media have become 'a form of religion in themselves' (media as religion).[144]

---

[141] Ibid., p. 25.
[142] Lövheim and Lynch 2011, p. 111.
[143] Stolow 2005, p. 125.
[144] Davie 2000, p. 114.

Chapter 2
Changing Media Portrayals of Religion and the Secular Sacred

In this chapter we consider the extent and nature of media coverage of religion and the secular sacred today, and how much it has changed since the early 1980s.[1] The principal sources for this analysis were three daily newspapers, *The Times*, *The Sun* and a local paper, the *Yorkshire Evening Post*, for one month, and three terrestrial television channels, BBC1, BBC2 and ITV1 for one week.[2] Although today's media is now more diverse, digital as well as analogue, in our view findings from these mainstream sources nevertheless paint an interesting and not unrepresentative picture of contemporary media portrayals of religion, and one that can be compared to those from our earlier study in the 1980s.

In October 2008, Britain was caught up in an international financial crisis, 'the credit crunch'. It increased the number of newspaper articles dealing with the morality of capitalism, some by Christian leaders, others by alternative moral commentators. October also saw the build up to the US presidential election in November, attracting discussion of religion and politics, and religious profiles of Barack Obama and Sarah Palin. The war in Afghanistan was ongoing and it drew media attention to Islam, to the Taleban and to Christian charities working in the area. Halloween and new information about UFO sightings were also covered.

At the time of our television research, the first week of February 2009, Britain experienced 'the Big Freeze', and snow dominated the news. Charles Darwin's bicentenary was commemorated (he was born on 12 February 1809) with documentaries and debates about religion and science, creationism and evolution. The anniversary of the 1979 Iranian revolution was marked with a new television series, *Iran and the West*, remembering the event and describing developments 30

---

[1]   For an interesting comparison, see Gill 2012, pp. 45–60. Gill analysed and compared stories about religion in eight British newspapers at three points, 1969, 1990 and 2011.

[2]   Newspapers were taken for October and November 2008, with the first month selected for quantitative content analysis; in 1982, the months analysed were February and March. At that time newspapers were a third the size they are today. Data from two months in 1982 were scaled down for comparison with findings from a single month in 2008. Data from one week's television (excluding children's and educational programmes) were collected from BBC1, BBC2 and ITV, the only available channels in 1982 (though Channel 4 began later that year). Television weeks were 19–25 April 1982 and 2–9 February 2009. Television recordings were supplied by the University of Leeds in 1982 and by the British Universities Film and Video Council in 2009.

years on. In addition, the world's many religions were featured in the long-running series, *Around the World in 80 Faiths*.

Thinking back to 1982, in addition to the greater incidence of formal religious broadcasting – including religious worship – the major event to affect the media's coverage of religious and secular issues was the forthcoming visit of Pope John Paul II (scheduled for June of that year). The centenary of the Society for Psychical Research was covered on television and in the press, and topical issues of intellectual debate included religion and education, and American-style televangelism. The first 'test tube twins' were born, reigniting ethical and religious debates around IVF. The media reported the international crisis between Britain and Argentina over the Falkland Islands/Malvinas (which led to war from April to June 1982), the 'Solidarity' movement and martial law in Poland, and events in Israel and Egypt.

This is what was happening in the world when we took our snapshots of religion in the media in 1982 and 2008–2009. Would other periods have produced significantly different coverage of religion? Despite our intention to avoid major festivals, it was impossible to select times when nothing out of the ordinary occurred. The landscape of media coverage is dynamic with new stories breaking all the time.

Religion and the Secular Sacred in the Media: An Overview

We turn now to how much coverage of these issues there was in the periods we selected, what it was about and what treatment religion and the secular sacred received in the newspapers and on television. It is not our aim to generalize on the basis of our two samples, but to show what these snapshots reveal and how they might be compared. Our analysis was based on the number and frequency of 'references' to various aspects of religion and the secular sacred. To us, a reference might be a single word, phrase or image. An extended examination of a religious topic would be likely to include a number of separate references, to the same or different topics. They might be one-off passing references or ones that contributed to an in-depth discussion. They might be literal or metaphorical.[3] We will quantify and give examples of such references later in the chapter.

In 2008–2009, a total of 4,370 references to religion and the secular sacred were identified in one month's copies of *The Times*, *The Sun* and the *Yorkshire Evening Post* and one week of television on BBC1, BBC2 and ITV1; in 1982, the equivalent number had been 2,454.[4] The rise is substantial, but the principal reason

---

[3]   For further discussion of what we mean by 'references' and how we coded them, see Poole and Taira 2013. In the early 1980s, we used a new database programme (Extract) to log, search, sort and count references. In 2008–2009, the Statistical Package for the Social Sciences (SPSS) was our preferred software.

[4]   For more information about media references to religion in 1982, see Knott 1984a.

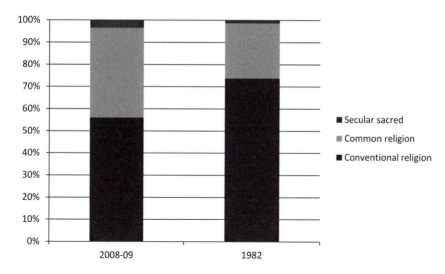

Figure 2.1   References by type, 2008–2009 and 1982

is practical: the increased size of newspapers. Changes to print technology since the 1980s, as well as the exponential growth of newspaper advertising, had trebled the number of pages. Typically, copies of *The Times* and *The Sun* in 1982 had 26 pages; by 2008, *The Sun* routinely had over 60 and *The Times* closer to 100 pages, often with additional supplements or inserts. Numbers of references on television were similar in both samples: 1,672 in 2009, compared with 1,630 in 1982.

In 2008–2009, the majority of references (56 per cent) were to conventional religious topics – to organized and official religions – with 40.5 per cent of references to common religion – to those beliefs and practices associated with the supernatural but beyond the churches and other religious organizations (Figure 2.1).[5] Just 3.5 per cent were to the secular sacred, to matters that were non-negotiable and inviolable but with no supernatural referent. (A full list of the conventional and common religious, and secular sacred categories and subcategories used in the research can be found in Appendix 1.) Back in 1982, conventional religion had dominated to an even greater degree, with nearly three-quarters of all references; common religion had accounted for most of the remainder, and the secular sacred just over 1 per cent.[6]

---

[5]   See Introduction for definitions of conventional religion, common religion and the secular sacred.

[6]   In the early 1980s we did not refer to the 'secular sacred'. However, data were collected on relevant themes, including atheism, humanism, the religion and science debate, and the term 'sacred' itself. References from the earlier sample have been reassigned to this new category (from conventional religion) to enable us to compare past and present.

In 2008–2009, more than 60 per cent of all references appeared in the newspaper month, with the remainder in the television week. In 1982, distribution had been more even: just over 50 per cent in the papers and just under 50 per cent of references on television. If we look more closely, we see variations, with more coverage in both periods of conventional religion and the secular sacred in the newspapers, but substantially more common religion on TV. The simple explanation for this is that advertisements contained a plethora of references to luck, gambling, magic, witchcraft and mystery or the unexplained. We will consider this in more depth later, but we begin by examining the newspaper coverage.

Newspaper Coverage in Depth

In October 2008, nearly 60 per cent of references in *The Times*, *The Sun* and the *Yorkshire Evening Post* were to conventional religion, 36 per cent to common religion, and less than 5 per cent to the secular sacred (see statistical summary in Appendix 2). Newspaper portrayals of conventional religion were dominated by two religions: Christianity, in its various guises, and Islam. In relation to the former, there were more *explicit* references to Roman Catholicism than Protestantism (the latter included the Church of England, Methodism, the Baptist church and other major denominations), but the two together accounted for over 7 per cent of all the newspaper references to religion and the secular sacred. However this was down significantly from more than 28 per cent in 1982. But these churches were also referred to *implicitly*. When analysing our data we were obliged repeatedly to categorize references as 'Christianity general' or 'Church general' because it was impossible to ascertain what denomination was intended. In photographs, as on television, there were visual references to church buildings which were difficult to code with any confidence: were they Anglican, Catholic or some other denomination? Equally, on most occasions, references to weddings and funerals were difficult to assign to particular churches. When denominations were alluded to, in addition to the mainline ones, the Religious Society of Friends (Quakers), the Salvation Army, Pentecostalism, Church of the Latter-Day Saints (Mormons) and Christian Science were mentioned.

The dominance of Christianity in both periods was not surprising. Despite considerable indifference to religion in the UK, it still has more adherents than other religious traditions, and the history and role of the Church of England in particular has been closely intertwined with British public life.[7] Nevertheless, it was clear that, in 1982, the two major denominations dominated newspaper coverage of religion, particularly in *The Times*. Although references to Roman Catholicism exceeded those to Protestantism in both samples, the coverage given to the former in 1982 was extraordinary, especially in a country where the state

---

[7]   See Chapter 3.

church is Protestant. It was explained by the celebrity status of the Pope at the time, and his pending pastoral visit.

Turning now to other religions, it was Islam that attracted significant media attention in 2008.[8] Given the percentage of Muslims in England and Wales (4.8 per cent in 2011), it was striking to see that it accounted for nearly 10 per cent of all newspaper references. There were more newspaper references to Islam than to all other non-Christian traditions and new religious movements taken together (see Appendix 2). The coverage in general was dominated by references to extremism, terrorism, violence and cultural differences. In addition, in light of their small numbers of adherents in the UK, Judaism and Buddhism were relatively well-represented in the newspapers. Judaism received 3 per cent of newspaper religious coverage in 2008 (a slight increase on 1982), which is understandable given its significance in British and broader European history. Three-quarters of references to Judaism were in *The Times*, often in obituaries or in articles referring to the Holocaust. Buddhism's relatively strong representation is explained by its presence in the *Yorkshire Evening Post*: more than half of all the newspaper references to Buddhism were on its announcements and events pages. Of other world religions, Hinduism and Sikhism were mentioned on several occasions in international and local news stories respectively; Zen, Taoism and Jainism were acknowledged, though infrequently. In terms of new movements, more than half were to Yoga, with others mentioned occasionally, including Krishna Consciousness and Scientology.

None of the established religious traditions were excluded from newspaper coverage, though some received more attention than might be expected in light of their numerical presence in the UK. Furthermore, the extent and frequency of such coverage had increased significantly since 1982. Just 6 per cent of newspaper references to religion concerned religions other than Christianity back then; by 2008 this had grown to over 15 per cent, reflecting the UK's increasing religious diversity and the visibility of religion in global politics. Given this state of affairs, when religious groups complain about the way they are treated in the media, it is not so much the absence of coverage that should be of concern as the wrong kind of coverage.[9] It is misrepresentation and negative reporting at the expense of a balanced portfolio of coverage, particularly in the case of Islam, that is deemed to be the problem.

Looking beyond references to the nature of the coverage, the figures suggest that religion was often represented through its concepts and practices. In 2008, there was significant newspaper coverage of religious cosmology (over 8 per cent of newspaper references to religion), religious practice (nearly 10 per cent) and religious concepts and doctrines (4.5 per cent) (see Appendix 2). A deeper examination, however, showed that many references were made in passing and were not intentionally religious. The category of religious cosmology consisted

---

[8]   See Chapter 4.

[9]   For debate on misrepresentation of religion by the British media, see Mitchell and Gower (eds) 2012.

largely of references to God, the devil and hell, and of various oaths and petitions, many of which were metaphorical. This is a reminder that media discourse is full of expressions with Christian origins which are not meant to be taken literally, such as 'Heavens above!', 'For God's sake', 'the devil's in the detail', and 'Hell's teeth'. In all three categories, with the exception of Islamic concepts such as *jihad* and *shari'ah*, the vast majority of references were Christian.

Turning now to common religion – to references to the supernatural beyond the remit of organized religions – in both 1982 and 2008 it was 'luck' and 'gambling' that dominated the coverage, with frequent coverage of the national lottery, betting and bingo. We were frequently asked why we included gambling in a study of religion. The simple explanation is that, when people bet, very few do so on the basis of statistical probability. Whether consciously or not, those who gamble or make reference to luck in betting and games of chance do so in the hope that 'the odds will fall in their favour', it will be their 'lucky day', or through some inexplicable divine intervention they will be singled out or 'blessed with good fortune'. Gambling is replete with references to luck, fate, destiny and fortune, all of which imply some kind of supernatural assistance.

Other popular categories were 'magic' and 'fortune-telling techniques'. References to magic were usually found in contexts where something positive and out-of-ordinary happened: a footballer scored a 'magic goal' or a reviewer considered a show 'magical'. Most of the references tell us little about actual belief in magic, but a lot about the use of language. The English language includes copious references to the supernatural, even though its speakers do not necessarily intend to say anything religious or spiritual.

The majority of fortune-telling references were to horoscopes, in *The Sun* and *Yorkshire Evening Post*. Even though few would claim to take them seriously, they are nevertheless part of our regular reading experience. Coverage of 'the unexplained', which had increased substantially since 1982 and provoked serious discussion, was dominated by references to mysterious occurrences and to UFOs, aliens and extraterrestrials.[10] The three mythological themes that stood out were Greek and Roman myths, dragons, and cannibalism. Folk religion and practice was dominated by references to Halloween, Native American religion and Paganism (including Stonehenge). Some of these occurred in editorials and opinion pieces and not merely news and adverts. Perhaps surprisingly, the relevance of Paganism and its relationship to the environment – a matter of contemporary debate – was not in evidence in the 2008 sample.

The main purpose of including the secular sacred in our study was to gather and analyse references to secularism, atheism and other deeply held philosophical perspectives which do not make reference to or depend upon supernatural agents such as God, Allah, spiritual forces or people. The distribution of references (see Appendix 2) shows that 'atheism' was more common in public discourse than 'secularism', which was generally used as a technical term reserved for articles

---

[10]   See Chapter 6.

on foreign politics or church-state relations. Very different kinds of issues were referred to as 'sacred' – the home, music, a library or civil birth ceremony – but most common were those that dealt with the sacredness of life, often in the context of ethical debates. In such cases, the importance of 'life' itself was the focus without any reference to religion, and arguments about its sacred nature were used both to support and oppose assisted suicide and abortion.[11]

References to immanent spirituality, the type that refers to nature and humanity but not to the supernatural, were not uncommon. The sub-category we drew on most frequently within the secular sacred, however, was 'religion-like'. It included those references where something unambiguously this-worldly or non-religious was referred to, but using religious terms. Examples included health, individualism, the environment, Marxism and Elvis, but the majority occurred during the financial crisis and were related to the market. The credit crunch prompted a response in the newspapers in which capitalism and its financial markets were understood as a religion-like system in need of more control and an injection of morality. Whilst the metaphor of religion was used – often negatively, in the sense of blind faith – in order to show the necessity for more economic regulation, Christian morality was also seen as a fitting counter to the problem of wild markets and greedy bankers.

In both 1982 and 2008 there were more religious references in *The Times* than in the other papers. In 2008, *The Times* accounted for 53 per cent of the references, *The Sun* 29 per cent and the *Yorkshire Evening Post*, 18 per cent. This was due in part to their relative size, *The Times* having the most pages. Nevertheless, a regular reading of all three would support our view that religion is higher on the agenda of *The Times* than the other papers.[12]

In both periods, conventional religion and the secular sacred were most in evidence in *The Times*, with *The Sun* being full of references to common religion (Figure 2.2). The *Yorkshire Evening Post* was evenly balanced in its portrayal of both conventional and common religion. *The Times* made far more reference to conventional categories such as Roman Catholicism, Islam, Judaism, modern religious issues and church history than the other papers, folk religion was the most frequently covered common religious topic, and secular sacred issues were given serious treatment. In *The Sun* references to religious cosmology were plentiful, but mostly metaphorical. In terms of common religion, folk practices (Halloween), gambling and fortune-telling (especially horoscopes) were all well covered in 2008.[13] The *Yorkshire Evening Post* offered more coverage of 'ghosts'

---

[11]   Cupitt 1999; Heelas and Woodhead 2005.

[12]   The continuity of space given to religious reporting in *The Times* in the last four decades is noted in Gill 2012, p. 50.

[13]   *The Times* and *The Sun* provided an interesting contrast. The former was seen as trustworthy in covering serious and traditional issues, whereas the latter was renowned for its sceptical humour and irony. However, *The Sun* did include serious stories, especially editorials and columns, with its implied readership – as in the case of other conservative British papers – deemed to be white Christian. Although it favoured sensationalism, gossip,

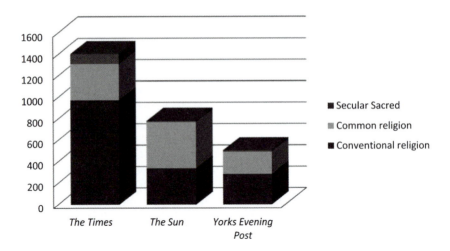

Figure 2.2   Newspaper references by type, 2008

and 'superstitions', such as touching wood and saluting magpies, especially in its advertisements. There were frequent references to religious practice, particularly life-cycle rites. Furthermore, in both periods, it made more reference to the smaller Christian churches, and to Buddhism and Sikhism than other papers, with fewer references to Islam and Judaism (which were in greater evidence in *The Times*). This brings the local dimension of the paper's coverage to the fore. It did not offer as much foreign news or elite history as *The Times*; rather, it focused attention on its multicultural and religiously-diverse local community.

If we turn now to different newspaper genres, we can see that, although religion was rarely front page news, it was covered throughout the papers, in every kind of genre (Figure 2.3). It featured frequently in news stories, but also in editorials and comments – signalling the significance of general debate about religion. Perhaps more surprisingly, it was often mentioned in the sports pages. These references were frequently but by no means exclusively to be found in *The Sun*, and mostly referred to common religion – especially to luck, gambling and magic – and also to religious cosmology.[14] Religion had a significant place in newspaper supplements, particularly in relation to culture, travel, jobs and health. Some of the references were about religion as cultural heritage and tourism, as well as to Greek mythology in theatre reviews. The 'other' genres, which included headlines without stories attached and other unclassified sections, reflected the general coverage except that they included more than 50 references to horoscopes. Religion was covered most

---

celebrities and witty stories, it should not be thought of as non-ideological. Allan 2004, pp. 102–7.

[14]   For more discussion of religion in the sports pages, see Chapter 6.

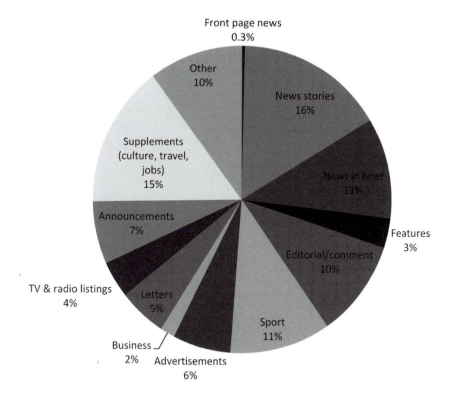

Figure 2.3   Percentages of religious references in different newspaper genres, 2008 (all papers)

in features and opinion pieces in *The Times*, in advertisements and the sports pages in *The Sun*, and in announcements and 'What's On' in the local paper.

Comparing coverage of religion and the secular sacred in the newspapers in 1982 and 2008, we may conclude that:

- There were more references in 2008 than in 1982 at least in part because of the increase in pages.
- In the two periods, in-depth literal coverage of both conventional religious and secular sacred themes was more in evidence in *The Times* than in the other papers, with more common religion and metaphorical references in *The Sun*. The *Evening Post* covered a broader range of religions, in conformity with its local context.
- In both periods, there were more references to Christianity – Catholicism in particular – than to any other religion, Islam accounting for significantly more references in 2008 than in 1982 (though many were negative and concerned extremism and terrorism).

- There was more newspaper coverage of religious diversity in 2008 than in 1982.

Whilst the extent of coverage of religion and the secular sacred was greater in 2008, there was less in-depth and informed treatment. In *The Times* in 1982, where a high degree of Christian knowledge on the part of readers was assumed, references to Protestantism, to named Christian denominations and Christian theology were not infrequent. By 2008, they had declined in number. Although there was greater coverage of religions other than Christianity by then, those religions rarely received in-depth treatment or informed analysis.

Television Coverage in Depth

We turn now to television. In our week of viewing in February 2009, more than half the references (51 per cent) were to conventional religion, but common religion was not far behind, with 47 per cent. If varieties of Christianity and Islam dominated the newspaper coverage in 2008, then the same could be said for the television coverage a few months later, even though the percentage of references remained lower and the nature of the portrayals was quite different (see Appendix 3).

In both 1982 and 2009, as in the newspapers, there were more references to Roman Catholicism than to Protestantism. The forthcoming Papal visit in 1982 accounted for the higher figure back then. In 2009, part of the explanation lay in the fact that the Church of England was referred to implicitly rather than explicitly, for example, in images of village churches or in non-specific references to 'the church'. We were forced to categorize such references 'Christian general' or 'Church general'. Christian denominations other than the Catholic Church and the Church of England were barely mentioned at all.

Of the other religions referenced on television in 1982, Judaism was the most frequently featured because of events in Israel, with Islam receiving far less coverage (less than 1 per cent) – it was hardly mentioned in the international TV news back then. In 2009, Islam was referenced more often than other established traditions, including Catholicism and Protestantism, but much less so than in the newspapers. The emphasis was again on violence, including references to the Taleban and al-Qaeda. Almost half the references dealt with Islam outside Britain, particularly in Afghanistan and Iraq, but also in Turkey and Iran. Other religious traditions were covered, especially in *Around the World in 80 Faiths* (BBC2), which briefly presented a plethora of different religions and their rituals. Of new religious movements, yoga was most frequently referenced, though others were mentioned, in historical documentaries and fiction series.[15]

---

[15]   Reference to alternative religions and spiritualities included a yoga practitioner in *Wanted Down Under* (BBC1, 4 February 2009), references to alchemy, magic, the occult,

Visually, religion was often represented by religious buildings, symbols, practices, and people in religious dress. Because of the difficulty of classifying such images with any certainty, they were often assigned to general categories. 'Religion General', for example, consisted of references to unspecified church buildings, to nuns and monasteries, priests and clergy, and material items such as crosses, rosaries and the Holy Grail. 'Religious Practice' included references to life-cycle rites, prayer, remembrance and meditation, whilst 'Religious Cosmology' included oaths and petitions as well as common idioms such as 'Oh my God', 'Bloody hell' and 'Jesus!' Indeed, only a quarter of references to religious cosmology were literal, most being metaphorical: they tell us more about our use of religious expressions than our actual beliefs.

Turning now to common religion, as in the newspapers, in both 1982 and 2009 references to 'luck' and 'gambling' dominated (see Appendix 3). With 'magic', these were often to be found in advertisements, but also in entertainment programmes and game shows. Ghosts were popular in 1982, and the 'unexplained' gained ground in 2009, particularly in mystery dramas. Despite their frequency, little weight can be placed on them because they were predominantly passing references and often metaphorical. References to mythology, however, were literal: more than half were to Greek and Roman traditions, and occurred in quiz shows such as BBC1's *The Weakest Link*. This suggests that, even though people do not believe in ancient mythology or practice its rituals, knowledge about them is important for a well-rounded education. Spirits and spiritualism, though not a dominant theme, were referred to more than many major religions, including Hinduism, Buddhism, Sikhism and Judaism. Nearly all such references were in television dramas and films, showing that the theme plays an important part in the western popular imaginary. Native American religions and Shamanism were also mentioned, stereotypically depicted, for example, in the figure of the wise old American Indian medicine man consulted for cures, clairvoyance and contact with the spirit world.

With more references in 2009 than 1982, secularism and atheism accounted for two thirds of the relatively small number of references to the secular sacred on television, with the religion versus science debate also represented. Although it would be easy to pass over these references in light of their numerical insignificance, in Chapter 5 we argue that there are good reasons to take them seriously.

Turning now to the different television channels, we see that in 2009 the majority of references (60 per cent) were on ITV1: 19 per cent on BBC1 and 21 per cent on BBC2; the comparable figures in 1982 had been 44 per cent for YTV,

---

demonology and witchcraft in a documentary about Shakespeare (*The South Bank Show*, ITV, 8 February), sofa-style chat about Harry Potter-esque popular mythology and the occult in *This Morning* (ITV, 4 February), and references to magic and astrology in *Scoop* (BBC2, 7 February), a Woody Allen film about a Tarot card killer.

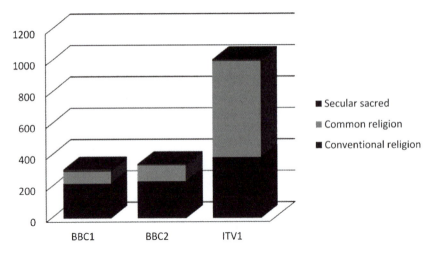

Figure 2.4   Television references by type, 2009

35 per cent for BBC1 and 21 per cent for BBC2.[16] There are several explanations for the higher number of references on independent television, the first being that airtime was greater, as both BBC1 and BBC2 broadcast educational and children's programmes which we excluded from our analysis. The second explanation concerns advertisements. In 2009, more than half of all ITV1's references were in adverts, making it by far the most popular genre for religion references on television (see Figure 2.5). However, even if we remove this genre, we find that the number of references on ITV1 still exceeded the numbers on other TV channels. We are left to conclude then that, in 2009 – despite a near complete lack of formal religious broadcasting – ITV1 was more likely than BBC1 or BBC2 to refer to religion.[17]

In Figure 2.4, a comparison between the types of references on the different TV channels shows that the BBC's profile was more on the conventional side, and common religion dominated on ITV1. This was partly because of the abundance of references to 'luck' and 'gambling' on the latter. Game shows, and the luck needed to succeed in them, constituted an important part of ITV1 programming, especially its day-time provision. In that sense ITV1 was more like *The Sun*, and the BBC more like *The Times*. It is noteworthy, however, that there were also

---

[16]   Note the independent TV channel names: Yorkshire Television (YTV) in 1982, and ITV1 in 2009.

[17]   By the time of our research in 2009, although documentaries on religion were aired on Channel 4, formal religious broadcasting on independent television was being phased out. In 2010, the post of Commissioning Editor for Religion at Channel 4 was axed, and only one hour of religious broadcasting was scheduled for ITV, with none on Channel 5. Beckford 2010.

more references to conventional religion on ITV1 than on either BBC1 or BBC2. Most, however, were general and abstract, and often related to religious practices and cosmology. In terms of common religion, ITV1 did not cover folk religion and practices as often as the other channels, but it had more references to most other aspects. Whilst *The Times* dominated references to the secular sacred in the newspapers, references were more evenly spread, though small in number, on television, with atheism mentioned on all channels.

Although, in 1982, BBC1 and YTV were not dissimilar in the extent and nature of their references to conventional religion, by 2009 the BBC channels differed quite considerably from ITV1, both in terms of in-depth treatment and expected level of audience knowledge.[18] They made more reference to Protestant churches, church history, religious texts and new religious movements. They covered most established non-Christian religious traditions. In terms of common religion, the emphasis was on folk religion and practices, spiritualism, spirit possession, gambling and the unexplained being covered less frequently. In relation to the secular sacred, the focus was on atheism, secularism and the relation between religion and science. The number of references to religions other than Christianity on BBC2 was exceptionally high in 2009 because of the series *Around the World in 80 Faiths*, a consequence being that religious concepts and doctrines were mentioned more often on BBC2 than elsewhere.

Turning to programme genres, in 1982, most references to religion were in the news and current affairs (34 per cent) and plays and films (31 per cent).[19] Perhaps not surprisingly, even though only 3 per cent of the airtime was dedicated to religious broadcasting, 18 per cent of the references appeared there. Entertainment produced 10 per cent of the references and sport, 7 per cent. No data were collected on the genre of advertising. By 2009, things had changed (Figure 2.5).

Most references were not in formal religious broadcasting: 5 per cent of the references appeared in just 1 per cent of airtime.[20] News and current affairs remained a key genre for religion references, with entertainment becoming more important than plays and films, and sport less significant than it had once been (with a reduction of airtime due to competition from satellite and cable channels). The most popular genre for religion references, however, was advertising.

In fact, the greatest differences between television and newspaper coverage of religion concerned these two genres. The sports pages in the papers were full of references to religion, whereas sports broadcasting – despite accounting for

---

[18] An analysis of Channel 4 at this time would have shown it to have had more in common with the BBC channels than ITV1.

[19] Knott 1984a, pp. 14–15.

[20] Of 315 broadcast hours in the week of viewing, the breakdown by genre was as follows: news and current affairs (111 hrs 5 mins), light entertainment (99 hrs 15 mins), plays and films (67 hrs 30 mins), sport (16 hours 15 mins), religion (3 hrs 15 mins), advertisements (17 hrs 40 mins).

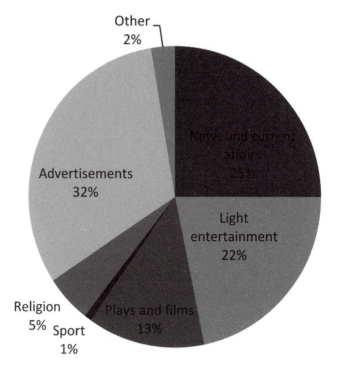

Figure 2.5   References by television genre, 2009

more than 16 hours in the first week of February 2009 – had very few references.[21] And, whilst religion was certainly evident in printed advertisements, it flourished in adverts on television. With just under 6 per cent of airtime, adverts contained more than 30 per cent of the references to religion. A closer look at the kinds of references revealed that the majority were to common religion, principally to the unexplained, magic, luck and gambling. Most of the conventional references in advertisements were to three themes: life cycle rites, prayer and meditation. Religious references were used extensively in advertising because they contributed to idealizing products and their uses – by demonstrating that ordinary people could overcome or control everyday problems with their help, and by connecting such problems to ideal or magical scenarios. This explains the frequent references to feel-good meditation, weddings, magic, mythology and wizardry. It is no coincidence that this kind of language was noted even in early theorizing about advertisements: Raymond Williams called advertising 'the magic system'.[22]

In the first week of February 2009, religious broadcasting was limited to 1 hour 35 minutes on BBC1, and 1 hour 40 minutes on BBC2, with none at all on

---

[21]   See Chapter 6.

[22]   Williams 1980, pp. 184–91.

ITV1. Nevertheless, despite just 1 per cent of available airtime (down from 3 per cent in 1982), it represented 5 per cent of the references (down from 18 per cent in 1982). Not surprisingly, conventional religion dominated (with 95 per cent of the references). In common with other genres, religious broadcasting highlighted religious practice, and referred to both 'religion' and 'Christianity' in general terms (without specifying denomination), but it differed in providing more coverage of other religions.

Although religious worship and music programmes had featured significantly in 1982, with *This is the Day*, *Morning Worship*, *Songs of Praise* and *Sing to the Lord*, there had also been two major religious documentary series, *Credo* and *Everyman*. During the first week of February 2009, BBC Religion and Ethics broadcast three programmes: *Songs of Praise*, *The Big Questions* and *Around the World in 80 Faiths* (the last of which was deemed by focus group participants to be a good example of the positive media portrayal of religion). These three programmes were very different, one being a long-standing traditional Christian music programme set within the format of a church service (*Songs of Praise*), the second a Sunday morning debate on contemporary religious and ethical issues (*The Big Questions*), and the third, an episode from a series about religious diversity in a global context, presented by a media-savvy Anglican priest (*Around the World in 80 Faiths*).[23]

A key transformation in religious broadcasting since the early 1980s has been the reduction in coverage of worship. This may explain in part why viewers do not always recognise a 'religious programme' (one produced by BBC Religion and Ethics) when they see one. They may classify it as a discussion programme or a documentary rather than a religious programme *per se*. In the 1980s, approximately 75 per cent of 'religious output consisted of acts of worship or programmes of hymn singing' a figure which, by the end of the 1990s, had dropped to 25 per cent.[24] Even today, religious broadcasting is more often than not on a Sunday, and has been pushed to the margins of the schedule (mornings, late afternoon or late at night, though religious documentaries are sometimes aired at peak times). Religious programmes are often stereotyped as the sole domain of the religious and elderly. However, viewing figures suggest that they often compete favourably with other special interest and debating programmes.[25]

The question of cuts to religious broadcasting was brought to the Church of England's General Synod in 2010, some ten years after a similar intervention had produced a vote of censure directed at the BBC.[26] In 2010, Synod softened its criticism but nevertheless expressed the view that more and better coverage of religion by all broadcasters was desirable. The BBC's Head of Religion and Ethics, Aaqil Ahmed, noted in response that, unlike other channels, the BBC was

---

23 See chapters 3 and 5.
24 Viney 1999, pp. 5–6.
25 Mark Lawson 2011.
26 Ibid. Holmes 2010.

not underselling religion in its schedule: 'The charter says we should do 110 hours. We're doing 164 this year.'[27]

Comparing coverage of religion and the secular sacred on television in 1982 and 2009, the following conclusions may be drawn:

- There were a similar number of references in both periods showing that coverage had not increased or declined.
- In both more reference was made to religion on independent television, than on either of the BBC channels, but the margin had increased by 2009 largely as a result of references to religion in advertisements. Many of these references were metaphorical.
- In both periods, Christianity – Catholicism in particular – was covered more than any other religion; the number of references to Islam increased significantly between 1982 and 2009.
- However, overall coverage of religious diversity was only slightly higher in 2009 than in 1982.
- The number of hours dedicated to formal religious broadcasting had declined, with no scheduled programmes on ITV1 in 2009, but three aired by the BBC.

Despite a similar number of references in the two periods, in-depth coverage had declined, with important exceptions.

References to Religion and the Secular Sacred:
Literal or Metaphorical, Main Issue or In-passing?

So far we have described and analysed the media portrayal of religion and the secular sacred in terms of the number and distribution of references, principal themes and media genres. In analysing findings from 1982 and 2008–2009 we also considered whether references were literal or metaphorical, and whether they were passing references or main items in stories or programmes. Such considerations are important because they tell us about how religion is deployed in the media and what status it is given. Literal references are made to actual religious groups, experiences, beliefs and practices, with metaphorical ones employed to create an effect by likening non-religious things to religious ones. Religious metaphors may lend weight, mystery or significance to a non-religious subject. They may be used to convey a negative attitude: 'blind faith', 'religious zeal' and 'fundamentalism' all being terms used of secular people or issues.

---

[27]   'Church of England concerned by "Religious TV cuts"', BBC News, 10 February 2010; but see Woolley 2012, p. 66.

Table 2.1   Literal and metaphorical references, 1982 and 2008–2009

	Newspapers 1982	Newspapers 2008	Television 1982	Television 2009
Literal references %	87	75	88	80
Metaphorical references %	13	25	12	20

In 1982, the majority of references to religion on TV and in the papers were literal (87.5 per cent), and just 12.5 per cent metaphorical; in 2009 the percentage of metaphorical references had risen to 22 per cent (see Table 2.1). In both periods, in *The Times* and the *Yorkshire Evening Post* literal references dominated, with a greater number of metaphorical references in *The Sun*. By 2009, almost half of *The Sun*'s references were metaphorical, religious terminology being used freely in non-religious contexts to create atmosphere or to indicate – often in a humorous or ironic way – the role of unexplained or magical forces, hope for a miracle, or the need for prayer.[28] The percentage of metaphorical references was higher on independent television than either of the BBC channels. Advertisements, comedy, entertainment, and sports reporting were key genres, and metaphorical references were more likely to draw on conventional religious topics than common religious or secular sacred ones, though there was a more even spread in 2009 than in 1982.

Given the widespread nature of references to religion and the creative use of religious language, it is not surprising that most references to religion (though not the secular sacred) were made in articles and programmes where religion was not the main issue: 95 per cent of all references to religion on television were of this kind, and 80 per cent of those in the newspapers. More than 20 per cent of references to religion in *The Times* appeared in articles where religious issues were the main subjects, compared with 15 per cent in *The Sun*. On ITV1, only 4 per cent of references appeared in programmes where religion was the principal issue, with this figure rising to 10 per cent for BBC2. We might hypothesize then that tabloid newspapers and commercial TV channels are less likely than others to report in depth on religion. Moreover, this may explain the widespread impression that there is little media treatment of religion: many religion references go unnoticed because those monitoring them focus solely on articles and programmes in which religion is the main subject. Such critics often miss the large number of passing references and discussion of religion in articles and programmes where it is not the major focus of attention. We would argue that such references are nonetheless important in reflecting the place and role of religion in everyday mediated experience, and in contributing substantially to media representations of religion, the subject of the next four chapters.

---

[28]   See Chapter 6 for further discussion of metaphorical references, particularly in sports reporting.

Media References to Religion

British media coverage of religion in the last thirty years has been dominated by Christianity, though this dominance has declined in recent years as greater attention has been given to other religions. Seen in relation to the relatively small number of Muslims in Britain in the late 2000s, Islam was the most over-represented of the established religious traditions, but its media image was predominantly negative, the majority of stories relating to terrorism and extremism (see Chapter 4). As other scholars have suggested, this tells us a good deal about Islam's increased political importance both nationally and internationally, as well as revealing many of the anxieties that surround it.[29] We would argue that none of the non-Christian religious traditions is under-represented as such, but also acknowledge that the extent of the coverage of Islam may overshadow the number of references to Judaism, Hinduism, Buddhism and Sikhism and thus give the impression that they are under-reported. References are by no means limited to established religious traditions, with extensive treatment of common religion, and some attention given to new religious movements, informal spirituality, atheism and secularism. Furthermore, the extent of the newspaper and television coverage of Christianity should not be taken to mean that it is unambiguously promoted. Rather, it tends to be in the background, embedded in Britain's culture.[30] This superficial treatment – of Christianity as wallpaper – is reflected in the many fleeting references and images to practices, concepts or buildings, and the relative paucity of informed analysis or theological discussion.

Based as they are on selected papers and TV channels, these results should be taken as hypotheses for future study rather than as representative of the nature and extent of religion and the secular sacred in the British media more generally. Nevertheless, what seems clear is that the view that the media coverage of religion is in decline was not borne out by the figures. Between 1982 and 2008-2009, there was a rise in the number of references overall, though with arguably less in-depth treatment, and an increase in media coverage of both religious diversity and the secular sacred. Religion was not always seen as a problem, though it was rarely celebrated. Frequently, it was simply taken for granted as part of the landscape, heritage and language, with religion observed more in linguistic motifs and visual images than in dedicated programmes and in-depth articles.[31]

---

[29]   For example, Poole 2002; Moore, Mason and Lewis 2008.

[30]   For further discussion, see Chapter 3.

[31]   For media celebration of religion, see Chapter 8 on the Papal visits; for religion in landscape, heritage and language, see Chapter 3.

Chapter 3

Media Representations of Christianity in Public Life

The irony of religion's place in British life was highlighted in February 2009 when *The One Show*, BBC1's early evening magazine programme, asked the question, 'Are we too embarrassed to talk about God?'[1] The public media examination of this intimate issue disclosed the success of secularism in Britain in making religion, or at least mainstream Christianity, a private matter.[2] The show's roving reporter, Anita Rani – embodying the confidence of Britain's minority communities in posing such a question to its majority population – met with predictable responses from interviewees who 'don't really talk about it', who discuss it 'only if I had to', or who would 'rather not answer'.[3] Set up to juxtapose white middle-class embarrassment on the subject with minority ease – 'I don't mind talking about it because I'm a Muslim' – the show toyed with discomfort and religious decline in equal measure, sensing a relationship between the two but unsure how to explain it: 'With every passing decade Britain becomes more secular. Any topic is acceptable in polite conversation except religion.'[4]

Against a backdrop of churches with empty pews and the image of an 'atheist bus' proclaiming 'There's no God so stop worrying and enjoy yourself', and a soundtrack of R.E.M's 'Losing my religion' and George Michael's 'Faith', the ten-minute segment adopted a common BBC strategy, of gentle mockery but with serious intent. It appeared to be neutral whilst being firmly situated in a particular normative position that is so deeply culturally embedded it is invisible to the eye: 'The secular is so much part of our modern life, it is not easy to grasp it directly'.[5] This media standpoint – of non-religious, pro-science secularism – set its report in the context of the decline in Christian participation (with empty pews and the statistics of secularization), using the foil of a demonstratively American Christian President, Obama, to expose the disquiet of Britain's political establishment

---

[1]   *The One Show*, BBC1, 3 February 2009. The show's presenters were Adrian Childs and Christine Bleakley; the resident reporter and interviewer was Anita Rani.

[2]   An Ipsos MORI poll for the Richard Dawkins Foundation in February 2012 found that 78 per cent of those polled agreed religion should be a private matter; 74 per cent said they did not want religion to have any special influence on public policy. Field 2012.

[3]   *The One Show*.

[4]   Ibid. Anita Rani, *The One Show* reporter and interviewer.

[5]   Asad 2003, p. 16.

who no longer 'do God' for fear of misinterpretation or accusations of bias.[6] The carefully selected, all-male interviewees – a black Christian theologian, a white inner-city Anglican priest, an author, and a moderate white pro-religion scientist (a BBC1 resident expert) – confirmed the show's findings, that the 'crisis' lies with white British middle-class Christians. Minority Christians, along with other religious minorities, are 'comfortable with their faith'. Religion in general has been 'othered' in Britain; it gets 'a bad press' from scientists and has become 'an issue of privacy' which exudes embarrassment.[7]

Anita Rani summarized the emotional tenor of the issue: as 'one woman said, it's like telling people you don't have a job! That's how people see religion'.[8] To interrogate this more deeply, we must ask why people don't mention their unemployment or religiosity – because it's embarrassing and you don't want other people to know these things about you. Why not? Because religion (a bit like unemployment) is viewed negatively and has been constituted in secularist discourse as a private matter.

The One Show's brief examination of this topic simultaneously explored and further endorsed the normative discourses of Christian decline and the secularist separation of private religion from secular public life. At issue were Christianity and class – particularly the white middle class – two aspects of Britain's legacy, along with its colonial past, which in recent decades have generated secular liberal unease and shame.

The One Show's portrayal is just one of many possible renditions of Christianity, some of which we observed in our research and others that were noticeable by their absence. It suggests several important themes to which we will return later. First, it highlights the role of media discourse on mainstream Christianity, its social significance, place in public life and location within a secular context. Secondly, it exposes portrayals of the relationship between Christianity, other religions, atheism and science, in the process inviting us to consider how other religious and ideological positions are used in the construction of media representations of Christianity. Thirdly, it highlights important associations between the nation, class, ethnicity, Christianity and religion more generally, and the way in which these are rendered and exploited in the media for different social, political and emotional effects. Finally, it raises the question of what media portrayals of Christianity suggest about media values and rhetoric, how Britain is being imagined in the early twenty-first century, and invites comparison with representations of Christianity and the image of Britain offered by the mainstream media in the 1980s.

We begin by examining some of the statistical evidence from our two studies before considering four themes in more detail: Christianity and the state; Christianity as cultural tradition and heritage; the clergy, moral responsibility and abuse; and Christianity, its 'others' and the 'othering' of Christianity.

---

[6]   *The One Show*, interview with ex-Prime Minister, Tony Blair.

[7]   Ibid. Quotations from Robert Beckford, Robert Winston and Anita Rani.

[8]   Ibid. Anita Rani.

Christianity and Public Life: Decline or Rise? Continuity or Change?

The One Show presented some widely-accepted statistics about decreasing church attendance and the predicted decline of congregational Christianity whilst also representing this fate visually and aurally. The use of two foils – God in American public discourse and the presence on UK streets of the atheist bus – reinforced the sense of a Britain where the Christian God has a shadowy and uneasy presence, if such a God has relevance at all. Although they cannot be entirely disentangled, it is useful to differentiate the *presentation of information* (in this case statistics) from *media representations* in order to appreciate that religion – like any other aspect of social and cultural life – once processed by the media appears as if 'through a glass darkly'.[9] This distortion effect is what excites criticism among religious commentators. Religious ideas, practices, symbols, experiences and statements that are taken up by the media seem, to critics, to undergo a change for the worse in the course of media reproduction.

What is important here is not so much whether such distortions constitute inaccurate portrayals as how such distorted effects are to be read and analysed. What do they tell us about religious change in Britain, about the media construction of contemporary religion, and the media themselves? Although, on the one hand, it is useful to draw on the analogy of mirrors and distortion in order to complicate the idea that the media merely reflect society; on the other, it creates an unhelpful distinction between so-called reality and its representations.[10] As we saw in Chapter 1, it is not a straightforward matter of there being an uncontested empirical socio-religious reality on which everyone can agree. Sociologists hold differing views about it. Religious commentators do too. Statistics, sociological interpretations, religious perspectives and media portrayals are all forms of representation with their own logics and associated distorting effects.

In this chapter we analyse newspaper and television portrayals of Christianity in public life in the 1980s and 2000s in the context of the sociological debates we introduced earlier on secularization, resacralization, mediatization and the new visibility of religion.[11] We test three trajectories identified by Guest, Olson and Wolffe in their account of Christianity's 'loss of monopoly' in Britain: the decline of church association; continuity, culture and identification; and changing Christian commitments.[12] Do media representations confirm these trajectories and

---

[9] *The Bible: King James Version*, 1 Corinthians 13:12. Gledhill 2012, pp. 89–98.

[10] Hall (ed.) 1997.

[11] In Chapter 2 quantitative content analysis was used to examine the extent of media coverage of conventional and common religion and the secular sacred. Here and in the following chapters, we use qualitative content analysis and discourse analysis to examine articles and programmes in more depth to uncover how religion and secular sacred issues are represented and what discourses are endorsed and constructed. Deacon et al. 2007.

[12] Guest, Olson and Wolffe 2012, pp. 60–73.

the apparent loss of monopoly? Indeed, do they contribute to the marginalization or even persecution of Christianity proclaimed and deplored by some Christian commentators?[13]

First of all, then, has there been a decline or rise in the number of references to Christianity in the media from the early 1980s to the late 2000s? What denominations, issues, beliefs and practices are featured, and what has changed? How can we explain new developments and continuities, and how are we to understand changes in the number of references in the context of sociological, religious and media debates?

In Chapter 2, we discussed the rise in references to Christianity, Islam and atheism/secularism. The Christian increase was the smallest in relative terms and was cancelled out largely by the growth in newspaper size. Nevertheless, it is reasonable to assume that, despite the decline in church attendance and membership across the period, there was no commensurate decline in the media coverage of Christianity.[14]

What was the nature of these references and how – if at all – had they changed?

As we noted in Chapter 2, in both studies, references to Protestantism were exceeded by those to Roman Catholicism, most appearing in the newspapers, particularly *The Times*. By 2008–2009, however, Protestant and Catholic references were exceeded by general references to churches, clergy and Christianity in which denomination was not specified. This differed considerably to the 1980s when the majority of Christian references explicitly identified one of the major denominations, interest in Pope John Paul II and his forthcoming Papal visit boosting references to Roman Catholicism. We might speculate that, by the time of the second study, the British public's knowledge about Christianity had declined to the point where mainstream denominational differences were no longer widely understood and, except where appropriate in news or documentaries, journalists, reporters and programme makers declined to mention them. Nevertheless, curiosity about religious as opposed to denominational diversity meant that a greater range of alternative Christian movements and groups were mentioned in 2008–2009 than the 1980s, including the Salvation Army, the Quakers, the Yoido Full Gospel Church, the Mormons and Christian Science.

References in several other broad categories – religious cosmology, religious practice, and religious concepts and doctrines – were predominantly Christian in kind. Although such themes have meaning and significance in other religious contexts, particularly Islam, in Britain their cultural origins are Judeo-Christian. When reference is made to them in the media – whether in text, spoken word or picture, and whether the reference is literal or metaphorical – the inflection is generally Christian, though readers and audiences are free to make their own interpretations.

---

[13]   Most Rev. Lord Carey of Clifton and other signatories 2010; Hutchinson 2010; Westminster Declaration of Christian Conscience 2010; Christians in Parliament 2012.

[14]   Gill's data supports this view. Gill 2012, pp. 45–60.

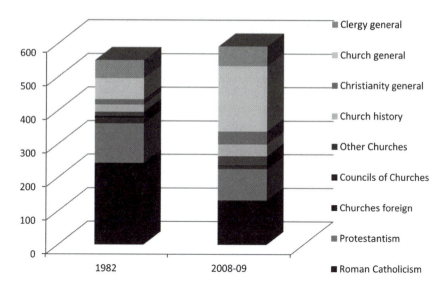

Figure 3.1 References to Christianity 1982 and 2008–2009

By 2008–2009 media references to ecumenism, church unity and church councils, not infrequent in the 1980s, had been superseded by those to inter-faith dialogue and encounter. References to religious texts and religious history extended beyond the Bible and church history to include other religions. But what was missing was any significant and in-depth reference to what Guest, Olson and Wolffe referred to as 'changing commitments'.[15] Evangelical Christianity, new Christian expressions, different forms of ethnic Christianity, particularly Pentecostal movements, were almost completely absent on television and in the press, despite their global – and indeed British – growth and vitality in the early twenty-first century. One story in *The Times* about the translation of the Bible into Jamaican patois and the response of the Jamaican diaspora in Britain and beyond, brief references to Polish Catholicism in reports on the murder of a young Polish women in the *The Sun* and *Yorkshire Evening Post*, and the depiction of Ugandan Christians, together with voodoo and ritual killing, in BBC2's crime drama *Moses Jones* completed an inadequate and partial representation of Britain's changing Christian commitments.[16]

All these occurred outside formal religious broadcasting and reporting. Whilst this reflected a general trend away from media protection of religion by the time of our second study, the commitment remained among selected media sources to

---

[15]   Guest et al. 2012.

[16]   Cohen 2008; brief news reports in *The Sun* and the *Yorkshire Evening Post*, 12 November 2008; *Moses Jones*, BBC2, 2 February 2009.

air and report religious programmes and stories.[17] Viney's survey, of the changing place and nature of religious broadcasting in 2000, showed that neither the mission to represent and serve Britain's diverse religious communities nor the number of scheduled hours on public television had changed in the twenty years from 1980 to 2000.[18] However, by 2010, although Channel 4 and the BBC remained committed, with the latter continuing to support a Religion and Ethics unit, ITV no longer supported religious broadcasting. A general decrease in hours was borne out by the decline in the number of dedicated religious programmes shown in a single week, from six across BBC1, BBC2 and ITV in 1982 to three in 2009.[19] Christian worship was no longer featured, *Songs of Praise* being the sole focus for Christian music and church life. Other religions and atheism, as well as Christianity, were represented in two of the three programmes.

The decline in media coverage of Christian association was not matched by an increase in attention to Christian innovation and diversity – what Guest, Olson and Wolffe called 'changing commitments'. However, the growth in the number of references to general non-denominational Christian matters in text and image reflects as well as endorses the notion that Christianity remains important in terms of popular identification.

Christianity and the State

In an interview in *The Times* in October 2008 the Immigration Minister, Phil Woolas, predicted the disestablishment of the Church of England within 50 years: 'I think it will happen because it's the way things are going … a modern society is multi-faith.'[20] Reform of the House of Lords, Britain's second parliamentary chamber, would lead, he said, to the Church of England being stripped of its special privilege as the Church established in law with the monarch as its Supreme Governor. Following his statement, the government denied it had any such intention, and sought to reassure the Church.

The issue of the status and privilege of the Church of England is one that is periodically debated by clerics, academics and the media, the cynical view being that it should remain 'established' because of the legal complexities that would be required to disestablish it.[21] But it is also the case that many religious groups and individuals support it, seeing an established church as a voice and protection for people of all faiths. In 2008, Woolas's comments led to the debate being reignited in *The Times*, with an editorial on 'Church and Nation' and a 'For

---

[17]   See Mutanen 2009, for journalist and editorial commitment to reporting religion.

[18]   Viney 1999.

[19]   See Chapter 2 for details. In the same week, Channel 4 broadcast *Christianity: A History*. However, it withdrew its commitment to religious broadcasting in 2011.

[20]   Ford and Gledhill 2008.

[21]   For a summary of arguments and a case for disestablishment, see Weller 2005.

and Against' piece.[22] Many papers ignored the subject, but as a liberal, right-of-centre paper with a close relationship with Britain's political class, *The Times* saw this as an issue it had a responsibility to explain and to express a view on. Its editorial supported the value of open debate, but stressed that 'the Church exists for the nation' in a role of service rather than privilege, a point that was reiterated several times in the days that followed: 'The Church is established to serve, sustain and encourage the establishment of the Christian faith as the ultimate point of reference for government'; 'the Church of England exists not simply for those who come to church, but for every single person who lives within our parish system … Our society and the Church have evolved together. It's part of the tradition of the country.'[23] The editorial was clear on one final point, however, that disestablishment is ultimately an issue for the Church not for politicians.

With *The Times* stating its support for the special role of the Church of England in October, the debate re-emerged two months later when the Archbishop of Canterbury was reported to have said that disestablishment would not be 'the end of the world'.[24] As a left-wing, secular liberal paper, *The Guardian* was quick to report this, quoting a spokesman for the Anglicans: 'To become disestablished would mean … a rethink and sharpening of the prophetic voice of the Church to the nation and this would be welcomed by many.'[25] Breaking the legal contract of church and state would free the former, as *The Times* had indeed noted in October, to become more distinctive and be 'more Christian'.[26]

Quickly picked up in *The Guardian*'s 'Comment is Free' section, opposing positions were voiced. Terry Sanderson, President of the National Secular Society, defended disestablishment and pressed the case for a secular state that would respect equally all interest groups, including religious ones, whilst Giles Fraser stated what he believed to be the Archbishop's true opinion, that, although a case could be made for disestablishment, this was not a position he actually endorsed.[27] Fraser wrote, 'I resist the call for the Church to withdraw from the public sphere. It won't be secularists who get together to organize next year's turkey dinner for the local elderly here in Putney.'[28]

Newspaper debate on what would generally have been considered to a distinctly un-newsworthy subject raised major questions about whether the Church should have a public role or remain a private matter, and on the relationship of Church, state and nation more generally. The issue had also been on the agenda at the time of our first study, in 1982. Then it had not been a single rogue Minister, but traditionalists in both Houses of Parliament who, according to *The Times*, had

---

[22]   *The Times* 2008b; Gibb and Herbert 2008.

[23]   *The Times* 2008a; The Rt Revd Christopher Herbert in Gibb and Herbert 2008.

[24]   Butt 2008.

[25]   Ibid.

[26]   *The Times* 2008b.

[27]   Sanderson 2008; Fraser 2008.

[28]   Fraser 2008.

criticized the Anglican Church for 'acting too much like a sect' in the interests of churchgoers alone and not 'the wider body of people who number themselves among its members'.[29] They had voted for a government Bill to reinforce use of the *Book of Common Prayer* and discourage adoption of the *Alternative Service Book*. The article, penned by Clifford Longley, *The Times* religious correspondent, referred to the Church of England as an 'historic folk church', whilst also noting the divergence of views between politicians and church leaders on key political issues of the day such as international aid and unemployment.

This tension, between the identification of church, nation and people and the prophetic Christian voice of the Church which drives it to speak out on matters of state, remains the crux of the debate about disestablishment today. Back in 1982, criticism was directed at the Church when it raised its voice against the Government's decision that Britain should go to war with Argentina over the Falklands: the Church was seen to be meddling in affairs of state. By 2008, the Church's place at the public table was sufficiently accepted that its potential disestablishment was represented as the withdrawal of a vital public role. What would such a move mean for the nation as a whole? Melanie Phillips, a conservative liberal commentator writing for *The Daily Mail*, summed up such fears: 'Disestablishment might not destroy the Church, but it would be a nail in the coffin for this country's beleaguered identity' and for the monarchy, its 'living embodiment'.[30] In what was an unusual religious reference for the *Mail*, she wrote that 'Protestantism is a core element of this country's identity' and 'infuses its institutions and values', a view shared by *The Telegraph*.[31] Its national status could not be left to the Church hierarchy, she insinuated, as they could not be trusted to put national identity first.

This strong view of Christian centrality will re-emerge later in the chapter, but we conclude this discussion on media representations of church/state relations by returning to the Woolas incident. Rachel Sylvester, one of two *Times* reporters to break the story, drew together many aspects of the debate about religion and politics.[32] Unlike the United States – covered in depth at the time because of the Presidential elections – Britain was not a Christian country, she wrote, but neither was it a secular state like France.[33] She acknowledged that 'its history, culture and constitutional settlement are based on the link between church and state'.[34] However, rather than concurring with Phillips on the idealized centrality of the church in the nation's values and identity, she noted what she saw as the sad reality, that 'the Government's statement of British values is unlikely to make

---

[29]   Longley 1982.

[30]   Phillips 2008.

[31]   Ibid. *The Telegraph* 2008a.

[32]   Sylvester 2008.

[33]   Ibid. See Jacoby 2008.

[34]   Sylvester 2008.

any mention of faith', focusing on queuing rather than Christianity.[35] Taking her lead from a church report, *Moral, But No Compass*, she depicted a government 'fearful of faith', that didn't 'do God', and that was religiously 'illiterate'.[36] This 'God-shaped hole' and abandonment of belief was out of kilter with a population in need of hope at a time of financial crisis.

Sylvester saw fit to criticize the government's religious illiteracy, but it was clear from interviews with other journalists and editors that they believed that criticism ought also to be extended to the Church if and when it crossed the boundary between private faith and public matters. As was the case in 1982, 'If the Church enters politics, you can attack it', noted the editor-in-chief of *The Economist*; Christian leaders could be 'lambasted' for their public views and moral breaches.[37] The separation between private faith and public religion remains significant for the media treatment of religious issues.

Taking these views together, there was a reasonable degree of consensus that the Church of England had an important role to play in national identity and public life, though at times this necessarily exposed it to criticism. There had been a change from the 1980s when the Church was frequently accused of political meddling, but when politicians had sufficient knowledge and interest to comment on Christian affairs. By the late 2000s, the Church was actively involved in social provision and its bishops voiced their views openly in the House of Lords. But few politicians knew much about religion, and those who were Christians found themselves awkwardly situated in an unforgiving secularist climate, in which a prime minister could not 'do God' in public and 'the creeping secularization of politics' pressed a Catholic cabinet minister to resign.[38] The press endorsed the role of the Church of England as a national institution whilst criticizing and at times marginalizing the views and practices of individual Church leaders and Christian politicians.

Christianity as Cultural Tradition and Heritage

In a letter to *The Times* on 25 October 2008, a legal academic likened the English Church to the National Health Service, 'a Christian nation's public religious provision'.[39] He noted that its assets constituted 'the ordinary Englishman's

---

[35] Ibid.

[36] Ibid. Von Hügel Institute, 2008.

[37] Micklethwait (*The Economist*) and Jonathon Wynne-Jones (*The Telegraph*) quoted in Mutanen 2009, p. 30.

[38] Sylvester. Tony Blair, Prime Minister from 1997–2007, was advised not to talk about God in public; Ruth Kelly, a member of Opus Dei, received negative press coverage for disagreeing with government policy on stem cell research on religious grounds and resigned in 2008. See also Christians in Parliament.

[39] Pearce 2008.

involuntary investment in his national cult', and that disestablishment – as well as complex legal changes – would require the Church to be disendowed of its buildings and other goods. This reference to the Church of England as custodian of the nation's cultural heritage highlights another important theme in the media coverage of Christianity in the late 2000s, one referred to often in newspaper travel, review and culture sections, in local as well as national stories, and not infrequently on television.

Churches as Cultural Heritage

That a substantial part of Britain's material religious culture belongs to the nation, to the British people, is something that few are likely to be aware of, and this was certainly the only media reference to it in our period of study. But this does not undermine the importance of Christian culture in the mainstream media representation of Britain as a country, its history and geography. Far from it: on TV, images of rural and urban churches abound. They contribute to the creation of a landscape that is inescapably British, one – like the rural landscape in general – cared for vicariously on behalf of the nation.[40]

In February 2009, in the week of our television research, the country was overwhelmed and incapacitated by snow. TV reporters were shown against scenic backdrops often centred on a church, and references to the local post office, shop, pub and church hall – all traditional markers of village life. Churches appeared in television dramas, as the site of a murderer's confession in *Inspector Morse*, and of dark village dealings in *Midsomer Murders*.[41] Symbolic of a traditional view of British town and village life, churches provide a convenient visual prompt or reference point to invoke a religious and moral ideal as capable of fall or inversion as of reification. They are the potential embodiment of the forces of darkness as well as light. Crucifixes and simple crosses too are used to represent purity and piety in the struggle between good and evil, as in ITV1's supernatural drama, *Demons*, though their desecration is as likely to be depicted, as in the spoof horror film, *Scary Movie*.[42]

Sites already deemed to be sacred as well as those that are spontaneously created may acquire special significance in and beyond the media at times of tragedy and celebration. Whilst churches and other places of prayer and worship may become a locus for grief, remembrance and the signing of books of condolence – then captured on television and in the press – the media are themselves producers of ritual, at times creating powerful, emotionally-charged events that are delivered

---

[40]   Davie 2000; Davie 2007, pp. 21–37.

[41]   *Inspector Morse*, ITV1, 7 February 2009; *Midsomer Murders*, ITV1, 3 February and 4 February 2009.

[42]   *Demons* and *Scary Movie*, both ITV1, 7 February 2009.

to huge audiences.[43] In the process they assign sacred significance to particular times and places, sometimes transforming local acts of offering and witness into major pilgrimage shrines. They invoke and celebrate particular media-oriented values such as live broadcast and mass participation in addition to prioritizing and endorsing more general norms and perspectives such as rallying round the flag, and the focus on religious and political leaders, celebrities and children.[44]

Remembrance, the Nation and Christian Civil Religion

In Britain, a significant example of the mediatization of a local ritual performance was the coverage of events at the village of Wootton Bassett in Wiltshire marking the passage of Britain's war dead from the local air-force base, RAF Lyneham, to the John Radcliffe Hospital in Oxford.[45] Beginning in April 2007, when the route of the funeral cortege was altered and its first journey along the new route coincided with a reunion of the Royal British Legion who came out on the streets to pay their respects, the event grew over the months to draw in hundreds, sometimes thousands of mourners and on-lookers. In October 2008, the Army repaid the honour by parading through the village. Covered by *The Sun*, it was the Army's Chief of General Staff, Sir Richard Dannett, who captured the mood by remarking that it was the things that cost nothing that really mattered, 'a friendly greeting in the street, a prayer in church … [but] the gestures shown by the people of Wootton Bassett surpass these at every level'.[46] However, this simple local generosity was arguably at odds with the growing media coverage. 'Was the town playing host to a "media circus"?', local people asked as the cameras and reporters grew to outnumber mourners.[47] But the lead role of the media in ensuring public awareness of the work and sacrifice made by the armed forces was also stressed:

> [If] repatriations hadn't been covered by the media in the past, would people who wanted to pay their respects, know where they could do so? Would we, the public, be aware of the huge sacrifice the soldiers had made, if the media didn't report their deaths and their homecoming?[48]

---

[43]   For studies of media ritual see Dayan and Katz 1992; Rothenbuhler 1998; Couldry 2003; Cottle 2006, pp. 411–32.

[44]   On media values, see Couldry 2003. Key media rituals include events memorializing those who died in stadium disasters and terrorist attacks, the celebration of royal weddings, jubilees and funerals, and visits of celebrities and dignitaries – such as Popes and Presidents.

[45]   The village was honoured with royal status in October 2011. It is now Royal Wootton Bassett.

[46]   *The Sun* 2008f.

[47]   BBC Wiltshire 2009.

[48]   Ibid.

The mediatization of this local ritual act was deemed to be justified in informing the public and guiding them in how to think and feel about this 'very British way of mourning'.[49]

Annual remembrance services, the laying of wreaths at war memorials and the wearing of poppies provide the principal opportunities for the integration of memories and sentiments about 'those who died to save us'. They too bring together religious tropes with those of the nation. Although the religious concepts and practices that are invoked are rarely specifically Christian – sacrifice, prayer, silent meditation, the honouring of ancestors, offerings, memorial acts, the ritual use of symbols such as crosses and poppies – they are generally given both a Christian and British inflection. As civil religious events, such performances are often sacralized by a member of the clergy, the repetition of a Christian prayer, or by their location outside a church; simultaneously, the Union Jack may be hoisted, and living members of the armed forces and, on particular occasions, royal representatives may be present. The Remembrance Day service on 9 November 2008 at the Cenotaph in London, which specifically commemorated 90 years since the end of the First World War, was appropriately covered in *The Sun*, but more telling of the paper's narrative and rhetorical style were two stories featuring poppies, one about an 'evil thief' who stole the proceeds of poppy sales, and the other about a 'royal staff ban' on the wearing of poppies at banquets in Buckingham Palace to avoid giving offence to international guests.[50] Representing honourable sacrifice for the nation, the iconic poppy was pitched against two classic *Sun* villains: the shameless petty criminal and the practice of political correctness.

In the local newspapers, the *Yorkshire Post* and *Yorkshire Evening Post*, the power of Remembrance Day to focus a locality's history of military involvement came to the fore, with articles on the placing of wooden crosses at a military cemetery, the sprucing up of a war memorial, and the sacrifice of one 'fallen VC hero from Chapeltown'.[51] These papers took the opportunity to explain what and who was being commemorated, not only those who had fallen during the two World Wars, but in more recent battles. The landscape of remembrance was evoked: 'in odd corners are smaller cemeteries, peaceful and unobtrusive. All contain a Great War stone carved with a text from Ecclesiasticus, "Their name liveth for evermore"'.[52] And readers were invited to participate in the process of commemoration by recording what the annual two minutes of silence meant to them.

With the coverage of repatriations and remembrance we see these newspapers operating as providers of historical knowledge as well as co-producers of commemorative ritual and discourse about the nation and its traditions. Christianity contributes symbolically to this civil public religion, and it is present

---

[49]   Jardine and Savill 2009.

[50]   Pyatt 2008; Larcombe and Spratt 2008.

[51]   *Yorkshire Post* 2008a; *Yorkshire Evening Post* 2008e; *Yorkshire Evening Post* 2008d.

[52]   *Yorkshire Post* 2008b; *Yorkshire Post* 2008c.

too in the language used, though its Christian origins are not consciously noted by the media. They are simply taken for granted and – as we shall see later – only become obvious and in need of defending when questioned, discriminated against or deemed irrelevant by secularist, politically correct critics. In the late 2000s no less than the 1980s, the vocabulary of remembrance was replete with references to the 'ultimate sacrifice' of those who had 'fallen' or 'perished' in a 'forgotten foreign field', to 'honouring the war dead' and 'paying respects', to visual images of wooden crosses, poppies, veterans, wreaths and war memorials, and to the reminiscent rendition of the Last Post by a solitary military bugler.[53]

The Judeo-Christian tradition, in its secularizing phase, has contributed the majority of what have now become generic terms in the English language for describing religion, religious institutions, beliefs and practices. It should come as no surprise then that these terms are now understood as inclusive, originating in one religious tradition but appropriated for religiously diverse contexts, such as those civil multi-faith remembrance services that have become the norm in British cities. The notion of Britain as 'multi-faith' is a product of a particular cultural formation based upon and informed by Protestant Christianity's concepts, beliefs and practices, but forged in a process of secular objectification and post-colonialist critique.

Christian History and Music

In *Redefining Christian Britain*, the authors noted that Christian knowledge is not the same as Christian language, the latter being prior.[54] It is possible to use such language without affirming Christian belief or knowing about Christianity as such. Despite this knowledge gap, 'the logic, syntax and grammar of the Christian language surely still shaped communication in post-1945 Britain' and arguably continues to do so today.[55] Their reminder, following Gadamer, that we are all situated in tradition and 'tradition is embodied in language', chimes with what we have seen in the media representation of remembrance tradition. But it is not necessary to await seasonal or festive occasions to see and hear Christian-inflected language in use in the media. Another telling example can be found in sports reporting. Predominantly metaphorical and humorous – though at times seriously literal – such language fittingly captures not only the highs and lows of competition and the status of sports celebrities, but the hope, fear and uncertainty associated with sport.[56] Drawing on tropes from common as well as conventional religion (magic and luck), the most frequently used metaphors involve the divine

---

[53]   *Yorkshire Post* 2008b.

[54]   Garnett, Grimley, Harris, Whyte and Williams 2006.

[55]   Ibid., p. 162.

[56]   Clark 1982, examined the link between dangerous or unpredictable occupations, uncertainty, religion and superstition.

(God, angels, the devil) and Christian practice (prayer and miracles). We discuss this further in Chapter 6.

The media's use of such language is evidence of the embeddedness of Christian concepts and practices in Britain's culture and traditions rather than a self-conscious expression of the nation's piety. Is this a case, as Hjarvard would have it, of Christianity becoming increasing 'banal' in the process of mediatization?[57] For that to be the case, Christianity must previously have been consciously known, understood and represented by the population at large and its popular media. Certainly, it was once more dutifully practised – as statistics on the decline of church attendance suggest – and, according to Brown, its culture was more routinely rehearsed in social life and discourse, but it may never have been deeply thought or widely understood as belief and theology.[58]

Although media use of Christian language during the research was not necessarily an indication of religious knowledge on the part of producers or audiences, there were times when such knowledge was taken seriously. As the nation's public service broadcaster, the BBC makes a commitment in its Charter to inform and educate as well as entertain, and religion continues to be an agreed part of its annual schedule.[59] We end this section on cultural tradition and heritage by focusing on knowledge about Christianity, through history and the arts.

At the very least, this knowledge continued to be recognized as an esoteric interest in BBC game shows such as *University Challenge* and *The Weakest Link*.[60] More importantly, Christianity provided an important historical foil in programmes celebrating the bicentenary of the birth of Charles Darwin and 150 years since the publication of *On the Origin of Species*.[61] It was an important element in a broadly secularist narrative about the development of the theory of evolution. Darwin's relationship with pious friends and family members, especially Reverend Alan Sedgewick, was explored, and Christianity was represented as both a brake on scientific progress and a body of belief and practice that was antithetical to science.[62] 'Can evolution and the Bible both be right?', the BBC asked in *The Big Questions*, with a former Archbishop of Canterbury, Lord Carey, offering a third way of 'theistic evolution' between secularist scientific evolutionists and evangelical creationists, and arguing for the compatibility of science and the Bible. However, in the same week there was also recognition of Darwin's own spiritual

---

[57]   Hjarvard 2011, pp. 119–35.

[58]   Brown 2009. In *Redefining Christian Britain* (p. 159), Garnett et al. cite the striking lack of Christian knowledge noted in Mass Observation's *Puzzled People* in 1947.

[59]   BBC Trust, *Charter and Agreement* (2005).

[60]   *University Challenge*, BBC2, 2 February 2009; *The Weakest Link*, BBC1, 4 February 2009.

[61]   *Charles Darwin and the Tree of Life*, BBC2, 7 February 2009; *The Big Questions*, BBC1, 8 February 2009; *Darwin's Struggle: The Evolution of The Origin of Species*, BBC4, 2 February 2009. For further discussion, see Chapter 5.

[62]   *Charles Darwin and the Tree of Life*.

and emotional struggle, his experimental journey being narrated as one of 'sacred' discovery.[63] Across these programmes we witnessed a 'mixed discourse' in which Christianity was represented variously in opposition to science, as an important part of Darwin's world view and environment, and as capable of theological change, with the secular sacred also portrayed.[64]

In the same week, Channel 4 – not formally part of our study – contributed to public information in its eight part series, *Christianity: A History*. The English Reformation was the subject, presented through the eyes of a surprising choice of commentator: Ann Widdecombe, Conservative Member of Parliament and a convert to Roman Catholicism. Despite the singular view – almost certainly at odds with the opinions of many British Anglicans – that the Reformation was one of the 'saddest periods in Christian history', the programme provided a detailed account of the religious politics, theological innovation, vernacular Bible translation and the lives of ordinary Christians at the time. Commissioned by Aaqil Ahmed, then Head of Religion at Channel 4, and later to become Head of Religion and Ethics at the BBC, the series was one of several produced at a time when the quality if not the quantity of religious broadcasting was said to be at its peak.[65]

A 'broadcasting institution' and mainstay of the BBC's religious provision, *Songs of Praise* was first aired in 1961 and is now a long-standing and respected part of the media's own heritage.[66] In 1982, one of several programmes featuring Christian worship and hymn singing, it had an audience of over 8 million viewers.[67] On 8 February 2009, some 3.5 million viewers watched an episode featuring the Church of St Martin-in-the-Fields, and its recent renovation, architectural significance and place in London's church history, its role in serving the homeless, as well as some fine hymn singing from a mixed white and black congregation and talented choir. The programme's regular format – honed over five decades – has reinforced the popular image of the importance to Christianity of church music and worship. Despite its appeal to older rather than younger Christians, and to those assured of their faith rather than to newcomers or sceptics, Mark Lawson, the cultural critic, nevertheless noted the likely irritation of 'anti-believers at the fact that '*Songs of Praise* has an audience of around three million, which at least equals *Question Time* and Grand Prix racing'.[68] 'There are other areas of specialist

---

[63]   Professor Jim Moore, co-author of *Darwin's Sacred Cause*, in *Darwin's Struggle*.

[64]   Grimley suggests that a mixed discourse is more typical of intellectual engagement with Christianity in Britain where US style culture wars (between evolutionists and creationists) have never taken hold. Grimley 2006, p. 273.

[65]   Mark Thompson 2008.

[66]   Aaqil Ahmed commenting at the time of the programme's fiftieth anniversary celebrations in 2011. Knott and Mitchell 2012, p. 253.

[67]   Knott 1984a.

[68]   Mark Lawson 2011.

broadcasting that are more in need of a mitigating sick note from the ratings matron', he suggested.[69]

As in 1982, it promoted a comfortable Sunday Christianity focused on practice and belonging – those very elements shown by secularization theorists to be in decline – whilst being attentive to changing patterns of Christian ethnic diversity, to musical shifts featuring Christian popular music as well as traditional hymns, and to the dynamic relationship between churches, their congregations and localities.

The Clergy, Moral Responsibility and Abuse

St Martin's new chapel, featured in *Songs of Praise*, was dedicated to Dick Sheppard (1880–1937), resident vicar during the First World War and responsible for developing the Church's mission to the homeless as well as for founding the Peace Pledge Union. As the current incumbent, Reverend Nicholas Holtam, pointed out, Sheppard became known as the BBC's 'Radio Parson' and was the first priest to broadcast a Christian sermon to the world on radio in 1924, establishing what was to become an important relationship between the British media and the Church.[70] By the 1980s, in addition to covering stories about and seeking moral advice from church leaders – Pope John Paul II and Britain's leading Catholic cleric, Cardinal Basil Hume, were especially respected, along with the Archbishop of Canterbury, Robert Runcie – television itself took on the metaphorical mantle of 'the new priesthood', in so far as it could deliver its message to a mass audience. But, in addition to the power of secular media to influence and popularize its own values, in the same period American Evangelical Christianity was beginning to use television for its own ends to preach the Gospel and solicit donations from a TV generation. Early in 1984, Luis Palau and Rex Humbard, two popular televangelists, were featured respectively in BBC1's *Everyman* and a BBC2 documentary *God-in-a-Box*, with the former stating: 'I like to believe that God allowed the invention of television, radio and mass printing, not to sell soap and cornflakes, but to present the truth of God to the millions and millions in the world.'[71] With tighter broadcast media regulation, the electronic church never took off in the UK as it did in the US, but British church leaders looked on in fascination and trepidation at this latest conjunction between the media and the Gospel.[72] By the late 2000s, however, the new frontier was digital media rather

---

[69]   Ibid.

[70]   Wolfe 1984.

[71]   Luis Palau, featured in *Everyman*, BBC1, 1 January 1984; *God-in-a-Box*, BBC2, 10 January 1984.

[72]   Fears were expressed in the Independent Broadcasting Authority's published report, *The End of a Road? Report of the Seventh IBA Religious Consultation* (London, 1983), and later discussed by Grace Davie, Davie 2000.

than television, with religious organizations and their representatives concerned to monitor and capitalize upon this novel technology.

If this aspect of the relationship between religious leaders and the media had shifted focus by the time of our second study, other aspects had remained largely unchanged. Serious treatment of the clergy could still be found, though with less deference shown and most editors and journalists seeing them as 'fair game', especially if clergy did not live up to expected moral standards.[73] Pope Benedict, for example, was openly criticized in the media for his views on Britain's equality laws and failure to respond to Catholic sex abuse prior to his 2010 visit.[74] Rowan Williams, the Archbishop of Canterbury, was frequently represented as inept or weak, though – like the Archbishop of York and many other Anglican bishops – his views were sought repeatedly on ethical and sometimes political issues such as assisted suicide and the financial crisis, and at times of annual festivals and national occasions.

The Times was the major source of serious coverage about the clergy: in autumn 2008 this included articles on Cardinal Newman in advance of his beatification, potential successors to Britain's retiring Catholic Cardinal, and a full page of clerical obituaries.[75] It was the obvious place to reproduce an exclusive extract from Rupert Shortt's biography of Rowan Williams.[76] The selection of content for both the extract and an associated article brought to the fore some of the governing interests of a secular newspaper covering a religious topic.[77] Although it was more attentive than usual to the spiritual aspects of the story – using Christian vocabulary including 'liturgy', 'Eucharist', 'homily', 'speaking in tongues' and 'intercession' – the focus was on the Archbishop as a charismatic, saintly and vulnerable figure, and on two traumatic events with immediate and widespread international appeal: 9/11, when he nearly died in a church centre on Wall Street just south of the twin towers, and the suicide of a young woman friend who had grown attached to him during his student years. These rhetorical motifs of crisis and celebrity illustrated clearly that religion, like any other area of human interest, can provide suitable substance for a successful media story. The key questions then – as they were back in the 1980s – were 'Will our readers be interested?' and 'How can the story be written in such a way to capture and retain this interest?'[78] On this occasion, the biographical extract was deemed sufficiently powerful in and of itself to be reproduced with no editing, and was accompanied by images of a pensive Archbishop, his marriage in 1981, and the devastation following the collapse of the twin towers. The central motif was his profound and sensitive but improvised response to the horror of the attack and its aftermath. It followed the

---

[73] Mutanen 2009, pp. 30–33, 37–8.

[74] For example, Butt 2010; BBC News 2010c; Salter 2010.

[75] Purves 2008; *The Times* 2008f; *The Times* 2008d.

[76] Shortt 2008.

[77] Brown and Gledhill 2008.

[78] Knott 1984a, p. 61.

form of an archetypal Biblical test of faith with a theodical resolution: We may doubt Him, but God has given us the free will to act, to take the consequences and to suffer. But He suffers with us.[79]

Although unusual in its theological depth, the article nevertheless fulfilled the rhetorical and narrative requirements of a good media story. Very different, but no less appropriate were *The Sun*'s clergy articles. Here the moral tone shifted from the pastoral and spiritual care exercised by the leader of the national church to the degenerate and sometimes criminal activities of lesser clergy (denomination generally not identified). This morbid media pleasure in the fall from grace of those who should know better was entirely in continuity with the paper's treatment of the clergy back in 1982.

> *The Sun* ... bombards its readership with headings such as "Gunman priest", "Art priest seized", "Betting priest" and "Vicar runs off with farmer's wife" ... *The Sun* reveals to us the more seamy side of the religious life: it reports on priests who like a drink or a visit to the dogs, and on clergymen who commit avaricious crimes while serving their church. It rarely goes into any detail about the explicitly religious side of a story. The denomination of a churchman is only occasionally mentioned ... and no religious terminology is used.[80]

In 2008, the offences were not dissimilar, though perhaps there was more sex involved: a 'naughty vicar' who committed adultery, a Swedish priest who downloaded porn, a priest who went to Accident and Emergency to have a potato removed from his bottom, a choir-master who attempted suicide hours before standing trial for sexual abuse of boys, and a vicar who was found to have joined the British National Party.[81] Several women were featured too: a 'swinging, boozy woman Rev banned from clergy' after 12 years of service, and a 'prim vicar's wife' who aided and abetted her sexually abusive husband by turning a blind eye to child pornography on his computer.[82]

The last being two out of only four stories about Christian women in prominent positions that were covered in the papers in our 2008 study, these articles reflect the paucity of media recognition given to this numerically significant group. In the remaining stories, one from *The Sun* and the other from the *Yorkshire Evening Post*, women clergy were presented as victims rather than perpetrators, the subject of a death threat in one, and of a theft in the other.[83] It was only in this last story that a woman vicar was presented without her gender being emphasized. In continuity with the parochial orientation of the paper, the focus was on the desecration of a local space rather than the clergywoman herself. There were no articles featuring

---

[79]   Shortt 2008.

[80]   Knott 1984a, p. 20.

[81]   *The Sun* 2008k; *The Sun* 2008g; *The Sun* 2008i; *The Sun* 2008e; *The Sun* 2008l.

[82]   *The Sun* 2008j; *The Sun* 2008b.

[83]   *The Sun* 2008c; *Yorkshire Evening Post* 2008a.

women priests in *The Times* during the research period, but references to the Virgin Mary reinforced one established gender stereotype, whilst an article on Muslim women leaders challenged another.[84]

With television coverage of prominent Christian women restricted to jokes about nuns and reviews of Meryl Streep as Mother Superior in the film *Doubt*, we may conclude that, despite earlier iconic representations of women clergy in the BBC's *The Vicar of Dibley* (1994–2007) and BBC Radio 4's *The Archers* (the Reverend Janet Fisher), the increase in women priests since the 1990s has not been appropriately reflected in the media portrayal of British church life. This may be explained by what we saw earlier: the media focus on a clerical elite and clerical degenerates, with women poorly represented in both categories.[85] Although few black Christian clergy were represented – with the notable exception of the media-savvy Archbishop of York, John Sentamu, and occasional references to Desmond Tutu – the explanation differs, there being no official obstacles barring black male clergy from promotion. In their case, it is the media focus on Anglicanism and Catholicism at the expense of Pentecostalism, Evangelical Christianity, African-origin and other new church expressions that explains their relative absence.

In 2010, the British media tradition of clergy 'sit-coms', of which *The Vicar of Dibley* was a prime example, was brought up to date with the introduction of BBC2's *Rev.*, focused on a London-based priest struggling with the secularization of the church, inner-city deprivation, the forces of consumerism and the media, and the fads of his clerical superiors.[86] Reverend Adam Smallbone (played by Tom Hollander) is 'explicitly a believer, who attends diligently to his congregation and whose voiceovers take the form of non-satirical prayers'.[87] According to Mark Lawson, '*Rev.* perfectly represents the current tone and position of spiritual television', by 'accepting the possibility of holiness' whilst taking seriously religious controversies.[88]

---

[84] In *The Times* the Virgin Mary was referred to on 1 November, and nuns on 4 November and 11 November 2008. The issue of Muslim women leading prayers challenged the idea that this is necessarily a male role in Islam, see Power 2008.

[85] Legislation to admit women as bishops of the Church of England was being prepared and debated in the 2000s, but was voted down by lay members at the General Synod in November 2012.

[86] *Rev.*, BBC2. A 'Sit-com' is a fictional television comedy drama situated in a domestic, work, rural or urban setting and based around a family or group of friends or work colleagues. Knott and Mitchell 2012, pp. 255–6.

[87] Mark Lawson 2011.

[88] Ibid.

Christianity, its 'Others' and the 'Othering' of Christianity

'A very British form of Christianity', Linda Woodhead has named it: cultural as much as religious, and 'part of the fabric of our towns, villages, families and lives'.[89] Most people are not 'Christian all the way through', but compelled by secular values whilst nevertheless believing in 'heaven, hell, the power of prayer, and fate'.[90] And this is indeed reflected in the portrayals of Christianity we have witnessed in this chapter, with the media responsible in part for shaping and guaranteeing this state of affairs. Reviewing the three trajectories identified earlier – decline of church association, continuity, culture and identification, and changing commitments – in the context of media coverage of Christianity, we may note that two are largely endorsed, and the other almost entirely absent from newspapers and television.[91] As we saw in the empty pews and statistics on falling church attendance in *The One Show*, in the decreasing number of hours dedicated to religious broadcasting, and the reduction in audience figures for *Songs of Praise*, decline in church association is both assumed and represented by the media, particularly television. Christian practice is nevertheless catered for as an important religious minority interest alongside others.[92]

British Christian identity is also accepted as normative, especially in the popular conservative press, but more generally at festivals and times of national crisis. Christian heritage and language is fundamental to the media representation of Britain's history, geography and culture. Continuity rather than change, and uncomplicated identity and practice rather than deep-seated commitment provide the general tenor of media Christian portrayals as they did in the early 1980s, though with less deference and a more overt challenge to churches and clergy.

This British media rendition of Christianity is not achieved in isolation, but as part of a broader engagement with issues of identity, ideology and culture in the process of depicting, debating and critiquing the nation. We discuss this further in the chapters that follow on minority religions, atheism and secularism, and popular religiosity. We draw this one to a close by considering the 'marginalization of Christianity', a media discourse that was gathering speed at the time of our research.

It only makes sense to talk about marginalization – or persecution, as some media commentators glossed it – in the context of the treatment of others, in this case secularists and Muslims. It was in coverage of cases where Christians found themselves opposed to Britain's new Equality Act on the grounds of religious

---

[89]   Woodhead 2012b. Woodhead was responding to a poll conducted for the Richard Dawkins's Foundation for Reason and Science. See also Field 2012; and, on nominal Christian identity, Day 2011.

[90]   Woodhead 2012b.

[91]   Guest et al. 2012.

[92]   See BBC Religion website. BBC Asian Network caters for interest in Indian music, with occasional programmes on Islamic, Hindu and Sikh festivals.

freedom (e.g. dress, prayer, refusal to cater for homosexuals) and in those where double standards were felt to favour Muslims over Christians that this discourse began to emerge, predominantly in the popular press.[93] *The Telegraph*, in particular, took on the role of exposing injustices, often citing the support of senior Evangelical clergy and Conservative politicians. In January 2008, for example, it printed 'Extremism has flourished as Britain has lost its faith in a Christian vision', by Michael Nazir-Ali, a former Anglican Bishop of Pakistani background and a leader in the defence of Christian Evangelicalism against the rise of Islam.[94] Other papers joined *The Telegraph* to cover the release of a report commissioned by senior Anglican clergy in June 2008, *Moral, But No Compass*. *The Sun*, for example, chose to place the stress on the threat of Islam: 'Britain's identity is being sacrificed by the Government favouring ISLAM over Christianity, the Church of England claimed yesterday'.[95] In this as in other articles, the Labour Government was cast as villainous, for favouring equality over freedom of religion, for political correctness and a failure of nerve in standing up to minorities (always Islam and Muslims) on behalf of the majority ('we', namely white Christian people).

It was Easter 2010 when sporadic coverage turned into an organized media campaign with a group of senior clergy, led by a previous Archbishop of Canterbury, Lord Carey, signing 'Westminster 2010: A Declaration of Christian Conscience' with sympathetic Christians being asked to affirm the Declaration online.[96] A letter by the group in *The Telegraph* on 28 March, and the Declaration on 4 April meant that the issues received widespread media attention, both from those who believed that Christians were being persecuted, and those who were sceptical or critical.[97] 'Are Christians being persecuted?' was the question asked in a special Easter documentary in the same period which had contributions from a range of Evangelical exponents of persecution theory, liberal Christian deniers, and secularist supporters of liberal egalitarianism.[98] The programme concluded that Christianity had not been entirely diminished, residual Christian identity remained important, faith-based organizations were hard at work, and religious groups fought against a tide of political correctness. The importance of debating

---

[93]　The Government introduced a new Equality Act in 2010.

[94]　Nazir-Ali 2008a.

[95]　*The Sun* 2008a. Paper's capitals.

[96]　Westminster Declaration of Christian Conscience 2010.

[97]　See in particular *The Telegraph* 2008b; Jamieson 2010; Peter Hutchinson 2010. Following an Easter sermon by the Archbishop of Canterbury in which he downplayed the problems of British Christians in light of global Christian persecution, Ruth Gledhill in *The Times* and Riazat Butt and Andrew Brown in *The Guardian* criticized the Declaration's stance.

[98]　*Are Christians Being Persecuted?*, BBC1, 4 April 2010. In 2012, a report by Christians in Parliament concluded they were not, but that they face problems living out their faith in times of cultural and legal change.

the issue was nevertheless stressed, the presenter, Nicky Campbell, predicting that otherwise 'we may find we've lost more than we've gained'.[99]

This mediated display of public Christian resistance to secular society was not new. In fact, in 1982 at the time of the first research project, *The Times* had pursued this theme following a speech by the Archbishop of Canterbury, Robert Runcie, to the National Society for the Promotion of Religious Education.[100] The catalyst then was not equality but pluralism, the Archbishop using the religious metaphor of sacrifice to bemoan the seeming loss of 'our native Christian tradition' on the 'altar of multiculturalism'.[101] The editor praised him for his timely defence: 'It was as if a halt was being called to the long, apologetic retreat of official Christianity before the advancing alliance of secularism and relativism.'[102]

Where freedom of expression is the norm there will always be disagreement and dissent. In 1982 not everyone shared this anxiety about multiculturalism's impact on religious education; in the late 2000s, despite being widespread in the popular press, the narrative of Christian marginalization was resisted by some religious correspondents as well as secularist commentators. But it is nevertheless striking that, in the longue durée of secularization, major national newspapers – *The Times* in 1982, joined by *The Telegraph* in 2008–2010 – took on the mantle of defender of Christianity and its centrality to the nation, its institutions and people against 'the demands of liberal orthodoxy'.[103] Situated within a government policy of the discourse of diversity, Christianity was increasingly represented as one religion among many in a multi-faith environment, and religion itself seen as one of several identity strands in a context of equality and human rights. Whilst this discourse was necessarily reflected in media news reporting, in the popular press fears were voiced about where this slippery slope might be leading the nation and its identity, and to a lesser extent Christianity itself.

As we noted in Chapter 1, in post-traditional societies religious traditions must learn to adapt and must be justified in public discourse. No longer taken for granted, they must fulfil the brief as traditions of cultural diversity or cultural heritage. In the media, as this chapter has illustrated, Christianity is represented in terms of both, with an emphasis on the latter. Implicitly, in terms of landscape, language and the arts, it is depicted as intrinsic to history and culture. Explicitly, it has become a vital component in the media's construction of Britain and Britishness, in the formation of 'our' nation and 'us', its people.

---

[99]   *Are Christians Being Persecuted?*, BBC1, 4 April 2010.
[100]   Geddes 1982; *The Times* 1982c.
[101]   Geddes 1982.
[102]   *The Times* 1982c.
[103]   Ibid.

Chapter 4

The Reporting of Islam and Other Religious Traditions

'I don't mind talking about [religion], because I am a Muslim', replied one Birmingham pedestrian when interviewed by Anita Rani for *The One Show*.[1] The findings of her street survey suggested that it was 'not minorities, but the white middle classes' who were too embarrassed to talk about religion. Their unwillingness was juxtaposed with the open religiosity of Britain's minority groups. That they had something positive to teach the wider population was a view held by guest experts. Biologist Robert Winston, for example, advocated both the value of spirituality and the healthiness of open discussion about religion. The programme reinforced the idea of Christianity as the dominant but declining religion, in conjunction with a British identity that is multicultural. In such a representation, although minorities were 'othered', they were simultaneously held up as a model of self-confident religiosity for the nation.

The One Show was one of only two programmes examining a range of faiths in our television week. It reflected the close link between coverage of religious diversity and Britain's minorities. Vox pop in style, it also included academic and religious voices and opinions. Does such coverage provide a counter to the largely negative newspaper coverage which so often reinforces a sense of 'us' (white British, Christian) versus 'them' (immigrants, Muslims)? Here we examine both newspaper and television coverage in order to answer this question and to establish the dominant frameworks of reporting on religious diversity in the late 2000s.

Increasing Diversity in Media Coverage

By 2008–2009, there had been a significant rise in the reporting of Islam by both newspapers and television from the time of our first study in the 1980s (Table 4.1), making it second only to Christianity. There were more references to Islam than either Roman Catholicism or Protestantism taken separately (Appendix 2; Appendix 3). Militancy and extremism were the principal topics in its media coverage.

---

[1] *The One Show*, BBC1, 3 February 2009.

Table 4.1   Media references to religions other than Christianity
              (1982, 2008–2009)

Religious tradition	References on television	Percentage of total references	References in newspapers	Percentage of total references	Total references 2008 (1 month)	Total references 1982 (1 month)
Islam	51	3.1	255	9.5	306	33
Judaism	10	0.6	81	3.0	91	54
Buddhism	15	0.9	28	1.0	43	2
Hinduism	6	0.4	29	1.1	35	4
Sikhism	3	0.2	10	0.4	13	6
Other religious traditions	14	0.8	6	0.2	20	6

Reporting of other religions also rose significantly, though less for Judaism which had received reasonable coverage in the early 1980s. Whilst the rise in references to other religions appears small by comparison with Islam, were we to remove those references to Islam in the newspapers that focused on extremism and terrorism (Table 4.2), the amount of coverage would be commensurate with that of other minority religions.[2] We would be left with just 73 references to Islam, fewer in fact than for Judaism (with 81), though this was less apparent in television coverage of Islam, which was more balanced. This illustrates an important point. Whilst the media acknowledged Britain to be a multi-faith society, coverage of religions other than Christianity was marginal except in cases where religion had a political significance.

The fact that more than a third of references to Islam on television occurred in news and current affairs programmes reinforces this. Although extremism was also a feature of the television coverage, its references to Islam were chiefly concerned with Muslims in Afghanistan, Iran and Turkey rather than those living in the UK (despite most programmes being domestic productions). This was in contrast to newspaper coverage which concentrated on the national scene, although *The Times* maintained some international focus (Table 4.2).

---

[2]   In Table 4.1 'Other religious traditions' included Shinto, Confucianism, Taoism, Jainism and Zoroastrianism. Kabbalah, popular among celebrities, was a feature of newspaper coverage.

Table 4.2   References to Islam in the newspapers in 2008: Sub-categories

Islam: Sub-categories	*The Times*	*The Sun*	*Yorkshire Evening Post*	Total number of references
Islam general	12	2	0	14
Muslims in Britain	3	1	3	7
Muslims outside Britain	18	2	0	20
Militant action	92	37	12	141
Satanic Verses Affair	2	0	1	3
Extremism	17	23	1	41
Adjustment to culture	8	2	3	13
Gender and sexuality	5	3	0	8
Art	3	0	1	3
Mecca	0	0	1	1
Sufism	2	0	0	2
Mosques	0	2	0	2
Total	162	72	21	255

On television, references to Islam and other religious traditions occurred mainly in BBC programmes, in part due to the series *Around the World in 80 Faiths*. Only 10 per cent of the coverage of Islam was on ITV compared to nearly 60 per cent on BBC2. Other religions, such as Buddhism, Hinduism and Judaism, appeared less frequently in the news, and more often in religious broadcasting and light entertainment. Turning to the newspapers, whilst *The Times*'s coverage of Islam, Judaism and Hinduism was higher than that of *The Sun* and the *Yorkshire Evening Post*, this was partly a reflection of the greater size of the newspaper. Islamic extremism, however, was more likely to be covered in *The Sun* (with its stories of 'Preachers of Hate' for example). The *Yorkshire Evening Post* gave serious attention to religions other than Christianity and Islam, particularly to announcements and listings for Buddhism and Sikhism, thus reflecting local interests.

Newspaper Coverage of Islam

Only once in October 2008 was a story on Islam deemed sufficiently significant to hit the front page.[3] Islam featured in news stories, news in brief and commentary, and only infrequently in sport, advertisements, culture, travel, jobs or reviews despite an otherwise high number of religious references in these categories. Already this hints at the type of coverage in which Islam was explicitly identified.

---

[3]   Wells 2008.

We analysed in depth three-quarters of all the articles from October 2008 in which Islam was the main focus: 51 articles from *The Times*, 26 from *The* Sun and 10 from the *Yorkshire Evening Post*. Nearly two thirds covered conflictual topics (terrorism, violence and extremism). Seven reported on anti-racism and community relations, and were broadly positive in their approach. The remaining articles showed Muslims in a predominantly negative light as a cultural threat. Whilst these topics could be found in both international and domestic news, some topics were more likely to appear in one rather than the other. The domestic focus of many stories represented a significant shift from the 1980s when Islam in the UK was barely covered. The focus then was on international conflict and Islamic beliefs, law and history, Islam being generally represented and understood within a Christian and ethnocentric perspective.

We turn now to the portrayal of Islam in the newspapers in the late 2000s. Five themes emerge as significant: terrorism, conflict abroad, extremism at home, the threat to cultural values, and discrimination, immigration and community relations.

Islam: The Terrorist Threat

It will come as no surprise that the dominant topic of newspaper coverage in 2008 was terrorism. What may be more unexpected is that all but two of the articles were about British Muslims. Whilst British Muslims had not been attributed with this label by the media prior to 9/11, it has since become the central framework for covering Muslims in the UK.[4] In 2008, stories included British Muslims on trial for planning terrorist activities, a Muslim convert's failed toilet bomb attempt, coverage of the trial of the perpetrators of the Glasgow airport attack, and accusations that terrorist groups were transmitting coded messages in child porn. In order to illustrate the common elements in the reporting of this topic, the focus will be on just two of these, the Glasgow airport trial and the 'toilet bomber'.

'Doctor on fire seen punching and kicking police' screams the headline in *The Times* following coverage of the trial of two men who drove a jeep filled with gas canisters into Glasgow Airport in July 2007.[5] They had been apprehended by police when the vehicle got stuck in the terminal doors. Coverage focused largely on the negative actions of the 'terrorists' in the build up to the attack in opposition to the less frequently featured but nonetheless 'heroic' action of the police and public. Aggression featured highly in the accounts as did the damage and chaos caused. The actors were explicitly categorized as 'bombers' and 'fanatics'. Defining someone in this way affects how their activities are understood and allows for action to be taken against them which does not have to be justified. Yet in the case of terrorism the discourse has been institutionalized and so appears neutral. Rather

---

4   Poole 2006.
5   Bird 2008.

than providing any historical or political context, the acts of terrorism were clearly linked to Islamic belief and practice. The defendants were described as 'strictly observant Muslims' who 'adhered to extreme Islamic beliefs' and yet were 'intent on murder'.[6] It was their Muslimness that was emphasized; other motivations, if mentioned, were dismissed. The only political motivation referred to was revenge (for the deaths of Muslims in Iraq and Afghanistan) but, with no further elaboration offered, this reference implied irrationality and a blind disregard for innocent victims.

It is important to note here the culturally embedded use of language and its implications for interpretation. With categories routinely established, replicated and exchanged in media discourse, one term is easily replaceable with another – 'extremist' with 'militant' or 'radical', for example. The meaning of one may thus be readily transferred to another. Whether 'extremist' or 'militant' is used, both may now carry the implication of terrorism. Islam is conflated with Islamism, the former as well as the latter becoming associated with irrational radical violence. 'Islamism', originally established in order to disassociate Islam from fundamentalism, is now used to describe myriad political groups and activities without reference to their 'actual practices' and 'discursive strands' and how these are articulated in particular contexts.[7] Added to this, the link to terrorism then criminalizes innocent groups and individuals.

Whilst the reporting of terrorism has become fairly homogenized, the main difference in the reporting of the Glasgow airport trial was that the defendants were doctors. Journalists puzzled over the contradiction between their training to save lives and the intent to murder. The answer was in their lineage. The defendants were othered by foregrounding their foreignness with reference to their background and birth. *The Sun*, for example, categorized one perpetrator as 'an Iraqi-born in Britain' and his accomplice as a 'Saudi-born pal'.[8]

A similar process was apparent in the reporting of Nick Reilly, a Muslim convert who made a failed attempt to blow up a bomb in a toilet but instead locked himself in. Since the London bombings of 7/7, when British citizens turned on their compatriots, a new strategy has emerged in press discourse to deal with this.[9] A process of othering takes place in which the perpetrator is individualized and so divorced from the wider Muslim community (thus countering potential accusations of racism). In this case, Reilly was represented as a criminal (e.g. through mug shots), and then, as with the doctors, linked to radicals outside the UK who had 'brainwashed' him with their 'extreme religious and murderous ideology'.[10] Thus the link was made to Islam, but also othered by being located outside the UK. This process was made explicit in this story where the central character was constructed

---

6   O'Neill and Bird 2008.

7   Kundnani 2007, p. 49.

8   Hughes 2008.

9   Featherstone, Holohan and Poole 2010, pp. 169–86.

10   O'Neill and Bird 2008.

as a naïve individual susceptible to brainwashing, and suffering from Asperger's syndrome (this vulnerability was offered as the only possible explanation for his conversion). Adopted in articles in both *The Sun* and *The Times*, this strategy was encapsulated in the opening sentence of the latter: 'A vulnerable Muslim convert was persuaded online by shadowy Pakistan-based extremists into trying to carry out a suicide bomb attack on a busy restaurant.'[11]

Significantly, it was technology which was marked out as central in this process: *The Times* referred to the process as 'Internet jihad'. In a supporting article, the paper's Crime and Security Editor concluded that Reilly had been 'radicalized from afar' and quoted the 'respected Jamestown Foundation' arguing that the Internet had 'become the easiest and safest way ... to reach young militants, who likely lack training, and steer them under al-Qaeda's general command'.[12] This focus on the Internet as a tool for immoral purposes was an example of the way in which new technologies are often blamed for society's ills and have consistently been a target for the conservative press (for example, films and computer games). A further example was evident several days later in *The Times*: 'YouTube left bombers page open despite police concern.'[13]

As Kundnani has noted, this discourse 'reduces widespread sociological trends occurring across a generation of young Muslims to a unilinear process of terrorist radicalization' and fails to acknowledge the multiple political and theological paths – predominantly non-violent – to which a 'new Muslim identity' can lead.[14] This homogenized radicalization discourse also reinforces the idea of collective responsibility, of leaders who should control their communities. Connected to radicals outside the UK, the responsibility nevertheless is seen as lying within.

Only two of the articles linking Islam and terrorism could be interpreted as critical and these were politically motivated, aimed at undermining the then Prime Minister, Gordon Brown, and his proposal to allow terrorist suspects to be held for 42 days without trial. All the articles analysed were hard news stories bar one, and this demonstrated the consensus around this interpretation of terrorism about which it was clearly felt little further discussion or debate was needed. Causes that might implicate the West were ignored, and no attempt was made to create a discursive space in which Muslims might speak back to power without being labelled 'terrorist'.[15]

---

[11] France and Coles 2008; Fresco 2008.
[12] O'Neill 2008.
[13] O'Neill 2008.
[14] Kundnani 2007, pp. 56–60.
[15] Kundnani 2007.

Conflict Abroad

Apart from reports on terrorism, which were largely domestic, stories about conflict tended to be international, and located in war zones such as Iraq and Afghanistan. Restricting our analysis to articles that made reference to Islam or the Taleban, we identified 22 articles, half of which were about the murder of an aid worker – Gayle Williams – in Afghanistan. Of the remainder, all but one came from *The Times*, reflecting its greater interest in international affairs.

This story was covered by all the papers but generated an extended analysis in *The Times*. The most significant point of debate was whether, as a Serve Afghanistan employee, Williams was a Christian missionary (as accused by the Taleban). This was refuted through a number of strategies: her categorization as an 'aid worker' rather than missionary; overuse of the word 'claim' (in relation to the Taleban accusation); the presentation of such claims in inverted commas, as in 'Taleban shoot aid worker for "preaching"'; and the assertion that the charity was, in fact, a secular organization (later refuted by the charity's Director).[16] This allowed for the construction of the Taleban as misguided and cowardly murderers.

In *The Sun*'s coverage of the story, however, Williams was clearly constructed as Christian (but not a missionary). Its explanation for her death was repeatedly because 'she was a Christian' and also British, 'a Londoner' (even though she had joint South African and British citizenship), marking her as 'one of us'.[17] This is part of a process of personalization, with a focus on positive attributes, to encourage empathy with the victim, and contrasts with the representation of civilian deaths in Afghanistan and Iraq caused by UK forces which usually only register statistically. This media focus on the persecution of Christians in Muslim countries was also the central feature of a letter to *The Times* and, since the 'Arab Spring', has become a more prominent feature of reporting as coverage seeks to identify the negative effects of the rise of Islamist governments.[18]

A further issue raised in relation to this story was the impact of the event on charities working in conflict zones.[19] Articles highlighting this stressed the risk to aid workers, and contrasted the moral benevolence of Western workers with the ideologically irresponsible and immoral actions of the perpetrators. A patriarchal and colonialist residue was discernible in such articles, the message being that the chaos in these countries required intervention from the West, as illustrated in the commentary 'Rescuing Afghanistan remains a noble ambition'.[20] Although, this was the only article that questioned the identity of Williams' killers, that differentiated between Taleban extremists and moderates,

---

[16] Coghlan 2008; Mukarji 2008.
[17] O'Shea 2008.
[18] Lyle 2008.
[19] *The Sun* 2008h.
[20] Linklater 2008.

and denied an imperial motive for a UK presence, the discourse of civilizing the uncivilized was also implicit.

As with articles on terrorism, there was a lack of contextualization. The Taleban were framed as outlaws (reinforced with repeated references to the drugs trade) whose lack of public support meant there was little need to justify action against them. Afghanistan was represented as a country in a downward spiral requiring intervention to contain terrorism.[21] Commentators tended to reinforce and justify the presence of Western troops and agencies abroad at a time when plans were being made for their withdrawal.

Extremism at Home: 'Preachers of Hate'

Other articles that focused on extremist activity were domestic stories featuring 'preachers of hate'. This term was coined by the British tabloid press to describe Muslim clerics who preached an anti-Western message, though on rare occasions it was applied to a non-Muslim if deemed sufficiently 'extreme', such as the leader of the Westboro Baptist Church.[22] Despite his propensity to 'hate speech', it was not applied by the British papers to the right-wing Dutch MP, Geert Wilders – though it was used of him in sections of the American press.[23] This representation of preachers of hate has parallels with other media coverage of extremism and terrorism which reinforces the sense of a generalized threat and thus increases support for repressive action.

Most of the relevant coverage – there were ten articles in October 2008 – was in *The Sun*, reflecting its populist approach to these topics. The obsessive pursuit of Omar Bakri Muhammad and Abu Hamza (the latter frequently referred to as 'Evil Hook'), as well as other stories that fit the framework, serves two further tabloid purposes: to reinforce an anti-immigrationist stance and to attack government spending. Abu Hamza's excessive welfare, legal and prison costs – '£3m bill as Evil Hook stays put for 5 years' – was a story that exploited the perception that immigrants receive unfair benefits.[24] This and other articles referred to specific examples of hate speech and associations with terror, and yet also demonstrated the individual's perfidiousness: e.g. Bakri Muhammad's divorce and new young wife, his pole dancer daughter and ex-wife's fraud. They operated as a positive representation of the in-group, in this case, the tolerance of the British compared to 'their' intolerance: 'People in this country do all they can to understand the Muslim way of life', yet 'they' object to the most innocuous things, such as the

---

[21]   Evans 2008a.

[22]   Widely reported in the press, the Westboro Baptist Church in the US was renowned in the late 2000s for its open intolerance, particularly of homosexuality.

[23]   Poole 2012a, pp. 453–68.

[24]   *The Sun* 2008d.

television show the *X Factor*.[25] Each recurring story confirmed the pattern of behaviour (and, in the case of Bakri Muhammad, repeated the previous charges against him), and served as a contrast to coverage of Geert Wilders in which the focus was on freedom of speech (see Chapter 7). This simplistic characterization constructed these Muslim clerics as bogeymen, easy to dismiss, hate and blame without any further contextual information, and often reinforced by establishment figures supportive of the paper's own line. Counter-discourse was noteworthy by its absence.

More generally, the construction of asylum seekers as scroungers, dependent on 'our' goodwill and with nothing to contribute, obscures the causes of their displacement in which Britain might itself be implicated. Instead of being seen as victims, they have become scapegoats for all the anxieties and uncertainties of living in a globalized world.[26]

Islam Within: Threatening Cultural Values

Prior to 9/11, it was within this framework, of a threat to the nation's cultural values, that British Muslims were most likely to be represented and understood.[27] The message was that Muslims, due to rigid beliefs at odds with UK culture and practices, posed a threat to the British way of life. Moore, Mason and Lewis suggested that such stories had moved back to the forefront of coverage on Islam following a decline in terrorist activity since 7/7.[28] This discourse positions Islam as a missionary religion and Muslims as those who seek to change British culture and practices, thus leading to a homogenization of 'them' and 'us' presented within an exclusive binary relationship. It naturalizes the censorious aspects of the religion, focusing on what is forbidden, in contrast to the representation of Britain as inherently liberal and tolerant.

As Table 4.2 showed, this played out in a number of articles in the autumn of 2008 (16 in all), including stories about women, relationships, religious practice and art. Eleven were in *The Times*, three in *The Sun*, and two in the *Yorkshire Evening Post*. Two stories were given extensive coverage, one of a couple being prosecuted in Dubai for inappropriate sexual behaviour in public, and a second which featured a Sony video game withdrawn for including a song that sampled verses from the Qur'an.[29] Overall, the topics covered were diverse: a couple trying to adopt a second Moroccan child but thwarted by British procedures and bureaucracy; the first female Muslim to lead prayers in the UK; Muslims and cohabitation law; young Muslims challenging traditional cultural norms (all in

---

[25] Letter from Christine Savage, *The Sun*, 24 October 2008; Wells 2008.

[26] Kundnani 2007, p. 88.

[27] Moore, Mason and Lewis 2008.

[28] Ibid.

[29] *The Times* had two articles on each story and *The Sun* one on each.

The Times). *The Sun* included a double page spread by Julie Burchill (a well-known feminist writer) on her preference for 'Page 3 girls' over women dressed in *burqa*s.

Most of these articles made a similar assertion, that Islam is prohibitionist, as the case of the Sony video game demonstrates. The tactic used here was to trivialize whatever offended Muslims and maximize the problems caused to those inconvenienced by their complaint. Both *The Times* and *The Sun* went out of their way to describe the game, *Little Big Planet*, as harmless: it was 'ultra cute' and 'funny' according to *The Sun*, 'cute', 'upbeat' and full of 'charm' in *The Times*.[30] For *The Sun*, the offending song was just a 'ditty', recorded in fact by a 'Grammy award winner who is himself a Muslim'.[31] This made Muslims look irrational in their demands: 'Sony have had to recall and dump millions of copies … because Muslims have taken offence.'[32] The headline 'Video games axed' disguised the fact that the launch of the game had in fact only been postponed. Muslims were conceptualized as 'hardliners' whilst Sony were depicted as apologetic and pro-active in responding to complaints. *The Times*'s portrayal, though more measured – the game only 'offending *some* Muslims' and presented as part of Sony's wider competitive strategy – nevertheless reinforced this view of Islam as censorious and Muslims as demanding.[33]

Elsewhere, *The Times* offered a more nuanced image of Muslims in an interview with a moderate Islamic leader.[34] However, by focusing on internal controversy within Islam, it nevertheless highlighted the negative repressive response from conservative groups. This is typical of the good Muslim/bad Muslim approach of coverage which delineates an 'acceptable' interpretation of Islam from others that are deemed beyond the pale. In this case, by juxtaposing the leader's pro-feminist views as the antithesis of a general Muslim response, Islam was shown to be misogynistic and backward with respect to women and equality.[35] Despite its positive overtones, this article made space for the repetition of negative views about Islam regarding women, headscarves at school, *madrasa*s, and freedom of speech whilst averting accusations of racism (by putting them in the mouth of a critical Muslim). The article also served as an attack on the Muslim establishment in Britain for not standing up to extremism and being dominated by 'Saudi theology'.[36]

Different again, the *Yorkshire Evening Post* demonstrated local news values in its representation of Islam. One commentator, through humour, used a softer approach to tackling discrimination by taking the stereotype of a Muslim woman in

---

[30]   Brown 2008; Ahmed 2008.

[31]   Brown 2008.

[32]   Ibid.

[33]   Ahmed 2008.

[34]   Power 2008.

[35]   Ibid. See also Burchill 2008.

[36]   Power 2008.

hijab and turning it on its head, thus challenging possible prejudices. Its empathetic perspective reflected local diversity and this was evident in its coverage.[37]

In general, in coverage of cultural differences, Islam was problematized, homogenized, essentialized and deemed obstructive. Whilst some of the coverage highlighted discrimination and diversity issues, overall, 'difference' was the central thread. Why this emphasis on difference? Important in maintaining power and superiority, differences that were once encouraged and preserved within multiculturalism are now to be feared as the need for integration and cultural protectionism is stressed. As we saw in the previous chapter, British values have been constructed and defined from the top down, often using minority cultures as a foil, thus further excluding Muslims. Emphasizing 'their' difference in opposition to 'our' tolerance places the onus on minority groups rather than wider society to change. Anyone failing to adopt these 'shared values' can be labelled 'extreme' and 'a threat to society'. As critics have argued, reifying the cultural masks the root causes of social problems – sociological, economic and political – as well as the inequalities in Western societies.[38]

Discrimination, Immigration and Community Relations

What about coverage that may be more sympathetic towards Islam? Articles varied in their openness towards Muslims with some appearing positive whilst nevertheless having an underlying agenda. One example was a double-page spread featuring an interview with the new Minister for Immigration, Phil Woolas.[39] Starting with a positive message – being tough on racism but also tough on immigration – the article then rehearsed various anxieties using Woolas's statements to support concerns about migrants' use of English, the *hijab*, 'health tourism' and arranged marriages (with Muslims implicated in several of these). *The Times* in general located the domestic integration problem within the Muslim community due to its lack of assimilation.[40] A more sympathetic approach was adopted, however, when the action was located outside the national context: for example, in one article the Danish authorities were criticized for failing to protect Iraqi interpreters.[41]

Articles with positive discourses could be found in the *Yorkshire Evening Post*. Two examples, featuring a charity football match between the police and a multi-faith team, focused on unity and working together through everyday activities like sport.[42] They emphasized positive community representations for the sake of

---

[37]   McPhee 2008.

[38]   Kundnani 2007.

[39]   Thomson and Sylvester 2008.

[40]   For example, Kerbaj and Gledhill 2008.

[41]   Kerbaj 2008.

[42]   Edwards 2008; Rosser 2008.

social cohesion. But in only one of four articles on anti-racism – also on football – did *The Times* acknowledge that Muslims do indeed suffer from racism (as opposed to always benefitting from positive discrimination).[43] Sport is one subject on which Muslims at times receive a positive press: high achieving individuals are celebrated, but often their 'Muslimness' remains unnoticed, as in the case of Mo Farah, rarely called Mohamed, who won double gold at the London Olympics in 2012.

Other Religious Traditions in the Newspapers: Victimhood, Aggression, Exoticism and the Invisible

The paucity of academic study of religious representations in the British media is particularly marked in the case of other major religious traditions, especially Buddhism, Hinduism and Sikhism. Although all these religions received some coverage in the autumn of 2008 (we analysed 50 articles), little attention was given to their internal diversity. As we will show, their treatment tended to be reductive and stereotypical.

Judaism

There have been more studies on media portrayals of Judaism than other minority religions, often focusing on anti-Semitism.[44] It has received more attention in the British media than religions associated with communities that have their origins outside Europe. As another Abrahamic religion, it is often denoted as closer to Christianity, whilst Asian religions are generally collectivized. Although, there has been an increase in the coverage of all religious traditions, the small rise in references to Judaism is probably explained by the increase in newspaper size, and does not necessarily relate directly to Britain's increasing diversity.

References to Judaism in autumn 2008 focused on the Holocaust, seven articles being commemorative, two historical and two on Holocaust denial. Four focused on politics in Israel. There were only two solely domestic articles, one examining Jewish schools in Britain, the other, in the *Yorkshire Evening Post*, reporting on an historic Jewish graveyard succumbing to subsidence. As well as being commemorative, these articles used current and historical events as a means of social commentary. For example, in a similar vein to its coverage of Geert Wilders (see Chapter 7), *The Times* distanced itself from the Holocaust denier, Fredrick Toben, and yet used the event to support an argument about British sovereignty (questioning the practice of extraditing people for activities, such as 'thought crime' that are illegal abroad but not in the UK).[45] Articles about

---

43   Barnes 2008b.

44   Cohen 2012; Finkelstein 2008; Gertel 2003; Harrison 2006.

45   Gibb 2008.

Israel represented the situation as a struggle between two 'opposing forces' (the secularists and Orthodox Jews). They were sympathetic to the secularist position and critical of 'ultra Orthodox parties' and their aggressive policies towards Palestinians. However, they were not labelled 'extremist', and more context and history was provided than in articles on conflict involving Islam.[46]

The only solely domestic issue in *The Times* covered a ruling that Jewish schools must open their doors to other faiths. It adopted an anti-segregationist position as with the reporting on Muslim schools, but was given comparatively little attention (featured in *News In Brief*).[47] 'Separatism' in the Jewish community is evidently not seen as problematic to the same degree as it is in Muslim communities.

Opposing anti-Semitism was a key narrative that runs through these articles. In terms of its treatment, anti-Semitism was largely located in the past and exclusively outside the UK (with more emphasis on what UK citizens and authorities did to save victims).[48] However, the parallel between this and the discrimination currently experienced by other minorities was made in four articles, including an editorial. The treatment of the histories of those who suffered in the Holocaust (personal narratives, witness reports) contrasted with the utilitarian coverage of the numerous civilian casualties in Iraq and Afghanistan. On the basis of our sample, Jews were cast either as victims (Holocaust) or aggressors (in Israel), the only exception being a case of inter-faith relations (between Dr Rowan Williams, the Archbishop of Canterbury, and Sir Jonathan Sacks, the Chief Rabbi, on a joint visit to Auschwitz).[49]

Buddhism

Buddhism appeared in several contexts: in terms of its cultural influence (here as part of the practice of liberal-minded celebrities), in travel news and advertisements, reporting on the Dalai Lama and the struggle for Tibetan independence, and local events. It tended to be positively represented as a peaceful, spiritual non-materialistic religion with an 'ancient' and 'majestical' history. Its adherents were depicted engaging in peaceful protest but also as victims of Chinese aggression.

The beliefs and practices of Buddhism, like those of other 'Eastern' religions, were subject to exoticization. The depiction of 'Buddha boy', who was thought to be a reincarnation of the Buddha, was a case in point.[50] His followers were portrayed as unquestioning, blindly following their faith. *The Times* took a rationalist sceptical position in relation to such stories.

The Times's coverage targeted international contexts whilst *The Sun*'s articles were domestic. The *Yorkshire Evening Post* coverage was local and event-focused.

---

46   Hilder 2008.
47   *The Times* 2008e.
48   For example, Jackson 2008.
49   Klein 2008.
50   Blakely 2008.

Hinduism

Coverage of Hinduism – which by comparison with references to Buddhism was very negative – comprised largely of *The Times'* reporting of religious violence in India. Five of its eight articles focused on 'brutal' Hindu violence towards local Christians in Orissa, India. The articles emphasized the persecution of Christians (through rape, burnings, forced conversions) in a similar way to the reporting of Islam by concentrating on the negative actions of the aggressors. The Hindu Nationalist movement (Rashtriya Swayamsevak Sangh, RSS) was referred to as a 'fundamentalist group' and 'extremist'. The aggressors (the RSS and opposing groups) were variously described as 'marauding mobs' and 'armed thugs', and were illustrated with images of worshippers with guns.[51] This was compared to the compassion shown by a local Christian humanitarian organization.[52] Other articles focused on similarly conflict-ridden events, intra- and inter-religious and ethnic violence, and the economic and social chaos arising from the mix of religion and politics. Only one article had a positive angle – the opening of a trade route through Kashmir – but equally made reference to its aim to 'help quell religious violence from separatists'.[53] All coverage of Hinduism was international, located outside the UK, as hard news. In this coverage, Indian society was depicted as hierarchical, conflict-ridden, corrupt and uncivilized. It reflected a wider pattern of coverage of the developing world which has become familiar in the reporting of the struggle between secular and religious forces following the Middle Eastern and North African uprisings. Underlying this coverage is suspicion towards religious movements that challenge or curtail secular attempts to create more progressive states.

Sikhism and Other Religions

Coverage of Hinduism was in sharp contrast to coverage of Sikhism, which was comprised only of domestic news stories. Sikhs were mentioned in passing as a feature of multiculturalism. Treatment was fairly benign with only the occasional reference to moments of tension in the history of their integration in the UK. Generally, they were held up as a model of assimilation, thus gaining little attention from the media. Accepting Sikhs within a notion of British identity has been deemed less problematic than is the case with Muslims. Most of the articles about Sikhs focused on arts and culture – entertainment, religious festivals, theatre productions, and a feature on the centenary of the first Sikh temple in the UK. Reporters used positive predicates, including 'wealthy', 'learned', 'faithful', and 'pride'; reference was made to Sikhs as 'soldiers' who had fought on the side of

---

[51]   Page and Blakely 2008.
[52]   Nazir-Ali 2008b.
[53]   Page 2008.

the British.[54] Coverage was located in *The Times* with some reference to local festivals in the *Yorkshire Evening Post*. This does not, of course, preclude negative coverage, as we have seen with Hinduism. One negative comment for example, occurred in a letter criticizing 'separatist' police organizations.

The two articles on other religions featured Shinto and Taoism, the latter exoticizing Taoist sex, but in the context of a rational interpretation of religious scripture.[55] Shinto was discussed, though incidentally, with reference to the Emperor of Japan who it was thought should 'atone personally for war atrocities' to the South Koreans in order to restore political relations in the region.[56]

To summarize, about two thirds of the coverage of religions other than Christianity and Islam was international with much of this located in *The Times*. Coverage in *The Sun* and the *Yorkshire Evening Post* had a more domestic focus and featured either local issues or popular culture and history. *The Times* shifted between a secularist rationalist position, when faced with extreme religious expression, and identification with Christianity, particularly when under attack. The articles covering inter-faith activity in the UK had a more positive tone but were few and far between in this particular sample.[57]

This analysis demonstrates that, as with any other topic, common news values apply to coverage of religious groups. The topics that dominated coverage of Islam equally informed the coverage of other religions, international news stories emphasizing conflict and domestic stories focusing on cultural values and multiculturalism. The media do not appear to be interested in religious diversity *per se*. Rather, the coverage of religion is limited unless it resonates strongly with these news values.

Television Coverage: A Wider Perspective

The exoticization of Eastern religions was also highlighted in television coverage. In the first week of February 2009, on BBC1, BBC2 and ITV1, there were just two programmes that featured minority faiths (other than Islam): *The One Show* (ITV) and *Around the World in 80 Faiths* (BBC2), both of which provided a microcosm of wider television coverage.

Religion abroad was typified by *Around the World in 80 Faiths*.[58] This popular series, part of the BBC's religious broadcasting provision, was presented by Peter Owen-Jones, a Bohemian Anglican vicar. In eight episodes Owen-Jones travelled the continents, reporting on and participating in the practices of a variety of religious groups and sects. Each hour-long episode featured ten religions and as

---

54   Binyon 2008b.
55   Godson and Stuttaford 2008.
56   Parry 2008.
57   See, for example, Binyon 2008a.
58   *Around the World in 80 Faiths*, BBC2, 6 February 2009.

such required careful selection and editing. As might be expected in a popular television format, it was the exotic and unusual that was featured: sword stabbing rituals in Indonesia, voodoo in Africa and whirling dervishes in Syria. The first episode in February focused on India and included items on Tibetan Buddhism, Hinduism, the Bishnoi of Rajasthan, Nath Firewalkers, Zoroastrianism, Sikhism and Jainism. With the religions presented not as collective, but as individual quests for enlightenment, the themes were devotion, dedication, hardship, sacrifice and tradition, all of which were appreciated by Owen-Jones. The spectacle of him participating in rituals and the direct address to camera invited viewers to share the experience, and to feel its emotional and spiritual intensity, the symbols of travel signifying his journey both literally and metaphorically.

Whilst the series constituted a positive portrayal of religious diversity and its complexity and depth that was unusual in media coverage of religion, it also emphasized the irrational, weird, strange and even extreme practices, and therefore inevitably contributed to othering them. Some religious stereotypes were challenged – by teenage Tibetan monks with familiar-looking bedrooms, for example – but Owen-Jones nevertheless depicted Indian spirituality as 'beautiful', 'incredible', as 'seep[ing] into everything'. The series also provided a form of visual tourism. Owen-Jones's own religiosity provided a reference point for viewers, but the incessant focus on diversity made it hard to differentiate between the religions, with exotic practices becoming indistinguishable from one another. In its positive approach these religions were represented as non-violent and self-sacrificing; Islam on the other hand was presented as the aggressor in relation to two of the groups featured.

How was Islam represented in the wider TV coverage? Six programmes mentioned Islam, including *The One Show* on BBC1 followed by a news item on Iran.[59] On BBC2, two documentaries, *Explore: From Istanbul to Anatolia*, on Turkey, and an episode of the series *Iran and the West*, marking the 30th anniversary of the Iranian Revolution, were aired.[60] On ITV1, coverage included a documentary on Afghanistan, *Doctors and Nurses at War*, and a feature on Ross Kemp's experience of filming in Afghanistan on *The Titchmarsh Show* (a teatime chat show) in which Muslims were portrayed either as either aggressors or victims. More interesting overall was the greater range and complexity of television reporting on Islam.

Iran and the West explored the history of political relations with the West, particularly the US, in three episodes. Despite its in-depth coverage, it nevertheless reproduced well-established discourses about Iran.[61] This first episode, 'The Man who Changed the World', presented the history of the Islamic Revolution in Iran from a largely American perspective (including the seizure of the US embassy

---

[59]   BBC1, 3 February 2009.

[60]   BBC2, 8 February and 7 February 2009.

[61]   Said 1981.

in Iran and the hostage crisis, followed by the start of the Iran-Iraq war).[62] Here, the US was represented as the victim of political manipulation by a devious and clever mastermind, Ayatollah Khomeini. The revolution was constructed as the political ambition of one man who manipulated his people and took advantage of an unsuspecting and ill-prepared American government. By supporting the siege, 'Khomeini had breached the basic rule that allows diplomats to work in a crisis. In doing so he had reversed the decision he had given to his Foreign Minister who had been at his side since his exile'.[63]

Employing the category 'the West' suggested an alliance against Iran, masking the differences between different countries' relations with Iran, and reinforcing the idea of a clash of civilizations. The construction of 'Iran' in the UK and America was shaped and fixed with reference to the Iranian revolution and there has been little deviation ever since, as was further illustrated by a BBC evening news item which reported on the launch of an Iranian communications satellite through a lens of suspicion about Iran's nuclear weapons programme. In this, as in other coverage, Iran was portrayed as menacing, an irrational, untrustworthy aggressor in the face of attempts by the West to make peace.[64] A later episode of the series did, however, offer an alternative construction by featuring Iran's offer to help the US and its allies in the war against Saddam Hussein. Such counter-discourse rarely occurs in mainstream television news (with the exception of Channel 4, renowned for its more oppositional perspective). Whilst to some extent this series represented an attempt to provide a more nuanced assessment of relations with Iran, it could not help but reinforce the perception that Iran is primarily of interest because of its relationship with 'the West'.

As a result of the variety of television channels and genres, there is considerable diversity of representations as well as some counter discourse. This was evident in the BBC2 travel documentary, *Explore*, which offered a more complex portrayal challenging both stereotypes and the homogenization of Islam, and providing a rare glimpse into the lives of a diversity of ordinary Muslims.[65] In the same week this was also demonstrated in the BBC4 documentary, *Rageh Inside Iran*, and in Omid Djalili's alternative comedy.[66]

This diversity provides a contrast to television programming from the early 1980s when coverage of minority religions was scarce. Religious broadcasting focused generally on Christian 'ecumenism, values and pastoral care', the exception being *Everyman*, a long-running BBC religious affairs programme

---

[62] *Iran and the West*, BBC2, 7 February 2009.

[63] Ibid.

[64] BBC News, BBC1, 3 February 2009.

[65] *Explore: From Istanbul to Anatolia*, BBC2, 8 February 2009. For further discussion, see Chapter 5.

[66] *Rageh Inside Iran*, BBC4, 7 February 2009; *No Age 14*, More4, 4 February 2009.

(1977–2005), and London Weekend Television's *Credo* (1978–1986), which occasionally featured other religious traditions.[67]

The Reception of Media Coverage of Religions

In order to understand what people thought of mainstream media coverage of religions, we commissioned five focus groups in multicultural urban centres.[68] They included adults from diverse social backgrounds some of whom were religious and others not. The participants were too few in number for the results to be generalized, but it is nevertheless noteworthy that there were no major differences between the religious and non-religious groups. Some general patterns were observed:

- Participants were generally liberal-minded and anti-racist.
- People felt that Muslims were poorly represented but within a wider negative representation and marginalization of religion, including Christianity. The news in general was thought to focus on the negative, controversial and sensational. One Muslim felt the media was responsible for 'tainting Muslims'.
- Although views across and within the groups were very mixed, the religious groups engaged in more passionate debate, even argument, about the specifics of their faith and beliefs that they felt had been misunderstood.
- People were aware of media bias and its role in influencing people's ideas, but tried to resist it.

When asked to think about religious representations the participants remembered from television, Islam did not feature that often. Some mentioned wars in the Middle East (particularly with Israel), the soap opera *Eastenders*, the documentary series *Dispatches* (which has been responsible for several negative programmes about British Islam), the film *East is East* (which was enjoyed whilst still being found to be stereotypical), the documentary *Around the World in 80 Faiths* (which was praised) and the British comedian, Omid Djalili (born to Iranian parents). Whilst humour and the ability to mock oneself was seen by most as a positive approach, one Muslim participant felt that this was inappropriate and demonstrated a 'lack of respect'. He argued that this was due to different 'cultural contexts', the lack of understanding of which led to tension between Muslims and non-Muslims.

---

[67]   Knott 1984a, p. 65; Knott and Mitchell 2012, pp. 252–4.

[68]   Five focus groups (one in Stoke-on-Trent, two in Birmingham and two in London), with 44 participants in total. McCloskey 2010. In the 1980s project, data on the reception of religious broadcasting and religion on British television was gathered by means of a survey carried out in the city of Leeds. Knott 1984a, pp. 25–34.

Homogenising Effect

The most significant finding was that, across the board, the participants clearly delineated between extremism and religion and were keen to emphasize the variation within religions. They were aware of how the media homogenize Muslims without explicitly saying so:

> The media do get things wrong, they always portray it as a religious group, but in actual fact it isn't, it's an extremist group. (Birmingham, non-religious)

> Something I've noticed, that is almost unique to Islam, in the sense that if you look at the media they always refer to it or brand it as the Nation of Islam … when really there are Islamic people everywhere, just like the Christian people. (Birmingham, Jewish)

Dominant Discourses

Some dominant discourses about Islam were repeated (by three people, two non-religious and one Christian). One second generation, non-religious Asian participant argued (with reference to Muslims) that people should 'abide by British rules': 'Our parents had to fit in and we'd have to do the same in their countries'. One Christian talked about the marginalization of Christianity and some people felt that this had led to political correctness (see Chapter 3).

Why did they think Muslims were represented negatively? The predominant reason given was economic – the commercial imperative to make sales which leads to a focus on the controversial and sensational.

> The media is always going to show the bad side of religion because that's what in the end gets the ratings, that's what sells the papers … they get more publicity if they show the shock stories. (Stoke, non-religious)

This reason extended from news about religion to news in general, and foreign news was mentioned as being particularly negative.

However, a number of people were also aware of the political context. Most non-Muslims talked about Islam being topical whilst a few Muslims explicitly linked ongoing coverage of Islam to the war on terror:

> If this guy came into the country and said stuff about the Bible, he would not have got no publicity, no nothing, that's the issue, there is a war on terror, so much media hype. (London, Muslim)

However, one non-religious participant went further:

> The war on terror is a war between Christianity and Islam, extremist, but that's essentially what it is. (Stoke, non-religious)

A couple of participants in this group also touched on the idea that negativity towards religion in the media could be due to the decline of religion in society.

Muslims were also critical of the sources used by the media. They had the knowledge to reject them as being non-representative, whilst the inclusion of Muslim sources to the non-Muslim participants was an indication of balance.

Other Religions

Although coverage of all religions was thought to be mainly negative, on reflection a number of people talked of the 'peaceful nature' of some religions (in particular Hinduism, Sikhism and Buddhism) that did not attract negative publicity (as well as being less connected to 'the West').

> There is no violence or nothing, like the controversial issues going on, in the Hindu people, that's why it is not in the media, unless someone ridicules a temple like an Eastern temple, then it comes into the picture. (London, Hindu)

> When you talk about religion the same three names keep cropping up, Islam, Judaism and Christianity, but I've read about other religions, like Rastafarianism, Buddhism, which is probably more of the spirituality kind of thing than the actual religion, and Hinduism, and I've seen those religions portrayed in a more positive way, probably because they are less idolising than, you know less do this, do that, less dictatorial. (London, non-religious)

It was suggested that the inclusion of positive stories may counteract the current negative press, and that local papers could be a possible medium for this. Other suggestions for positive change included avoiding stereotypes and emphasizing commonalities, engaging in socially responsible journalism including 'balance' and 'facts'. The media should also do more to show the human face of religion and real life situations, lives and beliefs of people.[69]

There is no doubt that coverage of minority religions, especially Islam, has grown considerably since the early 1980s. In the propositions posited in Chapter 1, we suggested that media professionals may be animated by religious values that relate to national culture, how religion is of major public concern and can be important in providing both subject matter and language for media narratives. In the media's current focus on topics of militancy, terrorism and cultural threat in relation to other religions we can see how coverage has its roots in the current political and economic context. Anxieties about cohesion, integration and national identity have led to a focus on extremism and cultural difference,

---

[69]   For similar suggestions, see articles by Hussain 2012 and Singh 2012.

especially in relation to Islam. Any behaviour that seems to contradict 'British' values is deemed extreme, and an integrationist discourse prevails. Despite the relatively small number of terrorist activities since 7/7, the media is saturated by images of Islamism, thus demonstrating a particularly intransigent journalistic approach. However, the research also shows, through an analysis of television, how representations can diversify in different media formats. The focus groups, although small-scale, indicate how far these interpretations are challenged by ordinary people. At a time of heightened economic and political sensitivity, these representations, nevertheless, establish an ethical challenge to journalists to produce more measured and responsible journalism.[70]

---

[70] This challenge was reflected in Lord Justice Leveson's report, *An Inquiry into the Culture, Practice and Ethics of the Press* (Leveson 2012), which was being publicly debated in late 2012. On the difficulties of harmonious reporting, see Gledhill 2012, pp. 89–98.

Chapter 5

Media Representations of Atheism and Secularism

In February 2009, in the studio with regular presenters of *The One Show* was Robert Winston, Professor of Reproductive Biology, member of the House of Lords and media celebrity in his own right.[1] From an Orthodox Jewish background, Winston was known for being a scientist open to religion. He had in fact presented a television series, *The Story of God*, some years before.[2] Asked to consider why people were too embarrassed to talk about God, Winston mentioned the bad press religion got from scientists, and named Richard Dawkins – whom he purported to admire – as one of the principal culprits. Dawkins's book, *The God Delusion*, was an outrageous and arrogant affront to religious believers, he said: science itself is just 'a version of the truth', not the truth itself.

As the audience pondered this thought, the screen cut to a shot of a bus emblazoned with the phrase: 'There's probably no God, now stop worrying and enjoy your life.' The atheist bus campaign had been organized by Britain's National Secular Society and launched a month earlier by Richard Dawkins and Ariane Sherine, a young atheist campaigner. Was this advertising immorality, one of the show's presenters asked? 'It suggests that if you believe in God, you don't enjoy life', said another, the two of them expressing a measure of doubt about atheism. Robert Winston – resident expert – followed this up by stating that spirituality had been genetically built into us for many hundreds of years. We shouldn't be too ready to dismiss it, he warned. Mirroring the atheist caricature of religion, these comments showed how atheists themselves were commonly portrayed in the media – as people of questionable morality who assume all believers are deluded and that religion and science are mutually exclusive.[3]

Whilst atheism was addressed explicitly in *The One Show*, secularism was a mere spectre – though an important one. A term with several distinct meanings, 'secularism' may refer to the separation of religion from the state, indifference to religion, and a humanist ideology and ethics. Secularism may also be linked to the idea of 'secularization' in which religion is held to decline in social significance

---

[1]   *The One Show*, BBC1, 3 February 2009.

[2]   Winston 2005.

[3]   Ibid. This is not the right place to question the validity of Winston's argument. However, it was a good example of how scientists and other experts at times use their authority in the media to present something uncertain and contested as unquestionably true, thus disqualifying the opinion of the – in this case absent – opponent.

as society modernizes. Secularization framed the introduction to 'Are We Too Embarrassed to Talk about God?', with shots of empty pews and statistics of declining church attendance. The secularist idea of separation was also implicitly present, with religion portrayed as a private matter. 'Broadcaster Jeremy Vine finds it difficult to talk about faith', the audience was told: it is 'socially unacceptable to say you believe in God'.

As well as the problem of talking publicly about religion, *The One Show* was also critical of the anti-religious public face of atheism. It introduced some of the issues we deal with in this chapter. We begin by showing the rise of atheist and secularist discourse in the British media, emphasizing that this occurs concurrently with a rise in discourse on religion. In the second part we examine the public campaigning of atheists and secularists and analyse their effect on media portrayals. We turn then to the media relationship between religion and science, and follow this with a discussion of the relationship between editorial opinion in the British press and actual content, arguing that the British media is less atheist and secularist than it is often assumed to be. In the final part we compare the normative role of secularism in both domestic and foreign news reporting, and consider its connection to Christianity. Together the themes and cases on which we focus provide a provisional map of media coverage of these two 'isms'.

Atheism and secularism can mean very different things in public discourse. Whilst atheism is understood as a non-religious and often anti-religious perspective, secularism may not necessarily be either. It can even be pro-religious; some religious secularists believe that the state should not interfere with religion, and others are committed to ensuring that no one religion can be allowed to control others.[4] In addition, whilst atheism is widely used as an identity tag, secularism is not. More often than not it denotes an ideological position on how society should be organized, or refers to normative statements about the proper location of religion in public life. Our principal interest though is on how the two are discussed in the media.

The Rise of Atheism and Secularism

The media are not obliged to cover different religions or world views in proportion to the number of their adherents. Other factors are influential, such as the perceived social, political or economic significance of the topic. Muslims, for example, are over-represented in the British media when compared with their relatively low numbers. In the population Census, people of 'no religion' constituted the largest group after Christians (25 per cent in 2011), and their number far exceeded the adherents of any of the minority religions. The 'nones' are not represented in the media as a group, however. Rather, their presence is felt *implicitly* either in references to the decline of religiosity or empty churches, or in debates on the

---

4   Bhargava 2007; Howe 2009, pp. 639–56.

relevance of religion, and *explicitly* in the campaigns of atheists and secularists. Nevertheless, there has been a general increase in the media presence of atheism and secularism and, more specifically, in new discourses on these subjects.

In our newspaper and television sample in the late 2000s, we identified 59 references to atheism, secularism and the conflict between religion and science, a rise from just eleven for the comparable period in the early 1980s. Admittedly, these topics hardly dominated the media, but in numerical terms they surpassed both Buddhism and New Religious Movements. The rise is well illustrated in *The Guardian* online. As Table 1 shows, in 2000 there were fewer than 50 references in *The Guardian* to 'atheism' and 'secularism' combined, but the number had increased six-fold to nearly 300 in 2008.[5] As it confirms, references to these subjects do not rise alone, but in parallel with those to 'religion' and 'faith' both of which doubled their incidence over the same period. The lack of any substantial rise in the number of references to two other identity issues, 'ethnicity' and 'racism' (not shown here), suggests that the increase in coverage of both religion and non-religion is significant.

Table 5.1   Incidence of articles referring to atheism, secularism, religion and faith on *The Guardian* website, 1999–2009

Year	'Atheism'	'Secularism'	'Religion'	'Faith'
1999	23	8	777	1,411
2000	29	19	978	1,775
2001	36	33	1,301	2,357
2002	24	34	1,272	2,324
2003	25	44	1,305	2,515
2004	75	70	1,588	2,822
2005	57	76	1,796	2,981
2006	88	109	2,050	3,330
2007	126	139	2,121	3,648
2008	143	148	2,343	3,813
2009	152	113	2,327	3,975

This rise is further illustrated if we compare the early 1980s with the late 2000s. According to our two samples, references to atheism and secularism increased more than references to all religious traditions other than Christianity and Islam. But an increase in itself is no necessary indicator of greater social importance. Two observations are telling, however. First, the discussion of atheism and secularism

---

[5]   Figures from search on www.guardian.co.uk, March 2010 (numbers have since changed, though general trends have not).

was largely an elite debate covered in the broadsheets rather than the popular tabloids. Most references were found in *The Times*, very few in the *The Sun* and *Yorkshire Evening Post*, though coverage was spread more evenly across BBC1, BBC2 and ITV1. Secondly, when they were discussed, atheism and secularism were not passing references but the main issue in articles or television programmes. They appeared generally in news and currents affairs or in editorials and comment, suggesting that this was a serious subject which was not taken lightly. When we juxtapose this to our other findings – that references to religious traditions were often made in passing, that Judaism was often referenced in obituaries in *The Times*, Buddhism in announcements and listings in the *Yorkshire Evening Post*, and psychic powers and witchcraft in television advertisements – it is clear that atheism and secularism were deemed important and worthy issues for discussion.

Atheism was not a common media topic back in the early 1980s. It was mentioned most often in *The Times*, where it was seen mainly as the enemy of Christianity. One article defended the doctrine of incarnation against the mindset and incredulity of 'modern man'.[6] This was directed toward Christian reformers who might be inclined to adjust the doctrine to make it easier for 'modern man' to swallow in the face of the 'onslaughts of secularism and atheism'.[7] Atheism also appeared in theatre and comedy reviews as well as in the context of Soviet ideology which was seen by one commentator as a common threat to both Islam and the Christian West.[8]

In the early 1980s there were some brief references to secularism as well as a few articles that considered it in more detail. Secularism had a double meaning. On the one hand, it was seen as threatening and an ally of relativism working against Christianity. On the other, it was considered a virtuous dimension of a state education system which was depicted as religiously diverse in composition but secular in tone.[9] Here secularism, as we will see again in relation to its contemporary treatment, was presented as worthy of approbation or approval, with Christianity as the yardstick. At that time the debate on religious symbols in public spaces was not organized – as it is today – around the distinction between religion and the non-religious secular. Instead, in one article, the debate about the banning of Christmas trees and carols was conceptualized as a clash between Pagan symbols and true Christianity.[10]

However, the presence of a letter in *The Times* in March 1982, prior to the visit of Pope John Paul II to Britain, reminds us that not everything in the current explosion of discourse on atheism and secularism is new.[11] Barbara Smoker, then President of the National Secular Society, addressed some well-rehearsed

---

[6]   *The Times* 1982a.

[7]   Ibid.

[8]   *The Times* 1982d.

[9]   *The Times* 1982c.

[10]   *The Times* 1982b; compare *Yorkshire Evening Post* 2008c.

[11]   Smoker 1982.

allegations towards the Pope, accusing him of underestimating the problem of overpopulation, of endorsing the sinfulness of birth control and abortion, of women's domestic role and clergy celibacy, and condemning homosexuality. She also contended that the Society she represented was 'deeply concerned about the excessive media coverage that will obviously be given to the reactionary sentiments of John Paul II during his four-day tour in Britain, with comparatively little argument on the other side'.[12] Evidently the liberal secular critique has been present in the media for a long time, but one sentiment in Smoker's letter suggests that something has changed. She claimed that the National Secular Society was not anti-Christian, and indeed sought allegiance with all liberal-minded people – religious or otherwise – against the Pope's conservative teachings. At the time of the Papal visit in 2010, there was no such evidence of a progressive alliance.[13]

Public Campaigning

The public campaigning of atheists and secularists has gained considerable attention in the media. One of its purposes has been to raise consciousness about the excessive role of religion in society and its repressive nature. Perhaps even more important has been the attempt to activate those who are indifferent, to encourage them to come 'out of the closet' and persuade them to declare their atheism. The assumption has been that those who do not believe in God or go to church would be prepared to join forces with campaigning atheists if only their consciousness was raised.[14] The most high profile initiative in recent times was the atheist bus campaign.

In January 2009, advertisements were placed on the sides of public buses. It would probably have been a minor local event in a couple of British cities had it not been for newspapers, television and the internet which helped transform it into a publicity stunt that went global and was later mimicked in other countries.[15] The idea for the campaign came from writer and journalist Ariane Sherine, who was shown in many images with Dawkins in front of one of the buses.

Rather than demonizing the campaign, the media strategy adopted by religious representatives was quite different. *The Sun* quoted Methodist minister, Jenny Ellis, who thanked Richard Dawkins for 'getting God on London buses': 'We are grateful to Richard for his continued interest in God and for encouraging people to think about these issues.'[16] *The Times* reported on how the Christian think tank,

---

[12]   Ibid.

[13]   Public atheist, Richard Dawkins, in advance of the 2010 Papal visit, was far more hard-line in his anti-papal opinions and offered no such olive branch. *The Sunday Times* 2010.

[14]   Taira 2012a, pp. 97–113.

[15]   See http://www.atheistbus.org.uk/press/.

[16]   Hagan 2008.

Theos, donated £50 to the bus campaign 'in the belief that talking about God is a good thing'.[17] A similar attitude had been recorded prior to the campaign by the Catholic author, John Cornwell, who said of Richard Dawkins: 'his views may do more good than harm: what an explosion of reviews, viewpoints, newspaper columns, debates, lectures, and seminars he has prompted!'[18] On the one hand, these examples can be interpreted as deliberate and clever responses devised to counter the reactionary representation of religious people in the media. On the other, they reveal a complex situation in which the only sure outcome was the intensification of a debate which ended up benefiting both sides.

Atheists and secularists appeared increasingly to organize themselves like religious bodies, with the two types often compared in the media. Presented as similar but different, atheist organizations were juxtaposed with religious groups in a media context where the distinction between religion and non-religion continued to be reproduced. The atheist bus campaign was a good example of the symbiotic relationship between the two having begun as a response to Christian bus advertisements (for example, for the Alpha Course).

Some months after the campaign, *Camp Quest UK* was launched. This so-called 'atheist' camp for children and young people aged 8–17 was run for the first time in the UK in the summer of 2009, modelled on an American venture originally developed as an alternative to religious summer camps. It was widely reported in the media, from the BBC news to a lengthy article in the *Daily Mail* which had the headline: 'Camp faithless: Is Britain's first atheist summer camp harmless fun or should we be worried?'[19] Neither option sounded promising. The heading implied a religious readership ('we') likely to be troubled by the idea of atheism. Religious metaphors were used throughout to slur and belittle atheism and its followers: Dawkins's *The God Delusion* was called the atheist 'bible', promotion of the camp, its 'mission', and its theme tune – John Lennon's 'Imagine' – the camp's 'hymn of choice'.[20] It was presented as a negative mirror-image of organized religion.

Similar traits were visible in the debate in July 2009 about whether BBC Radio 4's flagship *Thought for the Day* should open itself up to non-religious contributors.[21] The BBC invited public comment to 'Should Thought stay sacred?', and edited responses could be read online. Religious and non-religious

---

[17]   Bakewell 2008. At the time of the launch the Director of Theos stated: 'We think that the campaign is a great way to get people thinking about God. The posters will encourage people to consider the most important question we will ever face in our lives. The slogan itself is a great discussion starter. Telling someone "there's probably no God" is a bit like telling them they've probably remembered to lock their door. It creates the doubt that they might not have.' *The Times Online*, 6 January 2009.

[18]   Cornwell 2007, p. 18.

[19]   Brennan 2009.

[20]   Ibid.

[21]   BBC News 2009b.

people commented in remarkably similar ways, agreeing and disagreeing in equal measure. Some said it was the content that counted, not the identity of the speaker; but a few – presumably religious commentators – doubted whether atheists had anything of interest to say and suggested an alternative programme for atheists called 'Waffle for the Day'.[22] The debate nevertheless revealed the anxiety felt by some in and beyond the media that atheists and secularists should have equal rights even in traditionally religious domains.

The formative influence of religious groups on atheist and secularist organizations was not one way, however. Although religious advertisements led to the atheist bus campaign, the latter was soon followed by another round of religious bus advertising. The Christian Party simply changed the message to 'There definitely is a God; so join the Christian Party and enjoy your life', and the Trinitarian Bible Society adopted its slogan from Psalm 53.1: 'The fool hath said in his heart, there is no God.'[23] Christian Alpha course adverts were back on the buses by the summer of 2009, followed by another atheist advertisement in November, this time on billboards. It was called the 'Don't label me campaign', based on a theme covered in Richard Dawkins's book, *The God Delusion*: 'Please don't label me. Let me grow up and choose myself', the message read.[24]

The third point to note is that these public campaigns strengthened the peculiar relationship between Dawkins and the British media. By becoming *the* spokesperson of atheism – or 'megaphone atheist', as *The Times* once put it – Dawkins hijacked the media portrayal of atheists and of non-religious people in general. The representation of atheism was narrowed down to the views of Dawkins and a few like-minded companions. It is important to bear in mind that there were other kinds of atheists too, as well as humanists, agnostics and other non-religious people, whose voices were not heard in the media, partly because they were not interested in public campaigning but also because the voice of Dawkins was so loud. Although the mainstream media – both television and newspapers – offered plenty of criticism of Dawkins and the New Atheism, his celebrity status ensured that whatever he said continued to be widely reported.

Religion and Science: Conflict or Co-existence?

Our television research in February 2009 coincided with the bicentenary of Charles Darwin, as a result of which several programmes addressed the relationships between religion and science, and religion and evolution. They included *This Morning* (ITV1), *Charles Darwin and the Tree of Life* (BBC2), a documentary

---

22　Ibid.

23　BBC News 2009a.

24　Sherine 2009.

about the life and ideas of Darwin, and the debating programme, *The Big Questions* (BBC1), the latter asking, 'Can the Bible and Darwin both be Right?'[25]

The main guest on *This Morning* was none other than Robert Winston whom we had met the previous day in *The One Show* and who, on this occasion, discussed the importance of educating children about evolution. Evolution was introduced as 'perhaps the most important single idea in biology', but its veracity was established in contrast to the biblical Genesis and the literalist Christian conviction that the earth was created on 21 October 4004 BC.[26] When one of the programme hosts compared biblical creation and evolution, saying that the former ignores the dinosaurs, Winston was quick to respond that evolution does not in any way undermine religion. He gave an allegorical interpretation of Genesis and emphasized that the argument between science and religion is unfortunate, sad and unnecessary. The host suggested that perhaps science and religion might both have a role to play, to which Winston immediately responded, 'I absolutely feel we should be co-existing'; the polarization between science and religion is unhelpful and disturbing.[27]

A more extended treatment of evolution was given by David Attenborough in an hour-long documentary *Charles Darwin and the Tree of Life* (BBC2). Like the brief piece in *This Morning*, it also placed Genesis on the agenda when introducing the idea of evolution. Biblical creation was said to have been accepted literally by the whole of pre-Darwinian Western Europe as an explanation for the emergence of species.[28] Religion was presented as an obstacle in the public discussion of the origin of species. Attenborough suggested that Darwin knew that the idea that species may have come into being without divine intervention was dangerous, and that it was perhaps his wife's religiosity that explained his caution and reticence to publish his scientific work. Although any conclusions were left to the viewer's imagination, the implication was that Darwin was an atheist. It was stressed further in the allusion to the latter part of his life when he stopped attending church, but preferred to wait outside while Emma and the children went into the service. A serious and high quality documentary, it nevertheless gave a firm steer to viewers to see Christianity as both antithetical to and problematic for Darwin's work on evolution. First, the overarching narrative in the documentary concerned the paradigmatic shift from the Bible to evolution and natural selection, the two being presented as competing explanations and the latter assumed to be true without hesitation. There was no suggestion that the two might be seen as offering different levels of explanation; neither were problems in the evolutionary model mentioned for the sake of balance.

---

[25] *This Morning*, ITV1, 4 February 2009; *Charles Darwin and the Tree of Life*, BBC2, 7 February 2009; *The Big Questions*, BBC1, 8 February 2009. See also Chapter 3.

[26] *This Morning*, ITV1, 4 February 2009.

[27] Ibid.

[28] *Charles Darwin and the Tree of Life*, BBC2, 7 February 2009.

The depiction of Darwin's attitude to religion strengthened the documentary's implicit claim that caution explained Darwin's failure to express his opposition to religion in the public sphere. This representation, however, is challenged by Darwin's own letters, writings and life. He never identified himself as an atheist and, in fact, denied it in letters to the Professor of Natural History, Asa Gray, and the sceptic, John Fordyce, whilst, in letters to the socialist, Edvard Aveling, and the Revd J. B. Inness, he argued against attacking religion from the perspective of science.[29] Rather, he hoped and believed that scientific work would enlighten religious thinking. Furthermore, the documentary ignored the many positive responses to Darwin by religious people, and omitted to mention that responses to Darwin's work were generally mixed and not divided strictly between scientific supporters and religious opponents. Finally, the documentary was silent about the agnosticism that had prevailed in British elite circles before Darwin, thus overemphasizing the revolutionary impact of his theory. This absence enabled the documentary to portray a simple transformation from an absolute religious worldview to one of Darwinian evolutionism.

Both *This Morning* and *Charles Darwin and the Tree of Life* narrated the idea of evolution in contrast to Genesis, but they were very different in their general approach towards religion. The former denied any necessary incompatibility between religion and science, whilst the latter assumed it.

The third example from the same week was *The Big Questions* in which several different positions were represented.[30] The programme included Evangelical Christians sceptical of the power of Darwinian explanation and scientists who campaigned for atheism and secularism (such as Professor of Chemistry and Honorary Associate of the National Secular Society, Peter Atkins). Between these two extremes, there were the mediating figures of Lord Carey, former Archbishop of Canterbury, and Steve Fuller, Professor of Sociology, a dissenter from the neo-Darwinist synthesis and defender of Protestantism as a motivating force in science. The host, Nicky Campbell, framed the question 'Can the Bible and Darwin both be right?' by mentioning that one-third of British people believe that God created the earth less than 10,000 years ago, thus highlighting the acuteness of the debate between religion and science. Moving from the views of Evangelical creationism to scientistic atheism, Lord Carey then offered a third option, compatibility between the two. The Bible and Darwin are both right, he said, because they talk about two different entities. As a representative of the Church of England, his role was to mediate between the extremes.

Two observations are worth noting. The first concerns staging. The floor of the debate was divided in two with the extreme positions on either side and the host in the middle. The programme's main guests were on a podium (and were given more time to comment than other speakers and members of the audience).

---

[29]   Cockshut 1964, pp. 168–70; Darwin 2010, pp. 392–6; Desmond and Moore 1991; Spencer 2009.

[30]   *The Big Questions*, BBC1, 8 February 2009.

Not everyone on the podium was religious, nevertheless a clear message of the necessary coexistence of religion and evolution was voiced (by Muslim journalist, Fareena Alam, and non-religious writer and broadcaster, Bidisha, as well as by Lord Carey). Although such debates are not expected to end in agreement, with viewers left to make up their own minds, these consensual voices were made more authoritative by the staging. This revealed the implicit position of the programme itself, one that is in line with British media and society more generally: science and religion are both important, but campaigning atheism and creationism are unwelcome.

The second observation concerns competing attempts to guarantee the meaning of life. Evolution is generally presented as a theory that undermines Christian doctrine, but it is also seen as disenchanting the world or emptying it of meaning. That is why, in the narrative of co-existence, the suggestion is often made that religion still answers the 'why' questions whilst science shows 'how' something came into being. Partly because the non-religious world is sometimes seen as devoid of meaning, some atheists have sought to (re)construct meaning by referring to evolution's aesthetic dimension (its beauty), and its potential for re-enchantment. This was exemplified in *The Big Questions* when Peter Atkins described evolution as 'a miraculous process' in understanding 'the beauty of this world'.[31] Science was presented by its atheist and secularist protagonists as sacred (what we refer to in this book as 'secular sacred'), as taking the place of religion, not only by explaining the evolution of the species but by providing meaning and beauty in a world increasingly devoid of it.[32]

The bi-centenary of Darwin provided an excellent opportunity to analyse and compare how religion and atheism were represented in media accounts of evolution. Narratives of both conflict and co-existence between the two were traceable. What they had in common was the separation of religion and science. It was assumed but not explicated. In the conflict narrative, evolution equalled science, and both were linked to atheism. This narrative did not usually refer to atheism or atheists explicitly; it simply denounced a stereotypical creationist religious viewpoint. Even in this case, when linked to science, atheism was rarely represented in a positive light. In the co-existence narrative, the link between science and atheism was challenged. Here, atheists were generally represented as intolerant, arrogant, quarrelsome and eager to denounce religious people as wrong or 'lazy', as Peter Atkins provocatively stated in *The Big Questions*.[33] Whilst both narratives were present in the media, there was a tendency to favour the co-existence narrative which was at times accompanied by a negative portrayal of anti-religious atheists, even though the significance of science was taken for granted. This suggests that

---

[31]   Ibid.

[32]   Following the publication of New Atheist bestsellers, meaning-making and spirituality have become popular themes in atheist discourse: Antinoff 2009; Comte-Sponville 2007; De Botton 2012; Maisel 2009. For an analysis: Taira 2012b, pp. 388–404.

[33]   *The Big Questions*, BBC1, 8 February 2009.

media representations and the values that underlie them are not as anti-religious or secularist as is sometimes assumed. It is to this assumption that we now turn.

Rethinking the Idea of the 'Secularist Media'

Consider the following description:

> He [Dawkins] speaks to a significant minority – among them the 25 to 30 per cent of the British population who will declare in an opinion poll that they have no belief in God. Such people, it is worth noting, will be predominantly male; they will also be clustered in certain professions, notably the media.[34]

The suggestion here is that people who work in the media are often non-religious.[35] While media professionals are purportedly less religious than the British population at large, this does not reveal anything certain about their professional attitude towards atheism, secularism and non-religiosity more generally. It tells us even less about the content of the media. In the American context it has been argued convincingly that the media is 'unsecular', because the professionals who cover religion there are more religious than other media professionals and have generally positive attitudes towards the subject.[36] In the British context, as we have seen, the media publishes anti-religious and atheistic views, but it rarely endorses them.

According to interviews conducted by Annikka Mutanen, journalists and editors do not conform to their popular image as atheists who are indifferent or hostile to religion.[37] In fact, none of those interviewed said they openly supported atheism or secularism in their work. On the contrary, a few editors expressed their support for Christianity. For example, *The Telegraph* favours Christianity in general and the Church of England in particular. As the religion editor, George Pitcher, stated,

> I'm trying to be rather more pluralistic about it, but nevertheless I think that's starting from … the position of *The Telegraph* that has seen this traditionally as a Christian country, as a country that has an established church, a church that co-exists with the state and monarch who is head of them both, the church and the state. And therefore *The Telegraph* is going to start from that position. And it

---

[34]   Berger, Davie and Fokas 2008, p. 60.
[35]   See also Davie 2000; Holmes 2010.
[36]   Silk 1998; Winston and Green 2012, pp. 34–35.
[37]   Mutanen 2009.

has to be said it has often had quite a Roman Catholic input as well. The owners of *The Telegraph* are Roman Catholic.[38]

For the *Daily Mail*, religion was not considered a core element of their coverage, but the paper showed increasing interest in stories about secularization and the marginalization of Christianity.[39] Even *The Guardian* and *The Independent* did not express any explicit interest in promoting secularism: according to its editor-in-chief, *The Independent* opposed aggressive secularism.[40]

In order to assess the treatment of atheism and secularism, these editorial attitudes will be compared to the actual content of newspapers by focusing on their coverage of the case of the Dutch MP, Geert Wilders, whose entrance to Britain was denied in February 2009 on the grounds that his opinions were a threat to community harmony and public safety.[41] He had been due to show his inflammatory, anti-Islamic film *Fitna* to an invited audience in Britain's second chamber, the House of Lords.

In contrast with the prevailing image of a secularist media, the dominant position in the press was a fusion of Christianity and moderate secularism (with the emphasis on freedom of expression). This became visible in the complaints of media commentators about double standards. It went as follows: the British are surrendering to political correctness and the imposition of minorities in allowing Muslim 'hate preachers' to stay in the country whilst banning a white Christian male who opposes Islam.[42] Many of the most popular newspapers in Britain – *The Telegraph, Daily Mail, The Express* and *The Sun* – employed this discourse. *The Telegraph*, for example, used expressions like 'our Christian country', 'our Islamist enemies' and asked 'what of those who oppress Christians?'[43] *The Guardian* and *The Independent* were exceptions. Their political standpoint and reader profiles were very different from the other national dailies.[44] *The Guardian* hardly mentioned Christianity and *The Independent* was strongly secularist (with some evidence of an anti-religious stance).[45]

---

[38]   Ibid., p. 41. Gill states that *The Telegraph* is hostile to religion. This conclusion holds true for the paper's coverage of Islam, but is open to question on its treatment of Christianity. Gill 2012, pp. 45–60.

[39]   Mutanen 2009, p. 43.

[40]   Ibid., p. 51.

[41]   See Chapter 7.

[42]   Muir, Petley and Smith 2011, pp. 66–99.

[43]   Quotations from *The Telegraph*, February 2009.

[44]   *The Independent* is the paper most closely associated with the liberal democrats; of all daily readers of national newspapers, readers of *The Guardian* are least likely to vote for the Conservatives. Kuhn 2007, p. 214.

[45]   Hari 2009.

The Guardian emerged as secularist by a process of negation. Wilders was defined as 'the Catholic right-winger' and 'racist provocateur', not one of 'us'.[46] Furthermore, the paper strongly emphasized freedom of speech. Even though it did not endorse secularism as such, it published an article by a well-known atheist A.C. Grayling.[47] Moreover, in another article the paper suggested that conservative papers would not have spoken as stridently against the banning of Wilders had the case not been about a white Christian opposing Islam, thus distancing itself from other papers with a Christian emphasis. Despite the secular – and in some cases also pluralist – self-positioning of the paper, its coverage was not anti-religious. *The Independent*, however, published a strong defence of secularism and the freedom to criticize religions by Johann Hari.[48] The online copy of this article contained a postscript promoting secularist associations and provided links for further information. Nothing like this could be found in any other national dailies. Despite the strong emphasis on secularism and freedom of speech in *The Independent*, there was no defence of Wilders who was described as 'racist' and the source of 'ugly nonsense'.[49]

Coverage of the Wilders case revealed that the greatest divergence between editorial statement and actual content was in *The Independent*. Portrayed as a paper that opposed aggressive secularism, in this context it openly promoted organized secularism. But this was rare. Whilst the idea of a 'secularist media' is not nonsensical, because some secularist voices are indeed heard in the liberal, left-of-centre press, it is a narrow and misleading view of the British media landscape in general. It prevails because the media does not always report positively on religious matters and does not match the expectations of religious people. This view needs to be refined with reference to both the stated attitudes of media professionals on religion – especially those who have a responsibility for reporting on it – and their actual media portrayals.

Secularism in Domestic and Foreign Contexts

From the perspective of atheism and secularism, the case of Wilders turned out to be a minor controversy that people now struggle to remember.[50] However, it was an example of how secularism was understood, assessed and evaluated in

---

[46]   Quotations from *The Guardian*, 13 February 2009.

[47]   Grayling 2009.

[48]   Hari 2009. Johann Hari was a regular contributor to *The Independent* and some of his writings were anti-religious. However, his views were not indicative of those of the paper more generally.

[49]   Quotations from *The Independent*, 12 and 13 February 2009.

[50]   In focus groups undertaken a year after the event no one was able to put a name to Wilders's face. For some he was that 'Dutch guy'; others did not even recognize him at all. Once they began reading an article about him, the majority remembered the incident.

the context of national identity and religiosity. This can be pursued further if we ask what kind of ideological perspective dominates the media. As we will show, a moderate secularism with a relative separation of the religious and the secular seems to be the norm.[51] On occasions this moderate secularism is fused with Christianity, particularly in the conservative media. Although this norm makes space for moderate religious standpoints, it is Christianity that is represented as prototypical of a good and moral religion. In addition, Christianity plays a role in separating good and bad versions of secularism.

Paul Weller's description of Britain as Christian, secular and religiously plural is also the dominant normative position in the media.[52] In relation to secularism there seems to be a double standard at work: when juxtaposed with domestic Christianity, it is often criticized for being too narrow or strict; when treated in an international but non-Christian context, it is presented more positively, sometimes as the neutral basis for a society in which secularism guarantees the right balance between conflicting sides. This argument will be substantiated with examples from articles on Britain, India, the USA, Israel and Turkey. Reporting on Turkish secularism is exceptional and its specificity will be discussed.

We begin with five examples from *The Times* which focus on Britain. In the first it was argued that 'a bit of magic and fantasy in childhood is useful and helps you to grapple with your fears about life, death, peril and chance'.[53] This was targeted at Richard Dawkins who had warned about the pernicious nature of fairytales. In another case it was suggested that 'Myths have huge power! That's true even in our ultra-scientific, post-superstitious age'.[54] This was also directed against Dawkins who was assumed to believe that myths would disappear if challenged or countered with scientific rationality. The third example proposed that 'it is ironic that politicians in this country have abandoned belief – at the very moment that the people need hope'.[55] This story opposed the strict secularist separation of religion and politics, private and public, the writer complaining that British politicians were no longer able to express their religiosity in a professional context. In the fourth example, the commentator put forward an argument against the atheist bus campaign: 'My own fear is that, while this has started in a gentle and unconfrontational way, it may fuel the notion that people have to be antagonistic to those of other faiths … I am apprehensive that it may be seen by others as a move in the battle of faith-versus-science.'[56] Dawkins was also targeted in an article that advocated the compatibility of religion and science: 'God is outside the scope of science, unless you are Richard Dawkins.'[57]

---

[51]   Neither an 'absolute separation' nor 'no separation', see Modood 2010, pp. 4–14.

[52]   Weller 2008.

[53]   Purves 2008b.

[54]   Morrison 2008.

[55]   Sylvester 2008.

[56]   Bakewell 2008.

[57]   Barnes 2008c.

Although these examples do not oppose secularism as such, they suggest that good secularism makes space for moderate religiosity, especially Christianity, just as Christianity – which is supportive of morality and imagination – should be open to moderate secularism. Bad secularism and atheism do not allow space for imagination and fantasy, for the sense of mystery, myth and morality.

The understanding of the role and function of secularism is quite different in articles dealing with international issues. In reports on India, secularism was understood as a solution to conflict between religions, and also seen as protecting India's Christian minority. Furthermore, it was connected to democracy and the growing economy, and distanced from earlier bureaucratic and xenophobic government. 'Secular tolerance' was claimed to be the best of India's past.[58] In reports on religion in the US, secularism was seen as offering a positive framework for separating religion from politics.[59] Generally the reporting opposed the mixing of religion and politics, particularly when the religious view in question was 'conservative' or 'fundamentalist' Christianity. Stories related to Israel formed yet another example. In a story about Jerusalem's mayoral election, a value-laden opposition was constructed between the ultra-Orthodox Jewish community and secular Israelis. The former was strict, conservative and a threat to 'young entrepreneurs', whereas the latter were not anti-religious but capable of protecting Jerusalem, Israel and the Jewish people.[60]

Turkish secularism was an exception because it was not described as a neutral political settlement which protects religious and non-religious groups alike, but as an example of secularism gone too far. It was as if the limits of secularism were being negotiated in articles and programmes about Turkey, with 'Turkey' working as an example of bad secularism. This was exemplified in two articles in *The Times* and one television programme, *Explore: From Istanbul to Anatolia* (BBC2).[61]

The first of the articles was about the trial of a 'secret secularist network', so-called 'Deep-State'.[62] This group was depicted as an example of an overtly nationalistic secularism that uses legal and illegal means to prevent both Islamist developments in government and activities that 'insult' Turkishness. The group was described by the prosecutor, Mete Gokturk, as a 'backward entity' that should be banned to enable Turkey's integration into the wider world (the European Union).[63] The second article introduced *Mustafa*, a film that depicts Kemal Atatürk in an unflattering manner.[64] It noted that the film had upset many secularists, with

---

[58]   Maddox 2008.

[59]   Jacoby 2008.

[60]   Hider 2008.

[61]   *The Times*, 20 October and 8 November 2008; *Explore: From Istanbul to Anatolia*, BBC2, 8 February 2009.

[62]   Erdem 2008a.

[63]   Ibid.

[64]   Erdem 2008b.

Deep State described as an ultra-nationalist group which had brought about self-censorship in the media and had prevented freedom of expression.

Explore: From Istanbul to Anatolia portrayed Turkey expansively, commenting on its role between East and West, and its secular and Islamic traditions.[65] Turkish secularism was threatened, it was suggested, by the rise of the Justice and Development party (AKP) which – at local level – had demonstrated its Islamic 'fundamentalism' by banning the sale of alcohol. To emphasize the importance of the secular state and the separation of religion and politics, viewers were reminded of Turkey's secular constitution and its roots in the struggle for freedom, with Kemal Atatürk mentioned as its architect. The programme then turned to the 'darker side' of secularism. This version was militant and on a 'collision course' with 'conservative Islam': 'Any ideas that might undermine Atatürk's vision of Turkey are treated as dangerous'.[66] Providing evidence for this, the programme showed an interview with a publisher who had encountered problems because of his defence of free speech. Vulnerable Kurdish minorities were portrayed over against nationalistic and secularist Turks, the latter representing a bad and repressive form of secularism.

This focus on Turkey was almost certainly connected to its attempt to join the European Union. However, in our view, when the British media discusses Turkish secularism, it is also reflecting Britain and its possible futures. The problem of Turkish secularism is that it is seen as overtly nationalistic and exclusive. Turkey offers an example of a secularism which has gone too far, one that Britain should not follow: moderate secularism, like moderate Christianity, is what is needed. Applied to the British context, the media message is that secularism should be supported but it must remain diligent about avoiding intolerance towards Christianity and Britain's ethnic and religious minorities. Arguably, reservations about the New Atheists and their campaigns are part of the same dominant discourse in which some versions of atheism and secularism are conceptualized as unwanted and a potential threat to society – whilst a different version, of moderate atheism and tolerant secularism, is supported at the same time.

In the normal course of events then, domestic secularism was ridiculed or critiqued, but when secularism was applied to an international and non-Christian context, it was generally seen more positively. According to the media, if there was something amiss with secularism, the story was probably about Turkey or Britain.

---

[65]   *Explore: From Istanbul to Anatolia*, BBC2, 8 February 2009. Muslims were shown hunting wild boar, eating pork and drinking alcohol. A wide variety of habits and interpretations was depicted, and the overall impression was that Turkish Muslims were relaxed about their religion and its interpretation (the programme presenter, a British Muslim, noted that they would not be considered proper Muslims in the UK).

[66]   *Explore: From Istanbul to Anatolia*, BBC2, 8 February 2009.

Reporting Atheism and Secularism

Today the British media report on atheism and secularism far more than they did in the early 1980s. In addition to debates about the return of religion to public life in Britain or beyond, it is public campaigning by atheist and secularist groups that has prompted this interest. Religious campaigns are not a new phenomenon, but atheist campaigning has raised some objections and anxieties which have sparked widespread debate and a religious response. The overwhelming presence of Richard Dawkins in the media has silenced other non-religious voices. Not that the media sympathize with Dawkins, but he has celebrity status, causes controversy and can attract an audience, all qualities that sell papers and programmes.

The media representation of atheism and secularism tends to be dominated by white men who elevate the natural sciences as their guiding principle; as a non-white woman, Ariane Sherine was an exception. More broadly, the current polarized debate leaves out ordinary non-religious people. Quantitatively speaking there are many more of these than there are self-identifying atheists, but they offer nothing exotic that would make news, stimulate media debate, attract human interest or entertain.

The media's normative position is the middle-ground between a campaigning atheism and an evangelical or literalist Christianity. The media is rarely anti-religious, not even when defending science against creationism and biblical literalism: generally, it emphasizes the possibility of co-existence between mainstream religion and science. But, even when a scientific outlook is explicitly cherished, it is rare to find an overtly positive media representation of atheism and its supporters.

Although Christianity is occasionally mocked in comedy and cartoons, there are many articles and programmes about social and economic issues in which Christians are presented as moral specialists and representatives of the common good. Atheists are never seen in that role. And, whilst secularism is a more positively-loaded term than atheism, the media nevertheless criticizes it when it sees it as opposing Christianity. For these reasons the stereotypical image of the 'secularist media' should be challenged or at least refined. Although the coverage varies from one media source to another, it is more accurate to describe the dominant position as one of fusion between (domestic and national) Christianity and moderate secularism.

Chapter 6
Popular Belief and Ritual Practice, and their Media Representations

A busy Birmingham street. A reporter, microphone in hand, attempts to interview people for *The One Show* about their views on God and religion. They are shown running away and refusing to discuss it: 'I don't really talk about it', '...only if I had to'; 'We'd rather not answer'. Amidst this seeming embarrassment, the reporter distributes stickers saying 'Do God' and 'Don't do God'. At the end of her informal media survey she concludes that 'God is winning'. In itself this is interesting given the way the topic was introduced to viewers – with pictures of empty church pews and statistics about church decline. But we are none the wiser about what God means to people and what it is they do or do not believe. What is obvious though is that most people are reluctant to talk about it in public. For most, it is a private matter.

When people are willing to disclose their religiosity, their answers can be very illuminating. As part of our research we conducted focus groups to hear what ordinary people thought about the media treatment of religion. In addition to an initial pilot with students, we commissioned four groups, mixed in terms of age, gender, class and ethnicity. Two comprised people from a range of different religious backgrounds; two, those who self-identified as 'non-religious'. Here is what the 'non-religious' people said about themselves.[1] Their self-descriptions are organized in a spectrum from expressions of belief, through agnosticism to atheism.

> Believes in Karma, from a very religious background
> Believe in spirituality and karma
> Drawn towards spirituality
> Believe in some higher power, maybe planetary but not God
> Believe something is up there, but not 100 per cent
> Open minded and interested in Spirituality
> More of a freethinker – but does support family (Chinese) traditions
> Agnostic
> Still thinking about it all
> Thinks there is something greater than us, but not religion
> Thinks whatever happens happens
> Believes we are masters of our own destiny

---

[1]   McCloskey 2010, p. 22.

Non-religious, believe in the Big Bang
Atheist – parents very religious (Hindu)
Don't believe in anything
At 16, decided didn't believe
Dismissed her religion
Never had a religion and don't need one

What is striking about these statements by non-religious people is their variety.[2] A number of people profess to believing, but in a variety of different beings or powers, whilst some don't know what they believe or deny any kind of belief. Spirituality is mentioned by three people, karma by two, with three others mentioning something up there, higher or greater than us. Others refer to different kinds of agency: the big bang, humans as agents of their own destiny, or chance ('whatever happens happens'). A couple acknowledge their religious background, with others saying they never felt any need for religion or dismissed it at some point. If we add to these those who self-identify as religious – referring to themselves as 'Christian', 'Catholic', 'Anglican', 'Methodist', 'New Christian', 'Muslim', 'Hindu', 'Jewish', 'Sikh' – we see the extraordinary variety of professions of identity amongst just thirty-six people (admittedly selected for their differences).

The labels 'Do God' and 'Don't do God' clearly don't tell us much about personal beliefs and ritual practices, but the issue of privacy identified in *The One Show* is undoubtedly important. Not only do most people affirm in opinion polls that religion should be a private matter, but they live this out by keeping quiet on the subject unless formally prompted.[3] We know so little about whether the people around us self-identify as religious, spiritual, non-religious, agnostic or atheist, what they believe in and whether they act in accordance with their beliefs that it comes as a surprise when we hear the results of surveys and opinion polls on religion, spirituality, beliefs or superstition, or encounter people's professions of religion or belief on television or in the press. Looking at magazine-style programmes across our week of TV viewing in 2009, a range of beliefs and practices begins to emerge: people's beliefs about luck and the practice of gambling were aired; an alternative spiritual lifestyle in Wales was depicted; witchcraft was examined as part of popular culture; and monastic experience, faith healing and folk practices were all shown.[4] What is striking is that such matters are often presented as quirky, quaint or unusual, even dangerous or misguided, rather than part of the variegated but nevertheless everyday landscape of popular belief and practice.

In our first project in the 1980s, in addition to investigating portrayals of conventional religion of the kind we looked at in the chapters on Christianity and

---

[2] For a theoretical and empirical study of what it means to be 'non-religious' in contemporary Britain, see Lee 2011.

[3] Field 2012.

[4] Magazine programmes included *Breakfast* (BBC1), *The One Show* (BBC1), *GMTV* (ITV1) and *This Morning* (ITV1).

Islam and other religions, we examined 'common religion'. By this we meant those beliefs and practices that were associated with the supernatural but were non-institutional and not formally endorsed by religious authorities. They were often referred to in derogatory terms and included superstition, luck, magic, the paranormal, faith healing, fortune-telling and spiritualism.[5] Surveys suggest that these remain important areas of popular culture, and large numbers of people believe and sometimes participate in them as practitioners or clients. As historical studies confirm for earlier periods and as remains the case today, most people do not draw a hard boundary between conventional and common religion: their beliefs and practices reveal elements of both.[6] Furthermore, this is true of people of all religions and none, with Christians believing in karma and reincarnation, Muslims wearing amulets, warding off *jinn* and interpreting dreams for information about the future, and non-religious people affirming the power of psychics and the intervention of guardian angels.

Although religious organizations and leaders may seek to control what their members believe and practice, their powers to do so are fairly limited. Individuals find ways to subvert official teachings, to do their own thing – whether intentionally or unintentionally. Folk traditions are sometimes maintained in which local vernacular practices are continued alongside official religious ones. The spirit world is densely occupied by gods, angels, spirits, demons, ancestors, ghosts, aliens and other beings who derive their character from their cultural context and are drawn on variously according to need, time and place.[7] In surveys people may affirm a religious identity, but this tells us little about how they celebrate the stages of life, cope with misfortune, illness or the things beyond their control, how they explain what happens to them and seek to influence the future.[8] A full examination of people's personal beliefs and practices is certainly beyond the scope of this study; our more modest aim is to present and analyse how such things are portrayed by the media.

In this chapter, we focus on popular ritual practices and the paranormal, and the language of popular belief, and assess how the media reflect and shape them. We ask how their representations contribute to the broader depiction and construction of religion, society and culture in Britain. But we begin by examining the nature and extent of media references to popular belief and practice in the early 1980s and late 2000s. What, if anything, changed in the frequency and range of references to popular cosmology, mythology and religious practice, and to 'common religion'?

---

[5]   Knott 1984a; Towler 1974; Towler 1983; Toon 1981.

[6]   Obelkevich 1976; Clark 1982; Sarah Williams 1999; and Stringer 2008.

[7]   Stringer 2008, pp. 47–51. He disputes earlier accounts which suggest a conflict between official and folk beliefs, claiming that the two are held simultaneously by individuals but are drawn on in different situations. A similar point was made earlier by scholars of cognitive religion, see Barrett 1999, pp. 325–39.

[8]   For an analysis of what lies behind nominal census identities, see Day 2011.

Popular Belief and Ritual Practice and their Media Portrayals: Decline or Rise, Continuity or Change?

In his ethnographical reconsideration of what constitutes the elementary form of religion in Western societies, Martin Stringer identified three principal features: the situational, unsystematic nature of belief, the intimate association with the non-empirical, and 'the attempt to respond to pragmatic questions concerned with daily life and coping with everyday problems'.[9] These are at the heart of the media portrayals we discuss in this chapter. Clustered within them are a host of beliefs and practices, some of which are endorsed by religious institutions and are 'conventionally religious' such as belief in heaven or hell, and the practice of prayer, weddings and funerals, and others that are not under the dominion of institutions but are part of 'the underground religion of the common people' such as belief in fate or luck, fortune-telling and the paranormal.[10]

A number of surveys and opinion polls conducted over the last half century have included questions about this area of belief and practice. In 2008, *The Sun* commissioned a survey on belief in UFOs.[11] YouGov, the opinion pollster asked about belief in horoscopes in 2010 and luck in 2011.[12] The afterlife and the spirit world were the subject of an online survey in 2011 conducted to coincide with the UK launch of Warner Brothers' supernatural thriller, *Hereafter*.[13] These surveys and their media coverage revealed the ongoing popularity of these topics, with more than half of those polled believing in UFOs (though only 9 per cent claimed to have seen one) and 40 per cent believing it definite or possible that aliens had tried to communicate with Earth.[14] A mere 2 per cent were unfamiliar with their star sign though only 15 per cent read their horoscopes regularly; a third of respondents considered themselves to be lucky.[15] Two thirds believed in some form of afterlife and thought that our actions could affect what happens to our soul after death.[16] More than half believed psychics can communicate with the dead, more than 20 per cent having visited a medium, and 40 per cent believing in guardian angels.[17]

Surveys and polls over the last few decades also allow us to establish what has changed over the last 30 years. Clive Field, for 'British Religion in Numbers', has compiled a series of data tables and charts to illustrate changing patterns of

---

[9]　Stringer 2008, p. 108.

[10]　Towler 1974, pp. 147–8.

[11]　YouGov 2008.

[12]　Thompson 2010; Field 2010; Field 2011b.

[13]　Based on research on near-death experiences conducted by Penny Sartori. Field 2011a; for example, Jackson 2011.

[14]　YouGov 2008.

[15]　Thompson 2010; Field 2011b.

[16]　Field 2011a.

[17]　Ibid.

religious and superstitious beliefs, and from these we can see that the level of belief in the majority of aspects of popular religion has remained stable, though there has been an increase in some and decrease in others (Table 6.1).[18] Even in those cases where belief seems to be in decline, there is still considerable interest, more than half of respondents believing in extra-sensory perception, 30 per cent believing in religious miracles and 26 per cent in faith healing.

Table 6.1   Change in belief or practice of aspects of popular religion, 1980s to 2000s

Nature of change 1980s to late 2000s	Item of popular belief or practice
Increase	Belief in angels Belief that it is possible to communicate with the dead Belief in flying saucers (UFOs) Belief in ghosts and in sightings of ghosts
Broadly stable	Belief in afterlife Belief in astrology Belief in black magic Belief in the devil Belief in fate Practice of having fortune told Belief in heaven and hell Belief in horoscopes Belief in lucky charms Practice of possessing lucky charm Belief in psychics and mediums Belief in superstition
Decrease	Belief in extra-sensory perception (ESP, telepathy) Belief in faith healing Belief in religious miracles

Although there are differing views about their communal and public significance, the statistics show the resilience of many popular beliefs and some

---

[18]   Field 2009b. Figure 1 is based on time series information. Comparisons between data from different periods are subject to unreliability for the following reasons: information may have been collected by different research organizations; different questions asked; surveys and polls conducted at different times; different sample sizes used etc. For most items, data is available for the 1980s and 2000s, but for several there are data gaps because no polls or surveys were conducted at relevant times. In such cases, conclusions are based on data from nearest relevant dates.

associated practices.[19] They have changed, of course, with many that were popular in the nineteenth and early twentieth centuries no longer in evidence as a result of developments in lifestyle, working conditions and technology, and new ones – such as belief in UFOs – emerging. Most of today's beliefs and practices are more likely to be held by women than men (though belief in UFOs is a significant exception).[20] Privately – and with family and friends – they are important for coping with everyday problems, misfortune and crisis, for dealing with the unpredictable, death and the departure of loved ones, and for making sense of the unexplained. And, given that non-empirical beings are the subject of so many of these beliefs and practices, they are far from a-social.[21] They concern experiences and relationships between people in this world and with beings beyond it – angels, ancestors and aliens alike. They also bring people together – those who attend and participate in live shows and ghost hunts, but also 'armchair audiences'.[22]

Sarah Williams concluded her study of popular religion in Southwark in south-east London by stating that 'we need to understand how successive generations continued to construct, communicate, and adapt religious language if we are to appreciate popular religion as a distinctive system of belief'.[23] We turn now to how our own generation does just this in and through the media. We begin with how many references there were to popular beliefs and practices on television and in the newspapers, where they appeared, and how they had changed since the 1980s, before turning to an examination of several themes in more detail.

In Chapter 2 we noted that, in our first study in the 1980s, 25 per cent of references concerned common religion, with the rest relating to conventional religion. By the time of the second, common religion references had increased to 40 per cent. There had also been changes in the proportion of references to different topics. Luck and gambling remained very important, together accounting for more than 40 per cent of common religion references in both periods; there were relatively few references in either to fate or destiny. Ghosts were not referred to as often in mainstream media as they have been previously (but now there were dedicated programmes on minority TV channels, such as *Ghost Hunters*). However, 'the unexplained' (aliens and UFOs) received considerably more coverage, particularly in the newspapers. There was more interest in mythology too.

In the early 1980s the distinction between conventional and common religion seemed to make sense sociologically, the first referring to institutionalized religions and the second to all things supernatural that fell outside this official

---

[19]   Bruce 2011, on the secularization of superstition, and Sarah Williams 1999, on popular religion as a distinctive system operating within a 'loosely bounded interpretative community' (p. 11).

[20]   Trzebiatowska and Bruce 2012; Woodhead 2009.

[21]   For a discussion of the 'sensuous social supernatural', see Day 2011, pp. 98–114.

[22]   Hill 2011, p. 66.

[23]   Williams, p. 176.

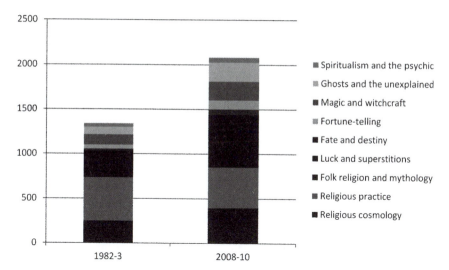

Figure 6.1   Media references to popular belief and practice,
1982 and 2008–2009

context. Today, it is clear that some aspects of what previously fell exclusively within the 'conventional' category may no longer do so, though there may still be some underlying residual traces of earlier religious connections. Marriage is a good example: a growing number are civil rather than religious in nature. When is 'yoga' Hindu, and when is it a secular leisure activity? Are 'prayers' always directed to officially sanctioned deities? Are 'angels' always conventional religious beings? In order to reflect the increasingly varied popular interpretations now held of many aspects of religious cosmology and practice (two of the conventional religious categories we originally used to code our data), we have discussed them along with common religion in this chapter on popular belief and practice.

The percentage of references to religious cosmology remained stable across the two studies at 9 per cent of all references, whilst those to religious practice declined substantially (from 18 per cent in 1982 to just over 10 per cent in 2008–2009). Figure 6.1 shows the changes in mainstream media coverage of the most important aspects of popular religiosity.

In Chapter 2 we distinguished between literal and metaphorical references. Those that were literal referred to actual religious groups, experiences, beliefs and practices, with metaphorical references employed to create an effect, by likening a non-religious object, sensation, idea or behaviour to a religious one. Literal references to 'God' can be found in hymns in the BBC's *Songs of Praise*, whereas the same term may be given metaphorical treatment in the popular press with reference to a revered and celebrated footballer. In the first case the subject-matter is explicitly and intentionally religious. In the latter the religious reference is used to draw attention to the player's status, and the hopes and expectations placed on him by fans (and possibly to signal his self-importance).

In 1982, just 12.5 per cent of references to religion were metaphorical; by 2008–2010 this had risen to 22 per cent. In both periods of research *The Sun* and ITV1 made more use of metaphorical references than other papers and channels, drawing on common religion – magic, witchcraft, aliens and other beings – but also on aspects of religious cosmology and practice such as prayer, miracles, heaven and hell. Advertisements, comedy, entertainment and sport were key genres for the use of religious metaphors. We will examine their use in sports reporting later. We begin though with life-cycle rites.

Popular Ritual Practices: Weddings and Funerals

In *Watching the English*, Fox noted the continued importance of rites concerning 'hatching, matching and dispatching'.[24] She observed that, like other rites of passage they featured ritual and alcohol, and that the experience of such occasions was often one of 'social dis-ease' alleviated by humour.[25] Such embarrassment and awkwardness – which has also been noted in relation to talking about God – is characteristic of English 'reserve' in public contexts where appearing not to care, not being too serious (e.g. not talking about religion or politics) and not expressing too much outward emotion are all important.[26] Nevertheless, everyone loves a good wedding or funeral, especially if they can watch it on TV with friends and family in the privacy of their own front room rather than having to be at the centre of things themselves.

The pinnacle of such mediated rites of passage – a successful global export and one for which the British are renowned – is the royal wedding or funeral, the most recent being the wedding of Prince William and Kate Middleton (now the Duke and Duchess of Cambridge) in April 2011.[27] The meaning and significance of such events has been discussed extensively by media theorists, from Shils and Young's work on Queen Elizabeth's coronation in 1953, through Dayan and Katz's 1992 book on the live broadcasting of media events, to more recent research by Couldry on Princess Diana's funeral and media rituals more generally.[28] In addition to the role of television in bringing together an audience around 'a common culture, an image of the nation as a knowable community', what is increasingly clear is the

---

[24]   Fox 2004, p. 353.

[25]   Ibid., pp. 398–99.

[26]   'Are We Too Embarrassed to Talk about God?', *The One Show*, BBC1, 3 February 2009.

[27]   The Royal Wedding, http://www.officialroyalwedding2011.org/. National television viewing figures were 24.5 million, with an estimated global audience of two billion.

[28]   Shils and Young 1956, pp. 63–82; Dayan and Katz 1992; Couldry 2003.

way in which the media construct rather than reflect national rituals.[29] Television, in particular, is 'the event's privileged interpreter' – offline and increasingly online – as *The Times* made clear when it described the coverage of Michael Jackson's funeral in 2009 as 'a made-for-TV event'.[30] The media's account is authorized then taken up by commentators and ordinary citizens who are guided in how to think and feel, as this woman's recollection of the TV commemoration of Diana suggests: 'I am not a royalist. I admired [Diana], but I never realised that I loved her. I wanted to be part of it all. It's the most moving thing that's happened in my lifetime.'[31]

Arguably, the media's constructive role is no less important in the production of ordinary weddings and funerals, particularly in conserving traditions, and drawing attention to normative practices and emotions. This was evident in media portrayal of these rites of passage in the 1980s in which church weddings and burials were the norm and civil marriages and cremations mentioned only rarely: 'On television and in the press the life cycle is shrouded in tradition. The white dress is the uniform of all TV brides, flowers are still thrown into open graves, and customary superstitions are still retorted and practised by those involved.'[32] We noted too the way in which the media captured the embarrassment and uneasiness brought on by such occasions – especially funerals – in their use of black humour.[33]

> A cartoon appeared in one of the corners of the back page of *The Sun* ... In it a small crowd is respectfully gathered in a churchyard. The vicar is portrayed chastising the bereaved wife with the words 'Mrs Tidwick, I said "a handful of earth ..."' as she hurls a large boulder into her late husband's grave. *The Evening Post* recorded the true story of the local clergyman who in his haste one busy day began to read the burial service over the bride and groom ..., and the *O.T.T* team were embarrassingly caught in the act of filming a wedding sketch outside a Midland's church just as a *bona fide* funeral service was about to begin.[34]

The significance of the treatment of weddings and funerals for the media representation of religion in the early 1980s was considerable. Nearly 20 per cent of all recorded references were to religious practices of one kind or another. They carried with them not only representations of the way the British marked the life cycle, but of the social role of churches and clergymen in framing events and conferring status.

---

[29]   Cardiff and Scannell quoted in Couldry 2003, p. 57; Couldry 2003, p. 70.

[30]   Ayres 2009.

[31]   Couldry 2003, pp. 68–69.

[32]   Knott 1984a, p. 22.

[33]   Ibid., p. 23.

[34]   Ibid. *O.T.T* – Over The Top – was the name of a television programme broadcast in the early 1980s.

With the percentage of media references to religious practices down to only 10 per cent of all references in the late 2000s, we can see that something has changed. Terrestrial television offered audiences no fictional weddings in early February 2009, though the burial of a funeral director in *Midsomer Murders* was treated with the usual dose of black humour alongside the customary practices we have come to expect from media portrayals of funerals.[35] Audiences of *GMTV* were promised a marriage proposal every day the following week (in the run up to Valentine's Day), and those tuning in to BBC2's *Working Lunch* were given advice on how to keep the cost of their wedding down during the credit crunch. The assumption of marriage as the desirable social norm was conveyed, though weddings themselves were curiously absent. Set against the popularity of recent TV series, *My Big Fat Gypsy Wedding* (C4), *Four Weddings* (Living TV) and Five's *Greatest TV Weddings*, 'charting our love affair with TV nuptials', this absence was an aberration, especially given that the newspaper coverage was no less extensive than it had been in the early 1980s.

Here, changes could be discerned. For example, in the local press, there were references to Sikh weddings and Muslim burials, and in *The Times*, to Shariʻa-based *nikah*, marriage contracts, and to forced marriages. Furthermore, the focus was not on clergy and other religious specialists, but on the way in which individuals and family and friends customized rituals to suit their own needs and interests. In 'My Little Angels', two murdered little girls were shown laid to rest in red and pink coffins, their favourite song playing, their mother dressed in cerise and mourners asked to wear bright colours.[36] In '172 Grandkids at Supernan Funeral', not only did we read about the devotion of Supernan Maggie, head of an Irish clan based in Salford, but of the release of balloons by her grandchildren at her Catholic funeral.[37] The sense of continuity was not lost, however, with local newly-weds depicted in classic poses, brides in white (or in the case of a Sikh bride, in red and gold), men in suits, flowers in abundance.[38] Even 'the world's fattest man', carried to his wedding on a bed on a flat-bed truck, was reported as marrying a bride in 'a traditional white satin dress [who] arrived in a more conventional vehicle'.[39]

The media portrayal of self-conscious traditionalism mixed with both religious diversity and individual innovation was not restricted to the representation of weddings and funerals, however. An analysis in 2009 of *The Times*'s coverage of religious festivals showed that the paper had significantly changed its content and treatment of these popular practices.[40] Numbers of articles on Christmas had grown from 850 in 1985 to 4000 in 2008, and those on Islamic, Jewish and Hindu festivals had risen substantially too. In his commentary, Jonathan Richards noted

---

[35]   *Midsomer Murders*, ITV1, 3 February 2009.

[36]   Pyatt 2008.

[37]   Patrick 2008.

[38]   Marriage notices, *Yorkshire Evening Post*, 15 October 2008f.

[39]   Wheeler 2008.

[40]   Richards 2009.

that the ritual and spiritual interests of the British now extended beyond their own traditions. He quoted *The Times* correspondent Ruth Gledhill: 'People now feel there's a smorgasbord of faith traditions they can dip into – even if the evangelicals don't like it.'[41]

Participation and enjoyment in the festivals of others is not a media construction in and of itself, but the result of wider public policies and practices of multiculturalism. What is clear, however, is that newspapers would not have intensified their coverage had the subject not been newsworthy, and had such an approach not contributed to building a more diverse consumer base. Festivals opened up possibilities for stories across a wide range of genres, including travel, culture, food and life-style as well as religion and news, as articles on Halloween and Christmas revealed in our 2008 sample.

Occasionally, as Richards' analysis and commentary demonstrates, journalists and media commentators directly address the question of religious change and its media representation. Cole Moreton's reflection on a celebrity funeral in *The Guardian* in 2009 was one such example.[42] For Moreton, the celebration of the life and death of *Big Brother* star, Jade Goody, exemplified the transition from Anglicanism and its 'old established God' to a new form of emotional and spiritual faith: 'Her service put the new faith of the people on display, live on television with white doves, party balloons and lots of tears. It was hosted by the Church of England in Essex, but was really Church of Everywhere.'[43] The media had a key role in this vignette on contemporary religious change, charged with communicating the power and emotional intensity of this public yet intimate spiritual moment to a wide and diverse audience, not of spectators but of participants. Church and clergy had a place too, though in Moreton's account it was the diminished role of host, the formal liturgy ignored as irrelevant.

This mass-mediated funeral – like those for two murdered children and Supernan Maggie – combined elements of Christian tradition and spiritual and cultural innovation, not only to celebrate Jade's public but iconic life (from brash media celebrity to brave and selfless victim of cancer), but to transform her into 'the brightest star in heaven'.[44] Like Diana, Jade's mortal passing represented her removal to a different place and role. It is to the media representation of that supernatural realm and its psychical and paranormal possibilities that we now turn.

The Paranormal: The Psychical and the Unexplained

Annette Hill, who conducted much of her research for her book, *Paranormal Media*, in the late 2000s as we were researching religion in the media, has

---

[41]   Ibid.

[42]   Moreton 2010. For other examples, see Mark Lawson 2011; Wilson 2010.

[43]   Moreton 2010.

[44]   Ibid.

argued for 'a paranormal turn in popular culture' illustrated by the explosion in consumption of books, magazines, websites, television programmes, D-I-Y kits and public performances featuring the psychic, unexplained, ghostly, spiritual and alien, and their shift from alternative to mainstream culture.[45] And indeed the number of media references to the paranormal had increased, with references to UFOs and the unexplained six times what they were in the early 1980s. At that time we concluded that interest in the paranormal was under-reported.[46] Now, we can say that people's enthusiasms are better served by the media than they once were, not least of all because of dedicated TV programmes on cable and satellite channels.

In 1982, in a documentary recognizing the centenary of the Society for Psychical Research, viewers were informed that 'over half the people in this country accept the paranormal as an established fact'.[47] But in our viewing week, in April of that year, broadcasters offered no entertainment programmes featuring it, just this one factual programme, and several light news items on sightings of the Roman ghosts of York and a Northumbrian poltergeist. Newspapers covered stories of one ghostly spirit who inhabited a churchyard and another who appeared to warn his son – a vicar – of an impending assault.[48] *The Times* offered a substantial article by the Archdeacon of Durham – also written to commemorate a century of psychical research – calling for 'thinking Christians' to become better informed about parapsychology and to dismiss it at their peril given the 'special pastoral and theological questions' it posed for churches.[49] Despite the remarkable presence of religion in these accounts – of clergy, churches and graveyards – a striking feature of the serious coverage back then was the role of science. Science, not the church, was presented as 'the final arbiter of truth', scientific method providing the yardstick by which to judge paranormal events.[50] To what extent was this still the case in coverage of psychical and unexplained phenomena in 2008–2010?

Most of television's allusions to the paranormal appeared in fictional programmes. In the first week of February 2009 the paranormal was given extensive coverage in murder mysteries (*Midsomer Murders*, ITV1; *Murder, She Wrote*, BBC2). It also featured in *Demons* (ITV1), the drama series centred on the activities of a vampire-fighting duo, *Pushing Daisies* (ITV1), an American comedy drama about a man who, by touching people, could bring them back from the dead, *Psych* (BBC2), the first in a US comedy series about a psychic policeman, and *Scoop* (BBC2), a comedy film starring Woody Allen, featuring magic, tarot and a

45   Hill 2011, p. 1.
46   Knott 1984a, pp. 17–18.
47   Ibid., *Credo*, ITV, 25 April 1982.
48   Ibid.
49   Perry 1982.
50   Knott 1984a, p. 19.

ghost.[51] The treatment was light-hearted and did not foreground issues of scientific truth, evidence or verifiability. Rather, the world of the psychic and clairvoyant was generally depicted as benign and useful, though at times fraudulent, a place where people sought answers to questions about their loved ones, the future could be foretold, crimes solved, justice secured, and even the dead brought back to life. In *Midsomer Murders*, for example, it was not the psychic but the vicar who turned out to be the murderer.[52] The spiritualist group, 'Spirit of Friendship', was represented as coexisting alongside the local Anglican church and 'The Crystal Goddess', a New Age shop, all three offering pastoral as well as ritual services – at a price – to villagers of differing spiritual dispositions.[53]

The value of helping the living by communicating with the dead was also presented in the popular press, especially by *The Sun* as part of its regular coverage of the supernatural. Along with astrology, it was portrayed as on the benign side – caring for those in need – and stories of UFOs and ghosts were on the dark side, featuring all things 'spooky', 'alien', 'scary', 'haunted' and 'oddball'.[54] Matching the publication of an extract from a new biography on the Archbishop of Canterbury in *The Times* in the same period, *The Sun* serialized the autobiography of 'ITV2's Star Psychic', Sally Morgan.[55] In two double-page features on consecutive days, and flagged up as an exclusive on the front page, Sally revealed predictions she had made to well-known people, particularly Princess Diana, and about major disasters including 9/11 and the Zeebrugge ferry tragedy. As with coverage of the Archbishop's life in *The Times*, the focus was on celebrity, relationships and crisis, and similar attention was paid to the details of her professional experience. It was not theology and liturgy that were foregrounded – as in the Archbishop's case – but the beliefs and emotions associated with contacting the spirit world and the drama of psychic demonstration to a public audience.

On television as in *The Sun*, far from being merely a matter of individual belief and practice, spiritualism was presented as a social arena, in which people gathered in groups to hear from the spirits, and participated in public performances of magic and the psychic.[56] It was also a place where charlatans might masquerade

---

[51]   Other channels carried films, *Sleepy Hollow* (C4), *Thir13en Ghosts* (Five), *Dungeons and Dragons* (Five), the series *Being Human* (BBC3) and *Ghost Hunters* (shown on Living TV).

[52]   *Midsomer Murders*, ITV1, 3 February and 4 February 2009.

[53]   Ibid. For accounts of alternative spirituality existing in parallel with conventional religious organizations, see Heelas and Woodhead 2005, and Bowman 2009, pp. 161–68.

[54]   All terms used in articles on the unexplained in *The Sun* in October and November 2008.

[55]   See discussion of *The Times* coverage of the biography of Archbishop of Canterbury in Chapter 3. From Sally Morgan (adapted by John Perry) 2008a, and Sally Morgan (adapted by John Perry) 2008b. See also Williamson 2008.

[56]   See Stringer 2008, pp. 68–72, for an account of women's shared experience of astrology and spiritualism.

as mediums or spiritual adepts. Spirits and their mediums came across variously as benign and useful, or scheming and unpredictable. Scepticism about this arena was the overriding discourse in *QI* (BBC2), a comedy panel game based on obscure knowledge about surprising and little known facts.[57] This episode focused on 'Frauds, Fakes and Fakirs'. Chaired by the comic actor and self-identified sceptic, Stephen Fry, it delighted in exposing the world of the paranormal and its practitioners as one of deception and sleight of hand. This was a rare example of its dismissal at the hands of scientific rationality.

In a foray into an earlier supernatural world, Melvin Bragg presented a cultural documentary on Shakespeare's *The Tempest* which illustrated the historical embeddedness of popular belief and practice, and explored the sixteenth century's fascination with alchemy and magic.[58] The interwoven social fabric of religion, science and the occult, and Shakespeare's representation of this in *The Tempest* are important forebears of modern esotericism and paranormal belief and practice, their juxtaposition vis-à-vis religion and science, and subsequent mainstreaming in popular culture. Interest in this area continues unabated, though not culturally unmodified. Take popular belief in ghosts and ghost hunting, for example. Far from being merely a safe horror thrill or response to the loss and grief experienced after 9/11, it is a long-standing part of 'the British psyche', according to Martin Jeffrey, founder of *Friday Nights*, a company that organizes ghost hunts.[59] Its persistence is such that Owen Davies in his social history of ghosts concluded: 'Neither science nor religion can exorcise beliefs generated by personal experience, and to be haunted by the dead would seem to be part of the human condition.'[60]

Nevertheless, the complex relationship between belief and scepticism remains central to popular experience of the 'paranormal media', whether of live demonstrations by magicians, mentalists or mediums, ghost tourism, paranormal reality TV such as *Most Haunted* (Living TV) or *Ghost Hunters* (Sci Fi Channel), or factual and fictional media representations.[61] As scholarly observers of this popular trend suggest, people 'construct an identity that contains both positions at the same time'.[62] Despite television's juxtaposition of religion and the paranormal (e.g. ITV1's *Midsomer Murders*), and of religion and science (e.g. BBC1's *The Big Questions*), ordinary believers do not always respect such discursive boundaries, working instead with a complex body of supernaturalist beliefs and practical ethics, and with both hope and scepticism. Neither is there any necessary conflict between official religious and/or scientific beliefs and folk or superstitious ones. This came across strongly in witness testimonies in the newspapers in the run up to Halloween in October 2008.

---

[57]   *QI*, BBC1, 6 February 2009.

[58]   *The South Bank Show*, ITV1, 8 February 2009.

[59]   Interview with Jeffrey in Dixon 2009.

[60]   Davies 2007, quoted in Hill 2011, p. 11.

[61]   Hill 2011, p. 43. *Most Haunted* was aired on Living TV in February 2009.

[62]   Ibid. See also Clark 2001.

Sparked not only by festive fervour – Halloween is always given extensive coverage by the popular press – but by preparations for an international UFO conference, and the declassification and release of Ministry of Defence files on UFO sightings in British airspace, the media went into paranormal overdrive. Between the 20th and 25th October, *The Sun*, *The Times* and the *Yorkshire Evening Post* all carried full page spreads on the unexplained and otherworldly, and the two national papers covered the story of a US airman who, in 1957, was ordered to shoot down an unidentified 'aircraft' visible on his radar screen only to have it disappear mysteriously.[63] Sworn to silence by the American National Security Agency at the time, his witness account was only made public in 2009. Both papers borrowed movie language – 'close encounter', 'ET' and 'Top Gun' – to capture the imaginary possibilities and thrill of the episode, and referred to recent testimony by the now 77-year-old airman. Superficially there was a difference between *The Times* article, which offered a scientific explanation by a university expert on paranormal media, and a linked piece on a UFO sighting in *The Sun* which ran with the title 'Best Proof Yet'. However, *The Sun* conceded that, of 11,000 sightings reported to the Ministry of Defence (MOD), just 5 per cent were unexplained, the rest being planes, stars, planets or satellites, whilst *The Times* explored the possibility of alien intelligence.[64]

Such pragmatism, combined with scepticism, about whether aliens have actually landed on earth, can be found in most articles on UFOs, but this doesn't take away from the media's fascination with this aspect of the paranormal. With *The Sun* commissioning a survey on UFO belief at the time of our research (which revealed that 52 per cent of people believed in their existence), its coverage included articles on sightings reported to the MOD, on the '100 per cent genuine' video footage of UFO images photographed in Turkey, the sighting of a mysterious craft by a mother and daughter in Bristol, celebrities who believed in aliens and a visit by the singer, Robbie Williams, to an American UFO camp.[65] In the same period, the *Yorkshire Evening Post* devoted two pages to an interview with a collector of amateur video footage of UFOs, 'The Truth is Out There'.[66] Citing the evidence of reported sightings from the 1950s and 1980s, the enthusiast suggested that the 'debunking' of such evidence was part of a conspiracy to cover up reports of the unexplained by police, pilots and the military. He was clearly used to having his beliefs questioned, and stressed his own scepticism (with the journalist confirming he 'doesn't come across as a nutter'). *The Times* too rehearsed related issues of belief, doubt and evidence in two articles on 21 October, one for children, the other an opinion piece by Lord Rees of Ludlow, the Astronomer Royal and President of the Royal Society.[67] Lord Rees brought his own enthusiasm to the debate,

---

63   Evans 2008b; Coles 2008.
64   Ibid. Rees 2008.
65   YouGov 2008. Topics covered in *The Sun*, October and November 2008.
66   Woodward 2008.
67   *The Times*, 'Is the truth out there?', Times2, 21 October 2008; Rees 2008.

discussing the physical and biological issues without joining the debunkers. 'I am open-minded about the possibility and would dearly like to know if they exist', he wrote, his words endorsing the seriousness of the quest for alien intelligence much as the Archdeacon of Durham had done for psychical research back in 1982.[68]

Media portrayals of the psychical and paranormal continue to be played out in the context of debates about belief and scientific evidence, though – compared to the early 1980s – science is not depicted as the final arbiter, nor is religious belief presented as more moral or superior to beliefs about communicating with the dead or encountering UFOs. When experts are called in, their media role is not to dismiss such beliefs, but to add alternative voices and explanations to those of faithful practitioners and witnesses.

The Language and Performance of Popular Belief

The *Daily Mail* did just this in its treatment of superstition in May 2010.[69] In its 'Life and Style' section it addressed the question of the continuity and prevalence of 'magical thinking' and superstitious rituals.[70] Presented as widespread and growing in popularity among an otherwise 'rational' and 'perfectly sensible' cohort (*Mail* readers are predominantly middle class and female), such practices were shown variously as rooted in the matriarchal line, a natural response to fear and loss of control, and an evolutionary hangover. A plethora of experts in mental health, natural selection and futurology offered compelling explanations for the phenomenon, the key message being that the real danger was not superstition itself but untreated anxiety and stress leading to Obsessive Compulsive Disorder. Moderate superstition, like moderate religion, was presented as harmless.

Despite this scientific rationalist frame, no reader could have missed the extraordinary level of detail about superstitious rituals themselves, the testimonies of the women who perform them, the allusions to luck, magic and tradition, and the connection of such beliefs and practices to the need to protect ourselves and our loved ones from danger, evil and misfortune. Twenty-three different superstitions were mentioned, practised by women as diverse as writers, celebrities, mothers, managers and a company director, several of whom felt the need to account for their actions: 'I can't explain it … it just makes me feel bad if I don't do it'; 'It's just something my mum used to do, and I suppose I'm a bit scared of what will happen if I don't do it'; 'I know I sound insane … but I feel as if something bad might happen to the children'.[71] With the article reporting the results of a recent survey, in which 77 per cent of those interviewed (men as well as women) admitted to engaging in superstitious behaviour, the overriding impression was not

---

[68]   Ibid.; Perry 1982.

[69]   Everett 2010.

[70]   Ibid.

[71]   Ibid.

only one of scale, but of the embeddedness of such behaviour in everyday routines beyond the reach of reason. These were not the periodic rituals of the life cycle or the annual celebration of festivals, but were ingrained in the habitus and tenor of daily life.

The *Mail*'s article was a rare rehearsal of an area of popular belief and practice that is generally ignored by the media despite its actual prevalence. Not that superstition is absent from newspapers and television – passing references abound now just as they did in the 1980s. But they are rarely the subject of analysis or discussion. At one level banal, their prevalence and repetition reveal something important about how we deal with our fears, our inability to control events, uncertainty about the future and hope that benign but distant forces will look out for, protect and advantage us and those we care for.[72]

Sport – the subject of so much TV airtime and so many newspaper column inches – provides a fertile field for the analysis of the media's treatment of superstition, luck, prayer and magical practices. No *viewer* of the television coverage of the 2012 Olympics, for example, could fail to have noticed the ritual displays, the touching and kissing of crosses and amulets before events, the winner's prayers and acts of thanksgiving, and the visual references to mascots and lucky items of clothing. But no *listener* to the commentary on either television or radio would have heard any mention of religious identity or practice, or of popular belief or superstitious ritual. Seen but not heard, such practices were either considered too intimate and private or too mundane, irrational and irrelevant to be noticed and commented upon by reporters. Or perhaps they were just insufficiently understood.

Such passing visual references are literal in kind: there was nothing metaphorical, for example, about Manchester City's Samir Nasri lifting his shirt after scoring a goal to reveal a vest emblazoned with the festive greeting, 'Eid Mubarak'.[73] Actual prayers are said and gratitude offered; hope and trust are placed in lucky and powerful objects. Such sincere religious gestures also grace the sports pages. Members of the Palestinian football team, for example, were photographed in prayer (*salat*) on the pitch before their historic first match on home soil in the West Bank, and the Chelsea manager, Phil Scolari, was reported to have prayed for God's help in avoiding injury to his star striker: 'I am religious … I asked my God, "Look out for this player".'[74]

More often, though, football references to 'miracles', 'prayer', 'God' and 'magic' are metaphorical, as two stories in *The Sun* – separated by 26 years – illustrate. Featuring an infamous football manager and a star player, they draw on popular religious metaphors to reify, celebrate and damn sporting celebrities. In the first, from February 1982, the 'curse' of Derby County Football team under ex-manager, Brian Clough, was discussed in a narrative that employed an array of

---

[72]   See discussion on believing in fate, in Day 2011, pp. 115–27.

[73]   This is a traditional Islamic greeting at the time of the festival of Eid. *Match of the Day*, BBC1, 18 August 2012.

[74]   Awad 2008; Wyen 2008.

religious, magical and paranormal metaphors to describe Clough's charm, power and unpredictability, and the tension he created in the Derby County dressing room.[75]

> The club was "haunted by the spectre of one man's magic spell", and ... Brian Clough "converted people with all the natural persuasion of an evangelist". The club was "bewitched", and to some people Clough was "God" while to others he was "more like the Devil".[76]

The Sun's pre-match feature from 4 October 2008 also employed a sustained and humorous metaphor of the divine, with references to 'worship', 'adulation', 'anointing', 'passion' and 'faith'.[77]
Britain's most expensive player, Robinho, was greeted with 'a reverence normally reserved for church': 'I am already a god and I didn't do a thing', he said.[78] The player was depicted hands together in genuine gratitude in front of adoring and expectant fans. The ambiguity of intentional heart-felt prayer and the witty metaphorical reference to God and other religious tropes is not uncommon in sports reporting.[79] In an exclusive interview with Sir Alex Ferguson in *The Times*, for example, the Manchester United manager's literal references to prayer were accompanied by the reporter's metaphorical ones to his 'Buddhist calm' and – in an accompanying cartoon – to his 'prayer mat'.[80] This combination of references to Christianity and other religions, in this case Buddhism and Islam, marks a change from the metaphorical references of the 1980s which were almost exclusively Christian.

The media's use of popular religious and superstitious language and gesture is complex. Deployed extensively in coverage of sport, it exposes a tension between the light-hearted and humorous use of religious metaphors to convey the beauty, significance and sacred nature of sport and its stars, and references to genuine commitment and practice. At times the two are intentionally combined, though more often literal religious references – usually performed rather than spoken – pass by ignored or unnoticed by reporters. Popular ritual gestures and the identities they reveal struggle for recognition *as religious*. At the same time, sustained metaphors are being crafted which reveal not only the creative skills but also the

---

[75]   *The Sun* 1982.

[76]   Knott 1984a, p. 10.

[77]   McGarry 2008.

[78]   Ibid. Robinho has since been surpassed as the most expensive player.

[79]   Among the most developed examples of this was an article in *The Guardian* on La Iglesia Maradoniana, the Church of Maradona, a new quasi-religious movement in Argentina, in which the literal and metaphorical were combined in a two-page analysis of devotion to this football celebrity, including the Church's ten commandments. Franklin 2008.

[80]   *The Times* 2008c.

religious knowledge of the journalist. In a change from the 1980s, these derive not only from Western culture and tradition, but from religions other than Christianity.

The language and performance of popular belief and its presence on television and in the newspapers suggest that processes of both embedding and disembedding are occurring. The continuity and stability of beliefs and their literal and metaphorical treatment across nearly three decades suggest their roots run deep in British popular culture, but unwillingness or an inability to recognize and name them as religious or superstitious signals an attenuation of language and gesture and the meanings and identities to which they once referred and – for many – still do.

Although psychical, paranormal and superstitious beliefs and rituals continue at times to be framed or interpreted in the media by science, medicine or some other form of rational knowledge, today those who hold, practise or witness such beliefs and rituals are given a greater voice than they were in the 1980s. Sought after for its narrative appeal, theirs is the voice of experience and authenticity rather than external authority. They tap into a resilient subterranean culture that continues to be believed and practised by large numbers of people in Britain, but also reflects the popularity and novelty of the recent 'paranormal turn'.

Customization of practices could also be observed reflecting a new confidence in designing and performing tailored rituals which nevertheless continue to be authorized and framed by churches and clergy. Although the media and their audiences still love a white wedding and the black humour of funerals, greater attention is now given to religious diversity and cultural innovation, and to the agency of non-specialist practitioners.

Chapter 7

The Case of Geert Wilders, Multiculturalism and Identity

Geert Wilders, Dutch MP and leader of the Party for Freedom (PVV), was banned from entering the UK in February 2009. In this chapter we examine how this became a controversial 'media event'.[1] It generated media commentaries on Islam, Christianity and secularism and their relationship to debates about freedom of speech, multiculturalism and national identity. One of two events we analysed across the British press – the second being the Papal visit of 2010 which we discuss in the next chapter – it provided an opportunity for further analysis of newspaper representations, but also of the media's role in constructing and managing an event that might otherwise have passed unnoticed with little interpretive embellishment.

Previously a member of the conservative-liberal People's Party for Freedom and Democracy, Wilders left to set up his own political party in 2004 after differences over Turkey's accession to Europe. He became well known internationally for his controversial anti-Islamic stance, and this brought him some success in Dutch politics. In 2008 he produced a short film *Fitna* (variously translated, but in the British press as 'discord' and 'strife') which juxtaposed media images of violent extremism with verses from the Qur'an. Widely viewed, it met with extensive criticism from Muslim and non-Muslim organizations and individuals alike.[2]

On 13 February 2009, Wilders was denied entry to Britain on public order grounds having been invited to a screening of *Fitna* in the House of Lords by Lord Pearson of the UK Independence Party.[3] The Home Office denied him entry under an EU law which allowed member states to exclude individuals on the grounds that they constituted a threat to public policy, security or health. The screening of the film, combined with Wilders' presence, was deemed by the Home Secretary to be 'threatening community harmony and therefore public security'. Despite being

---

[1]   For an earlier version of this chapter, see Poole 2012b, pp. 1–30.

[2]   For discussion of online video critique, see Van Zoonen, Mihelj, and Vis 2011, pp. 1283–1300.

[3]   The UK Independence Party (UKIP) is a Eurosceptic party with a strict policy on immigration. Its website calls for an immediate five-year freeze on immigration for permanent settlement.

aware of this, Wilders chose to fly into Heathrow knowing he would be turned back at the airport, thus creating a huge publicity coup.[4]

In this case study we focus on coverage of the prohibition of Wilders and the ensuing media debate. In February 2009 this event generated 159 articles in British national newspapers (including two local papers, see Table 7.1 below). They showed that immigration and diversity continued to generate anxiety and debate in Britain, in particular in relation to the hegemonic project of secular liberalism. In this chapter we see how press discourse represents an attempt by various elite groups to evoke and shape the nation and, in so doing, construct insiders and outsiders within a polarized identity politics.

The Wilders Case as a Media Event

In his typology of 'mediatized rituals', Cottle identifies six types, including those that are celebratory and conflicted.[5] He defines mediatized rituals as 'those exceptional and performative media phenomena that serve to sustain and/ or mobilize collective sentiments and solidarities on the basis of symbolization and a subjunctive orientation to what should or ought to be'.[6] This definition builds on Hjarvard's account of mediatization as that process whereby social and cultural activities are 'to a greater or lesser degree performed through interaction with a medium', the symbolic content and the structure of those activities being 'influenced by media environments which they gradually become more dependent upon'.[7] The Wilders event was performatively enacted, both by the principal actor himself and by the media in their readiness to cover and embellish the story. In doing so, they invoked solidarity by reaffirming a particular set of values, the chief of which was the sacred value of freedom of speech.

Media events may be conflictual or disruptive rather than effective in manufacturing consent.[8] Following Couldry, we argue that the coverage of Wilders constituted a conflicted media event in so far as it was a case of contested reporting whereby different groups struggled for hegemonic power, and competed for authority to speak on behalf of the social 'centre'.[9] It is such 'social antagonisms'

---

[4]   Since then a tribunal has overturned this ruling (October 2009) and Wilders has entered the UK twice to protests from Islam4UK, an organization which has since been banned under the UK's Terrorism Act 2000.

[5]   Cottle 2006, pp. 411–32.

[6]   Cottle 2006, p. 415. Although Couldry and Rothebuhler offer a critique of Cottle's analysis, there is nevertheless fairly widespread agreement around this definition: Couldry and Rothebuhler 2007, pp. 691–5.

[7]   Hjarvard 2008, pp. 9–26 (p. 9).

[8]   Couldry 2003; Cottle 2006.

[9]   Couldry, drawing on Shils' conception of the ritual construction of society's moral centre: Shils and Young 1956, pp. 63–82.

that give such events their 'electrifying charge'.[10] Other elements of media rituals were also present in the coverage of Wilders: the mobilization of collective fears against a symbolic other in order to police moral boundaries, and social integration through the building of specific solidarities. Although these elements were in evidence, as we will see later from readers' responses, it does not necessarily follow that the reporting of the Wilders' case was successful in enacting these processes.

As Fiske stated, 'A media event is not a mere representation of what happened, but it has its own reality, which gathers up into itself the reality of the event that may or may not have preceded it.'[11] The Wilders case became more than the sum of its original parts – the reporting of his arrival and departure, the Home Office ruling and public statement. It became a discursive struggle in the media for the moral high ground on issues of freedom of speech, multiculturalism and liberalism.

General Press Coverage

As Table 7.1 shows, although all the papers reported the Wilders story, the major part of the coverage came from the large national papers and, taken as a whole, a conservative interpretation dominated.[12] However, as the event was framed as an issue of freedom of speech, it was the two liberal-leaning newspapers – *The Independent* and *The Guardian* – that carried the most articles.[13] *The Independent*, which contained the most articles in print, many of them letters, was also the paper that endorsed freedom of speech most vigorously. The newspapers with the most articles online (*The Guardian* and the *Daily Mail*) also had the most commentary, reflecting the role of the Internet in extending analysis, debate and opinion. Demonstrating its importance for breaking news, all newspapers ran the story online at least a day before the main print coverage on 13 February 2009. Analysis online then continued for up to nine days, depending on the importance of the issue to the newspaper.

---

[10]   Cottle 2006, p. 419.

[11]   John Fiske cited in Cottle 2006, p. 419.

[12]   Articles from February 2009 that referred to Geert Wilders from all national newspapers and two local Yorkshire papers were analysed. Searches of hard copies of the papers, newspaper websites and the database Lexis Nexis were conducted to ensure all articles were retrieved.

[13]   In the UK, the press has a partisan bias with most newspapers leaning to the right (based on models of ownership), with the exception of two broadsheets, *The Guardian* and *The Independent*, and one tabloid, the *Daily Mirror*, which are liberal in orientation.

Table 7.1   Quantitative analysis of newspaper articles: Location and type

Newspaper	Total articles	Print articles	Online	News	Commentary	Editorial	Letter	Feature/Poll/ Review
Guardian	31	6	25	8	18	2	2	1
Independent	24	18	6	7	6	1	10	–
Telegraph	23	12	11	9	5	3	6	–
The Times	17	11	6	6	3	–	7	1
Daily Mail	16	2	14	5	10	–	–	1
The Sun	16	12	4	4	5	1	6	–
Daily Express	14	8	6	5	3	–	6	–
Financial Times	5	4	1	3	1	–	1	–
Daily Mirror	4	1	3	2	1	–	1	–
Yorkshire Post	4	2	2	4	–	–	–	–
Daily Star	3	2	1	2	–	1	–	–
Yorkshire Evening Post	2	–	2	1	–	–	1	–
Total articles	159	78	81	56	52	8	40	3

The story was largely narrated within a framework of freedom of speech versus censorship and illustrated the UK's identity struggle vis-à-vis multiculturalism and assertive religiosity.[14] The coverage tended to reinforce Wilders' stance. The press reaction to the story was to condemn his expulsion on the basis that it hindered free speech and smacked of double standards: Why should Wilders be banned when Islamic extremists were being allowed entry to Britain?

Categorization of Wilders

Despite media disagreement with his expulsion, Wilders was largely constructed as an outsider. However, views ranged from extreme distaste for his 'racist' views by the liberal press to a more favourable representation by the conservative papers. An example of the former was *The Guardian*'s first article online in which Wilders was discredited as 'virulently anti-Islamic' and his film as 'crude and vulgar' and 'shambolic'.[15] He was criticized for being a contriving opportunist. 'Hard right' Wilders (a term not used elsewhere) was given little space to air his views, the sole

---

[14]   For a critical review of frame analysis and its applications, see Vleigenthart and Van Zoonen 2011, pp. 101–15.

[15]   Fox 2009.

Wilders quotation being his description of the Qur'an as a 'fascist book', one that was to appear frequently in the media coverage.[16]

Although the conservative press also distanced themselves from Wilders, this was done by referring to him as a clown, as 'kooky', 'idiotic' and a 'weirdo'.[17] This highlighted his harmlessness, juxtaposed against the real threat to British society: Islamic extremists. In the majority of cases he was categorized as a 'far right' MP,[18] with more favourable definitions including a 'democratically elected Dutch MP' (*Daily Mail, Financial Times, Daily Express, The Sun*), 'anti-Islam campaigner' (*The Independent*) or 'Dutch film-maker' (*The Telegraph*). This afforded Wilders and his views legitimacy. Wilders was conceived as a victim receiving death threats and in need of 24-hour protection.[19]

This argumentative strategy constructed Wilders as a 'Dutch politician' in order to delegitimize the UK government's decision to deny him entry.[20] To add weight, the objection made by the Dutch Foreign Office was highlighted. The potential for a diplomatic row (which did not materialize) was emphasized, particularly by *The Times*.[21] This fed into a strong anti-government discourse that was present in all papers at the time. Then at the end of their third term, and subsequently ousted at the General Election in 2010, the Labour government was unpopular on both sides of the political spectrum. A number of newspapers were shifting their support from Labour to the Conservatives. In this context, the government was variously and negatively described as 'cowardly', 'hopeless', 'politically correct', 'idiotic', 'inconsistent' 'weasly', and 'hapless'. The most frequently cited quotation from Wilders was that the British government 'are the biggest bunch of cowards in Europe'.[22]

Despite a negative evaluation of Wilders, he was quoted excessively, thus giving credence to his views, and was distinguished from other banned individuals. For example, an article in the *Daily Express* suggested that, although the views in *Fitna* are highly questionable: 'Wilders is not Abu Hamza. His film doesn't preach hate, it preaches that tolerance of the intolerant will ultimately lead to the end of tolerance and, with it, our civilization. Wilders may be wrong about a lot of things but he's not wrong about that.'[23]

---

[16]   Ibid.

[17]   *Daily Mail* 2009a.

[18]   This label is questionable. Wilders seemingly combined a progressive political stance on women's and gay rights with a virulent anti-Islamic sentiment: he may be better described as a nationalist populist.

[19]   Traynor 2009a.

[20]   Moore 2009.

[21]   This initial framing of the story as a 'political row' demonstrates the importance of Britain's political activities and international relations to *The Times* and its readers.

[22]   For example, Charter 2009a.

[23]   Hartley-Brewer 2009.

Accompanying the text, Wilders' striking image was used repeatedly, becoming a visual signifier of the story and adding to its ability to provoke a response. Whilst many of the articles made reference to Wilders' peroxide blond hair, only *The Guardian* discussed it, recognising that his image was part of his projected identity and commenting on his hair as a racist symbol.[24] This article was supplemented by a profile of Wilders which awarded him considerable credence. Whilst presenting him as an attention seeker and making reference to his Catholic identity (but failing to disclose the fact that this had been renounced), it did not dismiss him as a mere 'populist' but recognized his influence: 'In the past two years his new Freedom Party has taken nine out of the 150 seats in the second chamber ... he has seen his support soar up to 15%. A little more than a year ago, Wilders was voted the most effective politician in the Netherlands.'[25]

Both *The Guardian* and *The Independent* acknowledged Wilders as self-promotionist, but there was little recognition that his violation of the ban constituted an act of provocation. Wilders, though not publicly supported, appeared to be a convenient mechanism for allowing the unsayable to be said (about Islam and Muslims) in the guise of criticism of 'double standards' or a defence of freedom of speech.

Freedom of Speech versus Multicultural Politics

The case against government policy was made here on the basis of freedom of speech. A major secular sacred value, it is regularly used by the press to reject favourable approaches to Muslims or policies to protect them, and goes back to the time of the Rushdie Affair when it became definitive in framing relations with Muslims in public discourse.[26] The Wilders event occurred just a week after its twentieth anniversary and became a conduit for the repetition of similar themes. But, in the reporting of Wilders, the Rushdie Affair was used to demonstrate the stark difference in the reaction of the government of the day, and thus added weight to the argument that British values were being eroded.[27]

That the story was formulated as such was a triumph for Wilders, as was the amount of coverage it received. The event could have been framed as an issue of the demonization of Muslims or the curtailment of Muslim rights, but this kind of reporting was absent from press discourse.[28] In this way the blame for social

---

[24] *The Guardian* 2009.

[25] Traynor 2009b.

[26] For discussion of the defence of secular sacred value of freedom of speech during the controversy surrounding publication of Salman Rushdie's *The Satanic Verses*, see Knott 2010, pp. 115–33.

[27] Johnston 2009.

[28] As was the case in America's *New York Times* and *Newsweek*: see Poole 2012a, pp. 453–68.

problems was shifted away from antagonists like Wilders to Muslims themselves. Other absences included any discussion of *Fitna* and its offensive content (it was simply referred to as 'controversial') or of Wilders' views more generally. The event became a debate about whether Wilders should be banned rather than examination of the wider issues.

The press were united in rejecting the ban on the basis of free speech, but with varying degrees of commitment, from the near-absolutist position of the liberal press (freedom of speech as unconditional) to the collective position of the right-wing press where the commitment appeared to be largely expedient.[29] If we compare it to coverage of 'preachers of hate' (see Chapter 4), this position emerges as a convenient mechanism for defending 'British values' against attack from outside.

At the liberal end of the scale was *The Guardian*, whose opinion poll revealed the paper's interpretive framework within the question it posed: 'On the grounds of free speech should he be let in?' Nearly 85 per cent of *Guardian* (online) readers voted 'Yes: It goes against the principles of free speech to ban him.'[30] Although *The Guardian* website sets an industry standard in online news, providing extensive debate on a range of issues, it is the unevenness of the online commentary in this case which is of interest. *The Guardian*'s position was that freedom of speech should be an absolute, with no exceptions: 'We cannot pick and choose what freedom we defend.'[31] In its editorials, this was made explicit: 'Opinions, however odious, cannot in themselves be criminal ... Britain's political establishment has in an unwitting, collaborative effort of stupidity and democratic illiteracy presented itself as an accomplice to extremisms and enemy of free speech.'[32]

The importance of the issue to *The Independent* was evidenced by the number of articles in its print copy, the position of the story when it broke (on pages 1–3), and the attention afforded to it (double page spread). However, freedom of speech came with limitations. Its editorial made plain the paper's view: 'Was the Home Office right to ban Mr Wilders from entering Britain? The answer is no. Freedom of speech and freedom of movement are principles that we tamper with at our peril.'[33] It went on to say, 'There are, it must be accepted, limitations on those freedoms. The Government has a responsibility to preserve the safety of minority groups in

---

[29]   The Danish cartoons controversy (which has parallels with the Wilders case) was found to present two possibilities for framing: 'A freedom of speech frame pitted absolutist and social responsibility positions on free speech against each other. Elaborations of this frame often equated socially responsible speech with religious tolerance, on one side, or with submission or "appeasement" on the other.' Craft and Waisbord 2008, p. 136.

[30]   *The Guardian* 2009.

[31]   Reidy 2009.

[32]   *The Observer* 2009. *The Observer* is *The Guardian*'s Sunday paper.

[33]   *The Independent* 2009.

Britain.'[34] In this case, however, it was argued that the line had not been crossed. It was noteworthy, though, that, whilst critical of Lord Ahmed for his selective approach to freedom of speech, the paper appeared similarly selective with regard to radical Muslim clerics: 'The radicalization in recent years of young British Muslims by extreme Islamist preachers has complicated such judgements ... The Government's decision to refuse to allow Omar Bakri Mohammed, the former head of the extremist group al-Muhajaroun, back into Britain from Lebanon was probably right.'[35]

Is it the case that the press only takes such an unconditional stance on freedom of speech when the values expressed are close to their own? For example, we saw no such appeals for freedom of speech in response to the Westboro Baptist Church, a virulently homophobic US Christian sect which threatened to enter the UK and picket a play about the murder of a gay man (a story that was in the news the following week). In this case all the papers included an extended quotation from the Home Office on how it opposes extremism of all kinds, in contrast to the shorter response used in the Wilders coverage.[36] Members of the Church were also referred to as 'preachers of hate', unlike Wilders.[37] The papers treated this story as an issue of consistency: will the government also prohibit these people?[38]

There was more emphasis on free speech in the conservative press in the Wilders case than had been evident in comparable cases in the past. In *The Sun* and the *Daily Mail*, some articles used it to attack liberal ideology, but the main thrust of conservative press coverage was 'double standards'.[39] Within this framework, the papers did not discriminate between the right to free speech and the right to publish, nor did they make any reference to the imbalance of power.[40] The freedom to practise one's religion was also absent from the media discussion.

The representation of Muslims as easily offended and quick to react ties into this discourse. The papers focused on the violent protests to *Fitna* across the Muslim world, and Pakistan's ban on access to the film via You Tube, at the expense of peaceful protest and open access.[41] As we saw in Chapter 4, the world was portrayed as subject to Muslim aggression, and its crisis as emanating from Islam:

---

[34]   Ibid.; but for an exclusivist liberal view (that was also anti-religious), see Hari 2009.

[35]   Ibid. Lord Nazir Ahmed was the Muslim peer who, according to the press, alerted the Home Office to the screening of *Fitna* in the House of Lords.

[36]   For example, Shepard 2009.

[37]   Ibid.

[38]   For example, Matthew Moore 2009, and *Daily Mail* 2009b.

[39]   For example, Laughland 2009.

[40]   As a politician, Wilders clearly had more power to speak and more opportunity to get his views across in the media (whether or not they were endorsed) than the religious community he disparaged.

[41]   *Yorkshire Post* 2009.

You may think he (Wilders) is wrong to say this; you may agree with him; you might, like the Lords who invited him to Britain, think it is something worthy of discussion, given the obvious problems caused around the world by radical Islamism and the violence perpetrated in the name of the religion. It is hard, in a free country, to understand why it is a view that must be suppressed.[42]

Within a discourse of modernity, rationality and history, Britain was portrayed positively, as free, accommodating and tolerant, with Muslims in this binary framework constructed as those who would not tolerate difference.[43] Muslims were represented as demanding, and in receipt of preferential treatment, and this was allied to accusations of government appeasement.[44]

Appeasement and Double Standards

In this framework, tolerance for Muslims was interpreted as submission, as a weakness which could not be tolerated: as illustrated in the title of Minette Marrin's article in *The Times* – 'Labour bares its appeaser's teeth to unbending Muslims'.[45] What the Wilders affair demonstrated for Marrin was the appeasement of a 'threatening minority' at the expense of consideration of the majority. 'We' cannot criticize Islam, however reasonable 'our' criticisms, whilst Muslims can speak out.[46] In its argumentative strategy, an event originally focused on one man's intolerance of Islam (in *Fitna*) was turned on its head with Muslims and, in particular the Qur'an, represented as intolerant and inciting hatred. This, for Marrin, was the principal reason the government should stand up to Muslims and allow Wilders entry.[47] This discourse had its strongest outward expression in *The Sun*, in 'Fanatics are on the rise and Labour has let it happen'.[48] Here, Wilders act was downplayed and capitulation to Muslims emphasized, in a sustained example of cultural scaremongering (with images of 'swamping', an emphasis on extremist violence and a negative evaluation of Islam).

The conservative press (in particular *The Sun*, *The Telegraph*, *Daily Express*, *Daily Mail* and *The Star*) used the event to accuse the government of double standards in refusing entry to Geert Wilders whilst 'preachers of hate' were allowed to live and teach their views openly in the UK. The term had become a convenient label to homogenize a group of disparate dissidents and, as these

---

[42]   Johnston 2009.

[43]   Nossek and Philips 2008, p. 113.

[44]   For a discussion of this representation – of Muslims as demanding – see Modood 2009, pp. 164–6.

[45]   Marrin 2009.

[46]   Ibid.

[47]   Ibid.

[48]   Kavanagh 2009.

are almost always radical Muslim clerics, the term had become associated with Islamic extremism. *The Sun*, like other conservative papers, selectively identified such 'radicals' living in the UK whilst failing to mention those who had been banned. One article began, 'Let's get this right then: Labour have allowed every Tom, Dick and Abdul into Britain in the past 11 years'.[49] Part of the strategy was to highlight their crimes whilst playing down the possible outcomes of Wilders' activities (e.g. 'Only five peers – and no MPs – were among the 30 people who attended last night's screening').[50]

This discourse also had a strong presence in the *Daily Mail*, with the well-known columnist, Melanie Phillips, defending Wilders for taking 'an uncompromising stand against the koranic sources of Islamist extremism and violence' and telling 'unpalatable truths'.[51] The event was presented in such a way that the Lords and Wilders were seen as principled and firm, as standing up for 'life and liberty', whereas the Muslim 'Lord Ahmed previously threatened the House of Lords authorities that he would bring a force of 10,000 Muslims to lay siege to the Lords if Wilders was allowed to speak'.[52]

Although on many occasions it was the government rather than Muslims that was deemed to be the villain of the piece, as the event continued coverage became more negative. In the early days, some Muslim writers were featured, for example, in *The Guardian*, *The Independent* and *The Sun*, but there were no Muslim voices in *The Times* or the *Daily Mail*.[53] But the discourse soon turned away from concern for offence to Muslims to the necessity of freedom of speech, in the liberal papers, and double standards and preachers of hate, in the conservative press.

Alternative Viewpoints

What counter discourse, if any, was present within the frameworks of reporting? In the conservative press it was scarce. Letters published in the *Daily Express* were set within a 'For and Against' format: for example, 'Is Expelling Koran Row MP a Source of Pride?' One Muslim respondent argued that he was proud to be British as 'we' do not tolerate discrimination. His representation of national identity ran counter to the dominant press discourse of Muslims as 'other', as outside the national frame. This could also be seen on *The Times* online 'Message Board' which included four texts: two opposing the ban, two supporting it. One of these, from the Netherlands, argued that the Wilders case was not about freedom of speech but the further restriction of the rights of Muslims. In its online

---

[49]   Gaunt 2009.

[50]   Hartley 2009.

[51]   Phillips 2009.

[52]   Ibid.

[53]   For example, Bunglawala 2009; Baig 2009.

commentary *The Times* also included a highly critical article about Wilders that focused on his publicity campaign and ability to 'escape scrutiny'.[54]

The majority of the counter discourse appeared in the liberal press (including the *Daily Mirror*). *The Independent* and *The Guardian* published four articles apiece which could be described as either supportive towards Muslims or in which the narrative ran against the dominant discourse that Wilders should not have been banned. In *The Guardian* this included a piece by Lord Ahmed which defended the ban, pointed out that Muslims too had been banned, and sought to demonstrate inclusivity by making reference to 'our country'.[55] In *The Independent*, Liberal Democrat MP, Chris Huhne, adopted a 'liberal pragmatist' approach, arguing that freedom of speech is precious but that in 'a civilized society there has to be a dividing line between freedom of speech and an incitement to hatred and violence'.[56] This was the only evidence of support for the government in acting to make this kind of racism officially illegitimate.

Although these papers provided some space for other views (chiefly online or in letters), their unequivocal position on freedom of speech eclipsed alternative perspectives. Opposing voices, included to provide a sense of balance, were pushed to the margins, and dominant discourse was prioritized centre stage.

Religion, Multiculturalism and Identity

In its representation of the Wilders event the press engaged in an internal struggle to imagine and define the identity of the nation in light of the majority's relation to its minorities. In the conservative press, the UK was constructed as 'Christian'. The dichotomization of Muslim illiberalism and liberal democracy – at the core of British identity – positioned Muslims as outsiders: 'Banning Wilders plays into the hands of our Islamist enemies', wrote Charles Moore in *The Telegraph*.[57] This was also strongly evident in *The Express* and the *Daily Mail*, and to some extent *The Sun*, whereas *The Times*, *The Financial Times*, and local papers tended to construct Britain first and foremost as secular, and Christian second.

For *The Telegraph* the main purpose of the Wilders coverage was to focus attention on what it saw as the impoverished role of Christianity and poor treatment of Christians in comparison to Muslims. The theme of six articles, this position was evident in its editorial, 'The priorities of a Christian country':

> Although many state officials seem determined to forget it, Britain still has a state religion … That is why the stories that we publish today are so surprising, for they suggest that there is a concerted attempt by some officials to marginalize

---

[54]   Charter 2009b.

[55]   Ahmed 2009.

[56]   Huhne 2009; Kunelius and Alhassan 2008, pp. 91–98.

[57]   Charles Moore 2009.

and to diminish the Christian faith … Christianity is and should be in a privileged position in Britain.[58]

The best example of this position was voiced in the *Daily Express*, 'Why Christianity is on the ropes in Labour's Britain', in which Leo McKinstry cited cases of discrimination against Christians followed by examples of government submission to Islam.[59] References to communism were used – as they were in other newspapers – to attack government 'authoritarianism', and convey a sense of its policy as ideological and an example of the centralized, heavy-handed state at work: 'Filled with authoritarian zeal, Labour now openly talks about creating "a new social order". In this Orwellian world, our history is forgotten, our identity traduced and our liberties destroyed.'[60]

Such metaphors were also used in relation to liberalism, which was held responsible for the preferential treatment awarded to Muslims and the 'Islamification' of society. In an ironic gesture the conservative press hijacked liberal ideals of tolerance and liberty to portray the government as illiberal in its curtailment of free speech (all the result of its policy of political correctness).[61] *The Times* used a discourse of democracy to debunk liberal ideology, and with it multiculturalism, whilst *The Financial Times* attacked immigration and multicultural policy as responsible for the 'retreat' from 'liberal beliefs' which 'provided the core of British identity': 'What has become of British liberalism? It has lost its nerve. It has been weakened by class conflict, immigration and the muddled thinking associated with multiculturalism.'[62] Here, liberalism was used to defend a conservative position excluding Muslims from participation in public life.

The threat to liberalism was also invoked in the left-wing press.[63] Here, implicitly, Britain was constructed as 'secular', religion – but not secularism – being invoked as an ideological identity position.[64] Past analysis of *The Guardian* has revealed an 'exclusive liberalism' in which religion was excluded from its positive approach to minorities.[65] The paper's secular world view found religious values to be conservative and at odds with its own.[66]

---

[58]   *The Telegraph* 2009.

[59]   McKinstry 2009.

[60]   Ibid.

[61]   Laughland 2009. Similar metaphors of totalitarianism were used by the liberal press to bemoan the loss of liberalism: see Knott 2013b.

[62]   Siedentop 2009.

[63]   For example, Ash 2009.

[64]   Ibid. We have distinguished here between the 'secular' as a space or condition (e.g. the nation as secular) and 'secularism' as an ideology or identity position.

[65]   Poole 2002.

[66]   Ibid.

These constructions – 'Christian' and 'secular' – constitute confirmed identity positions, with each paper convinced of the veracity and superiority of its interpretation. Whilst they appear to be competing, sociological analysis has found that '"secular" and "Christian" cultural identities are intertwined in complex and rarely verbalized modes among most Europeans'.[67] Do these varied media positions represent a struggle over Christian heritage and secular values or a fusion of the two? In this case, it seems that Christian and secularist interests were in alliance against Muslims rather than Muslims and Christians standing together to fight against the further erosion of religion in the public sphere.

In their analysis of the Danish cartoons crisis, Kunelius and Alhassan argued that the case demonstrated liberal ideology in action.[68] Press reaction showed how commentators used the resources of liberalism to make sense of what happened: 'The conflict challenged journalists in different political and cultural contexts by forcing them to take positions in this debate, by defining themselves, making distinctions between themselves and others, and elaborating their respective values.'[69] Here we can also see how different papers situated themselves within the discourse of liberalism. Liberal values were perceived to be at the core of British identity and were invoked – often in opposition to Islamic beliefs and values – even in those newspapers in which the UK was constructed as 'Christian'.

Readers' Responses

The reactions of readers to the Wilders case were captured in online commentaries on newspaper websites and in focus groups held a year later. Initial online responses demonstrated agreement with the press narrative in rejecting the ban. Here users constituted a community of shared norms and values. But in mixed focus groups more in-depth discussion of selected articles led to participants voicing their disagreement over the issue.[70] The dynamism of meaning-making was demonstrated as people revised their views in a dialogical context.

Commentary by users on the newspaper websites corresponded with the particular paper's content and discourse. *The Guardian* and the *Daily Mail* appeared to have the most activity, both regularly receiving over 100 comments per article (compared to under 40 for the other papers). Comments were moderated and several had been removed. *The Telegraph* included numerous journalist blogs (32 on Wilders) to which users responded, generally endorsing the paper's position.

---

[67] Casanova 2009, p. 144.

[68] Kunelius and Alhassan 2008, pp. 91–8.

[69] Ibid., p. 81.

[70] Articles used in the focus groups were Hartley 2009, Baig 2009, both from *The Sun*, and Tom Hutchison 2009.

Overall, online responses included little dialogue except in *The Independent* which featured more lengthy debates between individual users.[71]

Taking *The Guardian* and the *Daily Mail* as examples, the relationship of online posts to the newspaper coverage can be discerned. Of *The Guardian*'s posts, most were anti-Wilders but pro-free speech, with only a handful in agreement with the ban and only one defending Muslims. In the *Daily Mail*, of over 150 posts in response to its central report on the 13 February, 33 per cent accused the government of double standards, 26 per cent were direct attacks on the government or the Home Secretary, and 21 per cent were pro-freedom of speech, with less than 10 per cent supporting the ban. Users were invited to rate one another's posts, which had the effect that, when a message was posted that contradicted the dominant flow of discourse, it was rated negatively (shown by a red arrow facing downwards), as in the following case:[72]

> "Well done Jacqui Smith I say! This Dutch rabble-rouser has no place in our country!"
>
> – Joe Bloggs, worcester, uk, 11/2/2009 9:27
>
> Click to rate: Rating 3716 ▼

A positive rating was symbolized by a green arrow pointing upwards:

> A lot of these comments betray complete ignorance about Mr. Wilders and his film. I've seen the film, and it is nothing more than a plain statement of facts: passages from the Koran, and pictures of 9/11. There's no conclusion drawn, no political point made, no hate-speech, just facts. What's wrong with that? The Koran exists, 9/11 happened.
>
> – A.N. Other, Woodbridge UK, 11/2/2009 11:12
>
> Click to rate: Rating 2701 ▲

The direction of discussion was also influenced by the nature of the initial response. In most cases there was a clear relationship between the text, first post and subsequent discussion. However, *The Independent* followed a different pattern, provoking more heated discussion on the ban and the nature of Islam.

This level of debate was much more evident in the focus groups. Whilst having little recollection of the story, most people were initially in agreement with the first

---

[71]   One problem of analysing web content is that it is in a state of flux. *The Independent*, for example, removed initial commentary on Wilders from its website, thus compromising comparison with other websites.

[72]   For ethical reasons, names of posters have been changed.

article they read (from *The Sun*): Only eight out of 45 disagreed with the ban. The reasons given for rejecting it were in line with those expressed in the article, on freedom of speech:

> All debate is good debate, that's what people died for, freedom of speech, it doesn't mean to say you need to agree with it, but everyone should have a platform. (London, Presbyterian)

Participants argued forcefully that the ban had resulted in unwarranted publicity for Wilders. Only a few discussed the problem arising from freedom of speech when racism and violence are invoked. Those that supported the ban did so mainly on the grounds that Wilders' intention was to incite trouble. Others cited the need both to take a stand against his views and protect 'our' own (invoking the idea of a liberal, anti-racist Britain in opposition to the general position of the press).

The only apparent difference between religious and non-religious participants was that most of the latter thought the story would be more meaningful to religious people whom they judged more likely to support the ban, some surmising that Muslims would be offended by the story. However, this was not borne out among Muslim focus group participants. After the discussion some of those who had previously supported the ban changed their minds.

Participants' understanding of one of the articles – from the *Daily Star* – and their varied responses to it underscored the fact that media coverage generates multiple interpretations, a point acknowledged in one of the groups:

> This article could be interpreted in several different ways, same with the first one, because everyone here has said different things about the same article and that is important because ... nine people interpret it four or five ways. (London, non-religious)

Participants demonstrated confusion over details of the Wilders case, such as which religion was involved, and the identity of people in the story (confusing Hindus with Muslims, for example). They often struggled to articulate their views, a possible indication that they were not accustomed to think about or discuss such issues in everyday life. They denied the influence of the media on their own opinions, whilst suggesting it might influence others.

The Wilders Event: Muslims, Liberalism and the Identity of the Nation

According to Timothy M. Savage, the increasing European presence of Muslims has reopened debate on the following issues: 'the place of religion in public life, social tolerance in Europe, secularism as the only path to modernity, and Europe's very identity.'[73] Such issues underscored the media discourses arising from the Wilders event – that the Dutch MP should not have been banned, that freedom of speech and liberalism in general were in jeopardy, and that the country was subject to government folly, political correctness and double standards. Multiculturalism was under attack from all sides, and the conservative press also attacked liberal totalitarianism as an agent of censorship. In this framework the actual portrayal of Muslims and Islam was secondary: they were attributed with little positive agency. However, as 'preachers of hate', they were used as a foil to Wilders, and, more importantly, were fundamental to the narration of Britain's incipient 'Islamification' and the consequent marginalization of Christianity.[74]

The Wilders ban – which was generally interpreted by the media as an affront to freedom of speech and as evidence of the government's fear of Muslims – generated a conflicted media event in which different interpretations struggled for supremacy in defining the nation, its identity and direction. An event which could have othered Wilders and focused on the inflammatory nature of *Fitna* and its threat to community cohesion instead became an opportunity for only partially veiled discussion about the problem of Islam, and the unwillingness of Muslims to integrate. In the conservative press, this was understood to be a challenge to the future of 'liberal' and 'tolerant', but nonetheless 'Christian' Britain. In the liberal press, it was part of a narrative about increasing government authoritarianism, its failure to respond appropriately to the return of religion, and to recognize and protect the core values of secular liberalism.

---

[73]   Timothy M. Savage, cited in Saeed 2009, p. 203.

[74]   For further discussion of these narratives, see chapters 3 and 4.

Chapter 8
Reclaiming Religion in Secular Public Life:
The Media on the Papal Visit

In September 2010, Benedict XVI made the first state visit by a Pope to Britain, following Pope John Paul II's pastoral tour in 1982. Coinciding with our two studies of religion in the media, they gave us the opportunity to analyse and compare how the media portrayed, interpreted and constructed major public religious occasions. For most of the population, the media event – no less in 1982 than in 2010 – was the Papal visit 'as we know it'.[1] Media stories and pictures – selected, crafted and made available in the newspapers, on television, radio and online – constituted the event for the British public.

Following an introduction to the coverage of the visits, we examine the narrative structure of the media portrayal, and analyse and compare the visual images. Even though these dimensions reveal some variety, they nevertheless illuminate clearly shared and dominant features. The heterogeneous standpoints and attitudes of different newspapers become more evident in our analysis of newspaper editorials. In the second half of the chapter, we turn to the reporting of the Papal speeches. This allows us to return to the main themes discussed in earlier chapters: the media representation of religious diversity in its acceptable (interfaith) and unacceptable (religious extremist) forms, the public role of Christianity and its supposed marginalization, and the rise of atheism and secularism. We argue that, as a media event, the Papal visit endorsed current discourse in which the dividing line was not between different Christian denominations or between Christianity and other religions, but between 'faith communities' and 'atheists and secularists'. As we will suggest, this does not mean an end to the privileged position afforded to Christianity in the British media. Drawing attention to the interfaith aspect of the visit does not have the effect of making all religious traditions equal, but rather maintains Christian, particularly Anglican, hegemony.

Media Coverage of the Two Visits

Analysis of these events in 1982 and 2010 was based on relevant coverage in all the national newspapers (and one local paper) throughout each visit, as well as one

---

[1] For detailed analysis of the media coverage of the 1982 Papal visit, see Knott 1984a, pp. 34–59.

day before and one day after it.[2] A selection of Sunday papers, major weeklies and magazines was also consulted. Television programmes, especially live coverage and documentaries, but also news and talk shows, were examined before and during the visit. The official Papal visit website and the websites of interest groups were also monitored.[3]

On television, it was the BBC that carried the majority of the programming related to the 2010 visit (as it had in 1982); Channel 4 featured critical documentaries; ITV1 provided very little coverage.[4] The general public complained that the BBC was either too critical or not critical enough, but with almost 13 hours of live coverage as well as several more challenging pre-visit documentaries, the overall balance on the BBC was moderately positive.[5] The 'impartiality' of the BBC was construed as pro-Pope by those protesting against the visit and anti-Pope by the conservative newspapers. Back in 1982, public broadcasters had understood their role in reporting the visit to be the creation of a mass media event for the whole nation, one that would match up to the piety of Britain's Catholics, the ecumenical expectations of other Christians and the curiosity of non-religious viewers. Nevertheless, the BBC had been criticized by *The Daily Telegraph* for politicizing the event in its portrayal of His Holiness as critical of the Prime Minister, Margaret Thatcher, for taking the country to war against Argentina. *The Telegraph*'s urge to highlight and endorse the traditional link between Christianity and Conservative politics could be discerned, a standpoint which – as we shall witness – continues to be a defining trait of several contemporary right-of-centre newspapers.

---

[2]   In continuity with the rest of the research, the main focus was mainstream media, though we also consulted online sources, including websites, blogs and posts.

[3]   The Papal Visit, http://www.thepapalvisit.org.uk/; the websites of the British Humanist Association and the National Secular Society were monitored for their anti-visit stance and counter discourse.

[4]   Television coverage included documentaries such as *Panorama: What the Pope Knew* (BBC1, 13 September 2010), *The Trouble with the Pope* (Channel 4, 13 September), *Benedict: Trials of a Pope* (BBC2, 15 September) and *Vatican: The Hidden World* (BBC2, 18 September), some 13 hours of live coverage by the BBC, such as *Edinburgh: The Queen Welcomes the Pope* (BBC1, 16 September), *The Glasgow Mass* (BBC2, 16 September), *Evening Prayer from Westminster Abbey* (BBC2, 17 September), *Papal Mass from Westminster Cathedral* (BBC2, 18 September) and *Beatification Mass of John Henry Newman* (BBC2, 19 September), and reflection and conversation on the significance of the visit in *The Pope's Visit* (BBC2, 20 September). Moreover, the visit was debated beforehand in current affairs chat shows, such as *The Andrew Marr Show*, *Sunday Morning Live* and *The Politics Show* (BBC1, 12 September) and in pre-visit news items profiling Pope Benedict (BBC News, 13 September), and well as in news and current affairs programmes during the visit itself.

[5]   Plunkett 2010.

Table 8.1   Newspaper coverage of the Papal visit in September 2010

Newspaper	Articles/items	Front page	Pictures	Editorials
Daily Express	48	3	42	3
Daily Mail	58	2	52	4
Daily Mirror	50	3	82	4
Daily Star	25	1	31	2
Daily Telegraph	95	6	90	3
Guardian	91	3	66	2
Independent	74	3	68	3
Sun	41	3	54	4
Times	85	4	110	1
Yorkshire Evening Post	16	2	20	1
People (Sunday only)	4	–	4	–
Total	587	30	619	27

In September 2010, across six days of coverage, there were nearly 600 articles or other items, as well as several special supplements (e.g. a commemorative magazine in the *Daily Mirror*, and a 16-page supplement in *The Times*). The broadsheets provided extensive coverage, with only slightly less in the tabloids; only the *Daily Star* paid relatively little attention to the visit. *The Times* in 1982 provided nearly double the number of articles of other papers, but in 2010, it was overtaken by *The Telegraph* and *The Guardian* both of which gave more space to letters. The content of letters in these and other papers tended to support the general view of the newspaper itself, those in *The Guardian* and *The Independent* being predominantly critical, whilst readers of *The Telegraph* came across as more supportive of the Pope.

All daily papers published at least one story on their front page. *The Telegraph* had a relevant front-page story every day, accompanied by an image on all but one. This highlighted the importance of the visit for a paper with a pro-Christian stance and Catholic ownership.

From Doubt to Success

Today the media is a key institution for creating narratives which make news and stories accessible and meaningful. Television, newspapers and other media sources do not simply describe events but cast them in a narrative mould. In both 1982 and 2010, a compelling narrative structure emerged as the events took shape: first there were pre-visit problems and uncertainties that melted away during the visit, which was then transformed into an occasion of sympathy, relief and joy. The media narrative went from doubt to success.

More than half of Britain's six million Catholics wanted the Pope to visit in 2010, whereas only 14 per cent of the population as a whole supported the visit.[6] A major reservation expressed in letters to the papers was financial: many thought that at a time of deep cuts in public spending the money could have been spent more wisely (the cost was estimated at 20 million pounds, the taxpayer contributing more than half and the rest covered by British Catholics). Another was fall-out from the Catholic sex abuse controversy which had overshadowed the pre-visit coverage.[7] In addition, gay rights and human rights campaigners were dissatisfied with the Pope's strict attitude towards homosexuality. Pope Benedict had written that the very idea of gay marriage 'would fall outside the moral history of humanity' and that 'the basic structural pattern of human existence [would be] violated' were gay partnerships to be given status equal to heterosexual marriages.[8] Moreover, campaigning secularists and atheists used the media for provocation before the visit – the best known example being the widely publicized call by Richard Dawkins for the Pope to be arrested on arrival.[9] These voices were strengthened on the eve of the visit when one cardinal, Walter Kasper, warned of the rise of 'new and aggressive atheism' in Britain and suggested that arriving at Heathrow was like 'landing in a third-world country'. Taken as a criticism of Britain's liberalism and cultural diversity, his comments were widely reported and generally condemned: He was named 'the Pope's dope' in the tabloids and his stance was seen as 'a gift to … left-wing atheists', thus increasing misgivings about the visit in general.[10] When added to the critical pre-visit coverage on terrestrial television, such reporting reinforced the widespread sense of doubt about the occasion before the Pope's arrival. However, this evaporated when the Pope landed in Edinburgh. As the *Daily Mirror* put it, 'the warmth of his flock's welcome melted away all those fears'.[11]

BBC coverage changed from moderately critical to very positive once the live broadcasting began. A favourable documentary was aired; the mood lightened – in the newspapers as well as on television. The tabloids featured the Pope's shoes, reported that Fanta was 'fizzy Pope's' favourite drink, and claimed he enjoyed his 'holy roast' and Yorkshire pudding (in the case of John Paul II it had been an English breakfast). The broadsheets had fun too. A *Times* rock critic reviewed the open-air mass at Bellahouston park, Glasgow, giving it 2 out of 5 stars. On the same day a similar tongue-in-cheek review in *The Independent* gave 4 out of 5 stars because the event was superbly choreographed and celebrity singer Susan Boyle was kept 'out of sight during the service itself'.[12] The irony went largely

---

[6]   ComRes 2010.

[7]   Lewis 2010.

[8]   Jenkins 2007, p. 39; Shortt 2006, p. 99. See also Rowland 2010.

[9]   Horne 2010.

[10]   *Daily Mirror* 2010a; Graeme Wilson 2010.

[11]   *Daily Mirror* 2010b.

[12]   *The Times* (Turner 2010) and *The Independent* (Ingrams 2010).

unnoticed: Pope Benedict was known for his contempt of popular music because of its standardization, commercialization and mediocrity (he preferred Gospel, Mozart and choral music). However, humour proved to be a good way to relieve the pre-visit tension, and contributed to the narrative move from doubt to success.

After the success, the backlash. Six people were arrested, suspected of planning to kill the Pope. This turned out to be a false alarm, and only strengthened the Pope's image as he bravely continued the tour as scheduled. Yet fresh fears emerged as the visit progressed and the media worried about whether the Pope would speak publicly on the issue of Catholic child abuse. He finally did so, and met five victims, further confirmation of the positive nature of the visit.[13]

A key element of the visit's success was the media focus on personality. If Benedict was labelled more a Pope of content than image, it was partly because his predecessor had been represented as a charismatic celebrity. A major factor in the 1982 media coverage, John Paul II was a 'superstar Pope', 'super Pope', 'genuinely good and holy man' and 'one of the great Popes'.[14] This focus on the man and his charismatic image prevailed over the social and theological issues.

One commonly expressed doubt in 2010 was Benedict's rigidity and shyness. By the end of the visit, however, he was portrayed as a sympathetic, if uncharismatic, figure. No longer 'God's rottweiler', he had become 'a resounding success', 'warmer, more human and less rigid', 'beyond all expectations', a Pope whose 'trip won affection'.[15] *The Times* suggested that the visit would be recalled for the vitality of his message.[16] Some weeks later, one *Telegraph* columnist proposed that what had changed was the reputation of the Pope, from conservative and rigid to shy and thoughtful.[17] Even the most critical of the papers, *The Independent* – whose agenda was focused on victims of Catholic sex abuse – stated in an editorial that the 'visit passed off better, even much better, than might have been expected'.[18]

There had been doubts in 1982 too.[19] The Pope's pastoral visit to Britain was an historic occasion – Pope John Paul II was 'the first reigning Pope to set foot in England' – but it came at a time when Britain was at war.[20] The Falklands war had the potential to be divisive; the visit was nearly cancelled because of it, but went ahead on the basis that the Pope would not meet the Prime Minister. Furthermore, the ecumenical situation between Britain and Rome was unclear. But when the

---

[13]   This was variously reported with a focus in the liberal papers on the inadequacy of a remorse that does not lead to decisive action for change.

[14]   Knott 1984a, p. 34.

[15]   References to Pope Benedict made in *The Telegraph, The Independent, The Times,* and the *News of the World* during the Papal visit in September 2010.

[16]   *The Times* 2010.

[17]   Howse 2010.

[18]   *The Independent* 2010c.

[19]   Knott 1984a, pp. 34–59.

[20]   O'Sullivan 1982, p. 4.

visit took place, demonstrations were smaller and fewer than predicted.[21] Despite initial misgivings, the visit went smoothly. Certainly the narrative 'from doubt to success' was more visible in 2010, but the media emphasis on 'success' was nevertheless present in 1982. Pope John Paul was seen afterwards as 'the perfect guest', 'a man for our seasons', and admired for his 'extraordinary qualities of character and mind'.[22] He had been humble and had not offended people with his conservative moral theology. He had not criticized the government or encouraged a fanatical or tasteless popular response. The visit had not been 'evangelical, political or triumphalist', but suitably dignified, as befitted Britain.[23] More than 90 per cent of those questioned in a post-visit survey approved of the Pope's visit.[24]

Visual Coverage of the Visits

More than 600 photographs of the Pope and other aspects of his visit were published in the 60 newspapers we monitored in 2010. *The Times* and *The Telegraph* together accounted for a third of these, but even *The Guardian* and *The Independent* provided extensive visual coverage. In 1982, it had been *The Telegraph*, *The Sun* and the *Daily Mail* that had featured most images, but – with only 35 each across the eight-day period – it is clear that the role and significance of the visual coverage has changed. Technological developments have simplified the reproduction, purchasing and sharing of images, and the visual framing and illustration of stories has become essential to successful newspaper reporting in a way that it could not have been in the 1980s. In the case of the 1982 Papal visit, though, this was more than made up for by the television spectacle.

In both visits, the principal visual motif was the Pope himself: his arrival, his speeches, and meetings with the Queen and other dignitaries. The main image of 2010 was Benedict XVI with his hands spread wide. The 'pope-mobile' – the Papal vehicle, with its bullet proof windows – was often featured, surrounded by a cheering crowd. Photos also added humour to a story: the Pope's 'funky red loafers'; the wind lifting his cape over his head and blowing his cap off in Edinburgh.[25]

Five visual motifs were instrumental in establishing the image of success and constructing meanings of this media event. The *first* was the Pope kissing and blessing babies. Popular in both 1982 and 2010, this helped to create a positive image of the Pope and, metonymically, the Catholic Church. It also signalled

[21]   Baker 1982, pp. 475–81 (p. 45); Marshall 1982, pp. 481–5 (p. 481).

[22]   Knott 1984a, p. 43. References to Pope John Paul II made in *The Telegraph*, and *The Times* on 3 June 1982.

[23]   Knott 1984a, p. 43 (from *The Telegraph*, 3 June 1982).

[24]   A survey on conventional and common religion was conducted in Leeds in 1982; it included questions on the media coverage of the Papal visit. Knott 1984a, pp. 48–53.

[25]   Clench and Phillips 2010.

the affective economy of the visit and its impact on individuals and families. Captured in images, such Papal blessings constituted emotional peak moments, highly memorable, and often supported by interviews with mothers. The *second*, of teenagers and schoolchildren, was an altogether more surprising motif. Scenes of young people cheering and celebrating created a future-oriented and youthful image of contemporary religiosity and the appeal of Christianity. The *third* was the crowd.[26] Such images conveyed a sense of the scale and popularity of the event, and the solidarity of religious people. They drew attention to the fact that supporters of the Pope greatly exceeded the number protesting against him.[27]

Nevertheless, the demonstrations constituted an important *fourth* motif. Photographs of protests and protesters were a visual reminder of dissent, but what was interesting was their location in the papers. By comparison with the cosy images of the Pope and the crowds, they were hidden away near the bottom or margins of pages, and often featured unpopular celebrities of various ideological hues such as the Reverend Ian Paisley and Richard Dawkins. Despite the critical pre-visit commentary, there were few visual references to the victims of Catholic child abuse: most papers were keen to convey a different message once the visit was underway.[28] When the story broke on 18 September of the arrest of six people suspected of planning to kill the Pope, the visual images focused on a *fifth* theme, security. An important consideration in all news reporting since 9/11 and revitalized after 7/7, images supported text in reproducing the distinction between religion as a force for good (with Christianity as the prototype) and religion as a potentially disruptive force (focused on Muslim terrorism).

In general, as this brief analysis of the principal motifs shows, the visual coverage supported the overriding narrative of a visit that was successful in overcoming people's misgivings.

Divided Media: The Editorials

If the narrative structure and images tell a rather homogeneous story about the visit with only minor differences in the newspaper coverage, a closer look at editorials reveals the degree to which newspapers were divided in their interpretation.

---

[26]   According to the survey conducted five months after the 1982 visit, what people remembered best was the Pope holding babies, his vehicle and the crowd, not the content of speeches (Knott 1984a, pp. 48–53).

[27]   *The Independent* and *The Guardian* covered the demonstrations, the latter noting that the visit 'saw the biggest demonstrations against any Pope in modern times': *The Guardian* 2010d. This is significant bearing in mind that the Pope was seen live in 2010 by approximately 340,000 people while the number in 1982 was 2 million.

[28]   Emotive negative images could be found, for example on the website of the National Secular Society, but few were published by the newspapers.

All the daily papers published at least one editorial on the visit: *The Sun*, the *Daily Mail* and *Daily Mirror* had four each, illustrating the visit's importance for the popular tabloids. This was a change from 1982, when it was the broadsheets that gave the visit most editorial attention. In 2010 the tabloids used the event to defend Christianity and its role for the nation, and to reiterate their opposition to multiculturalism, political correctness and assertive atheism. Here, we give a flavour of the most distinctive editorial perspectives.

The *Daily Mail* revealed its unshakeable politically conservative and pro-Pope editorial position on the first day of the visit by classifying celebrity protests as 'pompous' and 'discourteous', and protesters like Stephen Fry 'egregiously self-satisfied' with 'venomous hatred'.[29] It mentioned more problematic issues, such as Pope Benedict's attitude towards homosexuality and the child abuse scandal, but added that, despite its faults, the Church 'promotes great good throughout the globe'. This was contrasted with the 'increasingly ugly and strident secularism being promoted by the BBC and left-wing papers'. Frequent reference was made to the opposition between Christianity and Nazism, by implication suggesting that atheists may be connected to the latter. In addition, it reiterated the idea of double standards – as seen in the case of Geert Wilders – stating that, if 'secularists' had targeted Muslim leaders rather than the Pope, 'the Left' would be 'screaming'. Finally, it was 'the politically correct Left-wing establishment' who, according to the *Mail*'s interpretation of the Pope's speech, tried to 'prevent the celebration of Christmas'. Throughout, the *Mail* generated a dichotomy between conservative Christians and Left-wing atheists, and made little reference to other religions. This was a position also voiced by *The Sun* which used strong language to ridicule the critical voices of 'atheist extremists', 'PC killjoys' and 'politically-motivated zealots who want to destroy Britain's cultural and religious identity'.[30]

The Telegraph drew attention to those values it believed were shared by Britain and the Holy See, and welcomed the flourishing religiosity generated by the visit, arguing that it was a good thing for people of all beliefs.[31] Like the tabloids, it attacked atheists and secularists, but focused on what it saw as the yoking of tolerance to a politically-correct liberal agenda, in contrast to the more open tolerance of religions, particularly Christianity. Eager to seize the opportunity, the editorials made the connection between Conservative politics and the renewal of public interest in Christianity (juxtaposing it to the 'bullying' of Christians under the previous Labour administration). If editorials in *The Telegraph* were eager to defend the Pope and religiosity against atheists and secularists, the only one published in *The Times*, though positive, made a plea for a less polarized debate between supporters and protesters.[32]

---

[29] *Daily Mail* 2010a, 2010b, 2010c, 2010d.
[30] *The Sun* 2010a, 2010b, 2010c.
[31] *The Telegraph* 2010a, 2010b, 2010c.
[32] *The Times* 2010.

Turning now to the liberal press, *The Independent* began by criticizing the timing of the Papal visit in light of massive public sector cuts, and in its next editorial focused on what it considered to be the inadequacy of the Papal response to Catholic child abuse. There was an acceptance, however, in its final editorial, that the visit had passed off better than expected, and that perhaps everyone – the Pope included – had learned something new.[33] *The Guardian*'s editorial contribution was interesting for its engagement – but from a liberal standpoint – with issues raised by the tabloid press. It argued that the marginalization of Christianity was not the fault of non-religious secularists alone. The Church should take some responsibility too, because of its internal problems. There was a plea for 'a little less preaching and a bit more humility' from the Pope. Whilst acknowledging the value of the visit, the paper was also critical in its assessment that 'the rapprochement required today is not so much between Protestant and Catholic as between the religious and the rest, and Benedict leaves without denting that divide'.[34]

The editorials followed quite clearly the general religious and political position of the papers, and disclosed the traditional fault lines between them. Reflecting our previous observations, it is instructive to note that the *Yorkshire Evening Post*, in conformity with its aim of addressing the local aspect of national news, succeeded by reporting on a story about a local children's choir that was to sing for the Pope.[35]

What the newspapers shared in stating their differing stances, priorities and attitudes was a discursive frame in which two groups – religious people (especially Christians), and secularists and atheists – were pitted against one another. There was a general failure to acknowledge that some pro-visit supporters were non-religious, and some protesters Catholic (for example, the victims and critics of clergy abuse). This discursive frame had not been invoked in 1982. The overall approach then had been much less divisive (though there had been public protests by Protestant loyalists), with most editorials welcoming Pope John Paul II as a 'genuinely good and holy man', and critical voices excluded. Editorial discourse had focused on the tension surrounding an Anglican and Conservative country at war and a Catholic Pope who epitomized peace, with right-leaning papers voicing nationalist sentiments, and left-leaning ones inclined towards criticism. This political fault line, however, did not reflect attitudes to religion as such. What had changed was that, by 2010, there was a greater identification between the political left, secularism, and criticism of religion, and – equally – between the right, a faith agenda (based on Christianity) and criticism of multiculturalism.

---

[33]   *The Independent* 2010a, 2010b, 2010c.

[34]   *The Guardian* 2010c, 2010d.

[35]   *Yorkshire Evening Post* 2010.

Reclaiming Religion in Public Life

In earlier chapters we examined how media representations constructed Britain variously as 'Christian', 'secular' and 'religiously diverse'. It was around these very poles that Pope Benedict developed his criticism of British society. What connected his speeches was the attempt to reclaim the role of religion – particularly Christianity – in public life. However, the media drew more attention to some of his views than others and added their own twist to the message. To explore this in greater detail, we focus on three themes – central tenets not only in coverage of the Papal visit, but in British media discourse on religion more generally: promotion of a diversity and interfaith agenda, anxiety about the marginalization of Christianity, and the attack on atheism and secularism. The themes are compared to the 1982 coverage, in order to assess how the discourse on religion has changed.

From Ecumenism to Interfaith

The 1982 visit was framed mainly in Christian terms. John Paul II took an ecumenical approach and talked about the 'restoration of unity among Christians'; with Anglicans and the leaders of other denominations, he signed a declaration for improving intra-Christian dialogue.[36] Even though he had spoken out during an earlier visit to Nigeria on the importance of Christian-Muslim relations, and had met members of the British Jewish community as part of his UK visit, he was described as 'a pilgrim of Christian unity'.[37] The Pope's visit was seen as a wave in the tide of the ecumenical movement, and was supported by all the papers as a welcome and inevitable step for overcoming disagreements between Catholics and Protestants. Even pre-visit television programmes focused on the ecumenical significance of the visit, in addition to the general arrangements. And, not surprisingly, the message that most people could remember five months later was peace and ecumenism.[38]

By 2010, the media focus had shifted from ecumenism to multi-faith and interfaith issues. BBC1 interviewed a Sikh who affirmed the visit's relevance. The Pope speaks beyond Catholics, he said: to be religious today is to be inter-religious.[39] BBC's *Look North* ran a story on Muslim children who, as members of a local school choir, sang for the Pope, and *The Times* noted the British Muslim welcome.[40] 'A Man for All Religions', wrote the *Daily Mirror*: the Pope 'speaks to us all … not just Catholics'.[41]

---

36   Knott 1984a, p. 41 (reference to a speech by Pope John Paul II, 30 May 1982).
37   Morrison 1982; O'Sullivan 1982.
38   Knott 1984a, pp. 48–53.
39   BBC News 2010d.
40   BBC Look North 2010; Wade 2010.
41   *Daily Mirror* 2010b.

Apart from local initiatives, the reason for this emphasis was by no means obvious. The Pope viewed multiculturalism as a challenge and, despite acknowledging the necessity for Christian-Muslim dialogue, his relationship to interfaith issues was ambiguous.[42] This was evident before he became Pope: as Cardinal Ratzinger, he had disagreed with Pope John Paul II over inviting interfaith leaders to pray for peace, and had spoken against Catholic involvement in yoga and Eastern meditation practices. As the current Pope, he had not only warned against non-religious attitudes such as atheism and the 'dictatorship of relativism', but also against syncretism and some forms of mysticism.[43] Neither his track record nor his speeches during the visit explained the media's interfaith emphasis.

This angle arose in part because politicians, Conservatives in particular, were eager to frame the visit a multi-faith event. The Prime Minister, David Cameron, was quoted as saying that it was a 'unique opportunity to celebrate the good works of religious groups' and 'to further intercultural and interreligious dialogue for the enrichment of the entire community'.[44] He added later that the Pope 'made us think', and endorsed the idea that faith was at the heart of a 'new culture of social responsibility' and 'part of the fabric of our country'.[45] This was effective political rhetoric from a Prime Minister eager to highlight the ideology and policies of the 'Big Society'.[46] The Papal visit gave the new Coalition government an opportunity to criticize the previous Labour regime – noted for 'not doing God' – by recognizing the public role of 'people of faith' and suggesting that the Coalition was on the side of religion. This was reported in many newspapers, but most visibly in those that were politically conservative.[47]

The promotion of religious diversity need not be based on a conception of the full equality of all traditions. Instead, it may operate by making a distinction between moderate (good) and extreme (bad) forms of religiosity. In Britain, where Christianity is discursively privileged, it is primarily Islam which has been deemed prototypical of extremism, though much has been made in discourse on Islam of the distinction between its 'moderate' and 'extreme' forms. We saw this at work in stories about the 'Muslim plot to kill Pope'.

On the 18 September the newspapers reported that police had arrested six cleaners suspected of planning to kill the Pope. Their homes were searched and they were soon released after nothing suspicious was found. Although the whole 'plot' turned out to be a false alarm, it served to reinforce the discursive connection between Islam and terrorism in media reporting.

---

[42]   Welborn 2009, pp. 107–28.

[43]   Shortt 2006, pp. 5, 85–6, 128.

[44]   *The Telegraph* 2010b; *The Guardian* 2010d.

[45]   *Daily Mail* 2010d.

[46]   In the 'Big Society', faith-based organizations were expected play a central role in supporting communities at a time of decentralization and the loss of state funding.

[47]   For example, the front page of *The Telegraph* 2010d.

Most papers made big news of the story, despite the lack of any hard information. Articles were filled with speculation about the ethnic origin and, in some cases, religion of the cleaners. *The Sun* printed a front page story claiming they were from North Africa, a region known to be a 'hotbed of Islamic fundamentalism', two days later noting they had been freed, but adding that they were 'believed to be Muslims'.[48] *The Daily Express* printed a similar story on the 18 September, speculating about Muslims, Islamic terrorism and al-Qaeda, whilst the *Daily Mirror* and *Daily Star* resisted labelling the suspects 'Muslim' directly though they implied it in references to the 7/7 bombers and the rise of Islam.[49] Other papers held back from referring to them as Muslim, but noted their ethnic identity. Once news of the false alarm had been made public, there were hints of embarrassment and back-tracking in the reporting (though no front page coverage), with the police being blamed for breaking the story too soon. By then, though, the genie of Islamophobia was out of the bottle.

Threats to security during the visit had undoubtedly been anticipated by the media. The disclosure of the 'plot' provided the perfect moment to release the story, though the final twist – of false alarm – could not have been foreseen. In 1982, there had been no such preoccupation, though threats had been made beforehand by Scottish Protestant loyalists to disrupt the Glasgow visit.[50] The 2010 'plot' was symptomatic of a different security context, the challenge of religious diversity, and the media's response to both. It afforded an opportunity for the distinction between extreme and acceptable forms of religion to be reiterated, and for the former to be associated with outsiders (migrant workers from North Africa) and the latter to be endorsed as a successful example of integration.

Marginalization of Christianity

The interfaith motif was not present at the expense of Christianity, however. According to the newspapers, the fate of Christianity was the Pope's main message to Britain: in his speech in Westminster Hall, he said he could not 'but voice [his] concern at the increasing marginalization of religion, particularly of Christianity' and continued that 'there are those who would advocate that the voice of religion be silenced, or at least relegated to the purely private sphere'.[51]

The main target of his complaint about marginalization was 'aggressive secularism', but the increasing presence of other religions was also addressed as an issue in his speeches and the media coverage. To the delight of those papers that had championed the cause of Christian marginalization, the Pope suggested that celebrating Christmas in a Christian way was under threat because it is seen

---

[48]   *The Sun* 2010a, 2010c.

[49]   *Daily Express* 2010; Blair 2010; *Daily Star* 2010a.

[50]   Horsnell 1982.

[51]   On its website, the BBC reproduced the Westminster Hall speech of 17 September 2010 in full; most newspapers quoted extensively from it.

as offending 'those of other religions or none'.[52] Some newspapers took the Pope's words as evidence of diversity gone too far, but more often it was turned against the political correctness of 'atheist Left-wingers'.[53]

Even though 'marginalization' was sometimes printed with scare quotes, indicating some disquiet at the expression, the Pope's message was nevertheless received with surprising agreement – particularly by more conservative papers – compared to the more cautious stance adopted several months earlier at the launch of the Declaration of Christian Conscience (see Chapter 3). The *Daily Star* captured the mood in an editorial: 'We have a strong history of welcoming all cultures to our shores. But there's a growing sentiment across the country that our traditions are being slowly lost.'[54] And a *Sunday Express* columnist stressed his support for a society which 'embraces all peoples and allows them to celebrate their many religions and enjoy their Hanukkah, Eid, Diwali or whatever else it might be, while all the time accepting that this is a Christian country with Christian core beliefs and values'.[55] These views make clear the difference and hierarchy between 'their' religions and 'our' Christian tradition, with the latter seen to be in need of defence.

More secular-minded journalists thought that such warnings were far-fetched given the realities of British political and religious relations, and dissenting voices could be found airing their views in commentaries and letters, but – as in the case of the fake terrorist plot – once the story was out there, it was hard to rein in.

The Pope's authoritarian voice and unashamed defence of Christianity's role in public life led to some calls for equivalent British voices. Pro-Christian conservative editorials stressed the need for a strong home-grown leader to defend Christianity against marginalization, and the comparison was made with the more liberal and equivocating Archbishop of Canterbury.[56] The *Daily Mail* was outspoken in arguing that the Archbishop is 'so cowed by the forces of secularism that he no longer poses any threat to their bleak vision'; 'if only the Archbishop dared to speak with a fraction of Benedict's authority'.[57] Despite assumptions about the decline in Christian participation in the 1980s, there had been no equivalent media discourse. Furthermore, the then Archbishop – Robert Runcie – was upheld as a strong leader and voice of 'Christian confidence'.[58]

One similarity between the two visiting Popes, however, was their uneasiness with the moral state of the contemporary secular nation: they both referred to the decline of morality, including sexual permissiveness. And John Paul II, in 1982,

---

[52]   *Daily Express* 2010.

[53]   Ibid.

[54]   *Daily Star* 2010b.

[55]   Ferrari 2010.

[56]   *Daily Mail* 2010c; *Sunday Express* 2010.

[57]   Glover 2010.

[58]   *The Times* 1982c; Prince Charles too was seen as an important defender of religion, *The Times* 1982e.

had worried about 'marginalization' but of the social kind, of the sick, elderly, handicapped and unemployed, not those in a hegemonic Christian majority. The differences in the two Papal speeches may be explained by the nature of the two visits – the former a pastoral, the latter a state visit – by the personalities of the two men, and the demands of the time. In 2010, there was a felt need to reclaim the position of religion and to justify it in public discourse against (real or imagined) threats posed by increasing diversity and a more audible atheism and secularism.

Unholy Warlords and Other Critical Voices: Atheism, Secularism and Liberalism

Media discourses on religious diversity and the marginalization of Christianity – which we have shown to be mutually imbricated – have generated a common enemy in atheism, secularism and liberalism.

Public discussion of atheism had increased and intensified and was expected to be a significant theme during the Papal visit because of pre-visit protests. Following Richard Dawkins's call on the front page of *The Times* several months earlier for the arrest of the Pope, an 'atheistic protest letter', signed by Dawkins himself, Stephen Fry, Terry Pratchett, Philip Pullman, Susan Blackmore, A. C. Grayling and 49 others, was published in *The Guardian* on the day prior to the visit.[59] It argued that Pope Benedict should not have been given the honour of a state visit, because the organization he led had been responsible for opposing equal rights, failing to address issues of child abuse and other issues.[60] This came on the same day that Cardinal Walter Kasper, the Pope's expert on Catholic-Anglican relations, was reported in all the papers to have referred to Britain as a 'third-world country' in which 'an aggressive new atheism' had spread.[61] This critical sentiment was picked up again by the media after the Pope's opening speech when he referred to 'atheist extremism of the 20th century'. Although the point was made that this referred to Nazi Germany, after the Cardinal's remark, it was interpreted as a comment on the current British situation.

The publication of the protest letter was widely referred to in the press. There were follow-up articles on these celebrities and public intellectuals, accompanied by others on ordinary protesters (principally the victims of child abuse and their representatives). The tabloids aired the topic, condemning the letter as 'spitting venom', a 'celebrity vendetta', written by 'the Left-wing chorus', and motivated by 'empty hatred': The *Daily Mail*, for example, referred to Dawkins, Fry and others as 'nihilists who have nothing to offer by way of hope to the young or anyone else'.[62] Critical voices were lumped together as atheist Left-wingers, multiculturalists and PC killjoys, though some columnists in the same papers were cautious about the Pope's reference to atheist extremism. Whilst earlier debates

---

[59]   Horne 2010; *The Guardian* 2010a.

[60]   *The Guardian* 2010a.

[61]   See, for example, *The Guardian* 2010b.

[62]   All phrases from the *Daily Mail* from 16–20 September 2010; Glover 2010.

on atheism and secularism had taken place almost exclusively in the broadsheets (see Chapter 5), the Papal visit provided a rare occasion for such discourse – albeit wholly negative – in the tabloids.

Even the broadsheets were ambiguous about ideological protesters (though supportive of critical victims of abuse). For example, Janice Turner, who chose to distinguish 'true secularism' – which she saw as open to an alliance with progressive and liberal religious groups – from less tolerant varieties, referred to Dawkins, Christopher Hitchens and Stephen Hawking as 'macho atheists' and 'unholy warlords'.[63] A similarly renowned atheist, Julian Baggini, bemoaned the impact on atheism of making a lot of noise without trying to 'find common cause' with dissatisfied Catholics.[64] This was reiterated by Dominic Lawson who argued that Dawkins gave 'us atheists a bad name' and called for harmonious co-existence between 'Catholics and unbelievers', and by Richard Ingrams, who suggested that 'atheism could do without Dawkins'.[65]

Even the most liberal of papers implied a distinction between 'good' (tolerant and open) and 'bad' (extremist, aggressive) atheism and, in this particular case, withdrew their support from the latter. The atheist cause was heard, but unfailingly it was associated with intolerance and provocation. On an occasion when empathy and support was reserved for the victims of Catholic child abuse, the self-promotion of atheist celebrities and public intellectuals was made to look more hollow than it might have done in different circumstances.

Neither atheism nor secularism had been issues in the Papal speeches of 1982, even though Pope John Paul II had complained briefly about materialism and consumerism. They were not seen as a threat or enemy of the Churches in the early 1980s; there was no discourse of 'atheists versus the faithful'.[66] In fact, the President of the National Secular Society, Barbara Smoker, struck a very different tone in her letter to *The Times* in March 1982, when she called on all liberal-minded people, religious or otherwise, to ally against the conservative teachings of the Pope.[67]

Protests about the Papal visit were not absent in 1982, and one protester in particular was singled out for media criticism because of his aggressive approach – just as Dawkins and Fry were to be some thirty years later. In 1982, however, the target was the Reverend Ian Paisley, outspoken critic and rude nuisance, whose form of Northern Irish loyalist Protestantism was reported to bear no relation to English religion with its 'dignified restraint' and 'undemonstrative piety'.[68] Although he continued his demonstration against the Pope in 2010, Paisley's mantle as the media's anti-Papal scapegoat had passed from Protestant to atheist

---

[63]   Turner 2010.

[64]   Baggini 2010.

[65]   Dominic Lawson 2010; Ingrams 2010.

[66]   Baggini 2010.

[67]   Smoker 1982. See Chapter 5.

[68]   Knott 1984a, p. 40 (from *The Telegraph*, 1 June 1982).

shoulders. The papers no longer felt a need to analyse or comment in detail on his vociferous protests.

More general criticism was directed against the Pope's conservative attitudes in 1982 than in 2010. They were portrayed as out of step with the views of most, apparently more liberal, British people. This uneasiness with conservative attitudes was obvious for instance in more left-wing papers like the *Morning Star*, the *Sunday People* and *The Guardian* which pointed out the relative silence of the Pope on important ethical issues such as birth control, abortion, divorce and remarriage. Classifying the Pope as conservative as opposed to liberal has been a continuing theme. The current Pope has been understood within a conflictual framework which highlights two sides – conservative and liberal – with Benedict labelled the 'conservative's conservative' by the media.[69] There are problems with applying this framework to the Papal visit, however. First, in his speeches Benedict distinguished instead between his own correct values and the misguided values of others (e.g. atheists, secularists, materialists, consumerists, hedonists and relativists). Secondly, the British media in general preferred to represent the Pope as a uniting force for all rather than a conservative exponent in a battle between conservatives and liberals.

These three broad themes from the coverage of the Pope's speeches in 2010, when compared to those from 1982, illuminate the dynamism of media discourse on religion: interfaith motifs replaced ecumenism, reflecting the need to cope with increased diversity; Christianity was portrayed as marginalized in a context where no religious tradition – not even the dominant one – could be taken for granted and all must justify themselves publicly; and the increased outspokenness and scapegoating of atheism and liberalism as the enemies of faith reflected the anxieties of religious people and secularists alike in their struggle for public recognition and the moral high ground. Overall, in reporting the visit, the media were favourable to faiths in general, and – given Britain's heritage and identity, and the Christian origins of its beliefs and values – to Christianity in particular.

The media transformed the Papal visits of both 1982 and 2010 into celebratory events. The extent and nature of published and broadcast material were evidence of the media interest and investment in the visits, with television in 1982 powerfully shaping the public experience and memory of Pope John Paul's pastoral tour.

> As the incredible blur of detail fades away, there is one general image that I'm sure will remain in people's minds as the essence of the Pope's visit to Britain … It is the television image – firstly of a vast, sunlit sea of humanity, singing, cheering, waving yellow flags so transfigured by warmth and joy that a tear sometimes came to the eye just to see them … And then, fading in and out of that huge crowd scene, the close-ups of a large, strong, loving face.[70]

---

[69]　Welborn 2009, pp. 123–4.

[70]　Knott 1984a, pp. 33–4 (from the *Daily Mail*, 3 June 1982).

But in 2010 too, there was recognition of the power of the media to shape the event. In the days that followed it, the BBC received hundreds of complaints: its coverage had been far too positive, said some; it was too critical, said others.[71] And – reflecting back on it – both were right. Before the Pope's arrival, television news and documentaries, like much of the press coverage, had focused on reservations about the visit, and negativity about the conduct and attitudes of the clergy; but over the visit itself, the coverage celebrated the Pope and created a visual record not only of crowds of joyful Catholics but positive and satisfied onlookers of all backgrounds. 'Although it lacked the panache of a British royal event', nevertheless, through their stories and images, the media transformed misgivings into success.[72]

---

[71]   Plunkett 2010.

[72]   Willey 2010.

Conclusion:
Religion, Media and Society Revisited

The One Show represented white, middle-class British people's embarrassment about religion framed by references to declining Christian participation, the assumed religiosity of those from minority backgrounds, the assertiveness of atheism, and the challenge to religion of science.[1] The show encapsulated some of the key media discourses we have identified and analysed in this book, and in a light way reflected, but also stoked, the discussion about the place of religion in contemporary British society. As we showed in Chapter 1, in the late 2000s, the renewed visibility of public religion, the importance of religious and increasingly 'non-religious' identities, the growth of religious diversity and the rise of political Islam were avidly debated by academics and other intellectual commentators, with differing conclusions drawn on how to interpret the evidence.

As we were concluding this book, the relevance of these issues was reinforced with the publication of data from the 2011 Census. Endorsing the narratives that we identified in earlier chapters, the new figures and population trends were met with some anxiety by the press. 'Now fewer than 6 in 10 say they are Christians as religion goes into decline', stated one newspaper.[2] The headline continued as follows, with the article rounded off with a photo of a *burqa*-wearing Muslim woman with her two children:

- Proportion of Christians in England and Wales down to 59.3 per cent
- Quarter of people say they do not follow any religion following rise of aggressive atheism
- Number of Muslims up to 2.7 million, 4.8 per cent of the population.[3]

It was a broadly similar story elsewhere, with another paper recognizing that 'whether you are delighted or alarmed … depends on your own experiences'.[4] As we saw in the chapters on the media representation of Christianity, Islam, and atheism and secularism, and on the Wilders ban and the two Papal visits, it also depends on where you get your news and comment. The British mainstream media as a whole came across as fairly pro-religion, but anxious about the crisis

---

[1]   *The One Show*, BBC1, 3 February 2009.
[2]   Doughty 2012.
[3]   Ibid.
[4]   White 2012.

of both Christianity and secularism, the rise of Islam (particularly the 'bad', extremist kind), and an increasingly vocal atheism. Nevertheless, there was considerable variability in how these issues affected the sensibilities of journalists and commentators, and how they were subsequently portrayed by different media sources. This was most obvious in the right-wing and left-wing press, with the former the more dominant and popular. Britain was constructed first and foremost as Christian in the former, though with a recognition of increasing diversity and a dislike of the supposed secularism of Labour politicians and public officials. In the latter, Britain was cast as secular and plural, with an accompanying discourse of Christian decline and irrelevance.

How the press handled data from the census, as well as other events in which religion featured, is a reminder of the difference between information and informed commentary. The Office of National Statistics supplied the data and provided a short discussion of the figures and the changes from 2011.[5] *The Guardian*, on its 'Data Blog: Facts are Sacred' page, reproduced much of this without comment, although readers were invited to share their thoughts, with the first response the most telling: 'Goody, some more statistics for people to twist to suit whatever agenda they're pushing.'[6] Coverage elsewhere in this and other papers and news websites ranged between basic repetition of the data and editorials or personal interpretations of what the figures might mean for British religion and society and their future direction. The idea of 'twisting to suit their agenda' – although itself rather negatively expressed – aptly identifies what newspapers do in editorials and commentaries, and is a key reason why they continue to be popular and to attract loyal audiences. This is true too for television companies: 'independence, impartiality and honesty', and 'diversity, innovation and nonconformity' – associated respectively with the BBC Trust and Channel 4 – also constitute agenda that determine policy, programming and editorial approach.

At a time when the numbers of people who participate regularly in religious practices and have access to religious knowledge is declining, the media's role as an information provider, even educator, is potentially important. But this role is complicated by the medium of delivery. The task of the media is not merely to provide information, but to do so in a compelling and engaging way so that audiences are attracted to articles and programmes. But inevitably, much that goes on in religious organizations and the lives of the religious, agnostic or atheist fails to meet the criteria for a good story, lacking the necessary focus on personality or celebrity, on events or breakthroughs, or on controversies or conflicts. Census data is important information, but it is the story it generates that gets it into the paper or onto television news. Thus, much that is important to religious communities and organizations – and indeed to other social and cultural groups and individuals – is ignored. Furthermore, commercial pressures and declining resources in the media make researching stories and events a luxury for which there is little time or money.

---

[5]   Office of National Statistics, 'Religion in England and Wales 2011'.

[6]   Comment in White 2012.

The consequence is that knowledge about religion obtained from media sources is inevitably partial. Some things are included, others left out. Those events, stories, issues and debates that do make it do so because they conform to media priorities. Once accepted, they are not merely reported, they are crafted into something that conforms to the discourse and values of the paper or channel and that is attractive and accessible to loyal readers and viewers. For those for whom religion is not a lived experience, who do not participate actively in religious organizations or have not had recent exposure to religious education, this creative media process is responsible for generating religion 'as we know it'. Although other sources may be available, for the majority, media representations of religion – and increasingly 'non-religion' – and their discourses on its social role and fate constitute the extent of public knowledge.

Religion and the Secular Sacred in a British Media Context

In the first study of media portrayals of religion, we distinguished between 'conventional religion' and 'common religion', the former, institutionalized, and the latter, unofficial and unorganized, but both directed towards the supernatural. Back in the 1980s, this distinction had represented an important step in recognizing the significance of beliefs and practices beyond the remit of the Churches, major religious traditions and new religious movements. It troubled the rational, scientific boundary between that which was normally defined and approved as 'religion' and that which was classified and delegitimized as 'superstition'. These broad types, subdivided into various categories and subcategories, had formed the basis of the coding frame we developed in 1982 as we collected data from newspapers and television. Operationalizing religion in this way had helped us to see what was favoured in the media coverage and treatment and what might have been excluded or misrepresented. It was apparent, for example, that conventional religion received greater coverage in *The Times* and in BBC programmes, with common religion more in evidence in *The Sun* and on commercial television.

In the second study, as well as collecting and analysing new data, we were keen to make comparisons with the earlier project and to see what had changed since the 1980s. This required us to revisit 'conventional religion' and 'common religion'. By 2008, however, both the public climate and sociological discourse about religion were changing. Religious diversity – Islam in particular – and a vocal New Atheism were forces to be reckoned with, church attendance was in continuing decline and Christianity on the back foot, mired in internal controversies, public scandal and criticized for being out of touch. In part, we were able to respond by adding new categories and sub-categories within our conventional and common religious framework, but this could not do justice to the growing interest in beliefs, values, practices and spiritualities which did not have the supernatural as their focus (except possibly to deny or critique it). It was important to make space for the media representation of new as well as resurgent expressions of atheism, humanism and secular liberalism, and for emergent individualized spiritualities focused on 'life', music, healing, nature and anti-capitalism. In response, we added a third strand, the 'secular sacred' (with its attendant categories and subcategories), in order to reflect changes in the ideological, philosophical, ritual and experiential landscape, and to recognize that there is much that is valued in the lives of *non-religious* people and in the *secular* sphere that is powerfully significant and meaningful, deeply-held and non-negotiable, as well as a source of personal and social identity.[7] Our decisions to retain the conventional/common distinction and to include the secular sacred were borne out by what we found. In addition to a growing number of references to diverse religious traditions, those on common religion had increased since the 1980s, showing its importance in popular culture, and – though the amount of coverage was relatively small – discussion of atheism, liberal secularism, evolution, ethical and equality issues was provocative and impassioned, reflecting the intensity of debate on matters of secular sacred concern.

The lived realities, identities and institutional discourses of conventional and common religion and the secular sacred appear 'through a glass darkly', as and when they appear at all in the media. The absence of things, as well as what is present and how it is represented, tells us something about media priorities, knowledge and values. We will return to this later in the chapter, but it reminds us that this *cannot* be a straightforward account of contemporary religion; it is as much an examination of what the newspapers and television find important and how they construct society and the place of religion within it as it is a discussion of conventional and common religion and the secular sacred as they are refracted through the media.

Media Religion and the Secular Sacred

What does mainstream media religion in twenty-first century Britain look like?

Although media religion does not exist as a single formation, but is rather the sum of a variety of discourses and representations produced by different media sources, it is possible to make some generalizations about it – including saying what it is not. We have ascertained that it is not simply a reflection of the institutionalized religion of churches, mosques or gurdwaras; neither is it the lived everyday practices and beliefs of ordinary religious or affirmatively 'non-religious' people. By definition, it is also not that which it excludes and ignores. Important aspects of religion were absent including intra-religious diversity (different Christian denominations or the variety of Buddhist groups), innovation within religious institutions, women's participation and leadership in religions and in atheism, and the complexity of contemporary religious and/or spiritual commitments, which are often a pragmatic and creative mixture of beliefs,

---

[7]   Knott 2013a; Day, Cotter and Vincett (eds) 2013.

practices, values and forms of expression informed by different sources. Media religion is no mere reflection of the current state of religion and the secular sacred in Britain or beyond.

What are the major elements then of British media religion? In our discussion of media Christianity, we noted two concurrent representations. Christian material culture, language, history and rituals were shown as embedded in Britain's dominant culture, traditions and national interest. But Christianity – of the committed, believing and church-attending variety – was portrayed as in decline and as one of a number of religious minorities in a secular context. This tension was at the heart of media attitudes and feelings towards Christianity, and indeed towards other public institutions, including the nation and the flag. As contesting newspaper representations showed, for some people, these were seen as central, significant and definitive for belief, practice and morality; for others, they were peripheral, past rather than future-oriented, a private rather than public matter, with reason rather than faith the principal moral and cognitive arbiter.

The identification of the majority of British people with Christianity was accepted as normative, especially in the conservative popular press, but more widely at Christmas, times of national crisis, commemoration and celebration. Even when a multi-faith presence was recognized by the media, as in Remembrance Day services, much of the iconography was Christian, and the structure Anglican as much as civic. Furthermore, Christian heritage, particularly its contribution to the landscape and language, was shown to be inextricably bound up with Britain's history, culture and environment. This was presented not as a dying heritage, but a living one which continues largely unselfconsciously but nevertheless unabated; one cared for and protected vicariously by an active minority of lay Christians and church leaders.

Early twenty-first century representations of Christianity were marked by the continuity of nominal religiosity, heritage and tradition, rather than innovation and change, and portrayed as fair game for both humour and criticism. This media rendition was not achieved in isolation, but as part of a broader engagement with issues of identity, ideology and culture in the process of depicting, debating and critiquing the nation. Other religious traditions and, increasingly, non-religious beliefs were also drawn on.

Despite at times being portrayed as one religion among many, and as a minority interest, Christianity – particularly the established Church of England – was seen as underwriting and enabling the idea of Britain as a multi-faith nation and the realization of this idea in shared events and interfaith projects. Nevertheless, it was Islam that attracted the greatest increase in media attention, as Chapter 4 showed. Depicted as 'bad' religion, through its continued association with violence, conflict, extremism, terrorism, and failure to integrate, in the late 2000s Muslims (especially 'hate preachers' and 'Islamic extremists') were constructed as expansionist and demanding, favoured by a weak and politically-correct Labour government. They constituted the principal foil in the portrayal of Christianity as endangered and marginalized, even persecuted.

The reporting of minority religions was rooted in contemporary political and economic concerns, both local and global: New Labour and multiculturalism in crisis, a post-terrorism environment and economic uncertainty. Any beliefs or practices that seemed to contradict 'British' values were deemed antithetical and problematic. Anxieties about cohesion, integration and national identity, about the wars in Iraq and Afghanistan and other global events led to a focus on cultural difference, extremism and violence, especially in relation to Islam, but to some extent to Hinduism and Judaism too. In a minority of cases, in local media coverage and in some reporting of the Papal visit, minority religions were celebrated as part of the multi-faith city and nation: for example, where children formed the subject-matter, interfaith or intercultural initiatives provided the focus, or so-called 'peaceful' religions, like Buddhism, were depicted.

As we saw in Chapter 5, atheism and secularism and their supporters (commonly described in the conservative press as 'aggressive', 'strident' and 'left-wing', but also 'extremist') provided a further foil in the process of differentiating between good and bad, acceptable and unacceptable. Richard Dawkins was the chief scapegoat, though he was joined by others during the Papal visit. Even though the liberal press, *The Times* and the BBC often gave time and space to atheist ideologues and commentators, they too were critical of over-zealous anti-religious expression. According to these media sources, the principal ideological rift was not between Christianity and Islam, but 'between the religious and the rest', and it was here that a 'rapprochement' was thought to be needed.[8] Religious representatives and atheist or humanist exponents were often juxtaposed in TV debates or in 'For and Against' columns, with a favoured subject being religion versus science, especially arguments about the theory of evolution. Although this dichotomy was repeatedly reinforced, journalists and other commentators tended to endorse the middle ground: a moderate stance, not anti-religious, but certainly not pro-atheist. Those on the right were more explicit in favouring religion (Christianity), and those on the left in favouring liberal secularism.

In chapters 7 and 8, in case studies on the banning of Geert Wilders in 2009 and the Papal visit of 2010, we saw how these media representations of religions and other ideological positions, constructed for other purposes at other times, could be drawn on and further developed in relation to different news events. Despite fairly widespread – if somewhat superficial – criticism of Wilders' inflammatory Islamophobic views, his ban took on a life of its own in the media, becoming a focus in the conservative press for anxieties around the 'Islamification' of Britain and 'marginalization of Christianity', and – in *The Guardian* and *The Independent* – around the threat to liberalism posed by the affront to freedom of speech. Although some of the same discourses were emphasized in coverage of the Papal visit – the scapegoating of 'aggressive atheism', Christian 'marginalization', and the fear of 'Islamic extremists' (the latter in association with the fake terror plot) – the visit itself was narrated as one of transformation from doubt to success, and provided

---

8   *The Guardian* 2010c.

an opportunity for the expression of a positive and politically-endorsed multi-faith discourse. Furthermore, it generated a media event without which neither the visit nor the visitor (and his message) could have been communicated and constituted as public knowledge. Comparing this event with the one in 1982 allowed us to see how media discourses on religion had changed, with the hope of ecumenism replaced by that of interfaith, Christianity requiring public justification in a way that had not been necessary previously (and helped in the conservative press by the threat of Islamic extremism), and a new fault line in evidence, not between Protestantism and Roman Catholicism, but between religion and the rest.

Reflecting our interest in common religion as well as conventional religion and the secular sacred, in Chapter 6 we analysed the extensive coverage, language and representation of popular beliefs and practices. Their continuity and stability and literal and metaphorical treatment from the 1980s to the late 2000s confirmed that, like Christianity, their roots run deep in British culture. As we noted, though, the unwillingness or inability to recognize and name such beliefs and practices as either religious or superstitious suggests that the link has now been cut between the language and gestures of common belief and ritual, and the meanings and identities to which they once referred. Psychical, paranormal and superstitious beliefs and rituals continued to provide popular subject matter for the media. Although they were often framed or interpreted by science, medicine or some other form of rational knowledge, in the late 2000s the media gave greater space and voice than previously to ritual practitioners and those with authentic personal experience of the spirit world, with innovation and customization applauded. Although some motifs gave way to others – telepathy and religious miracles covered less, and UFOs and angels more – a resilient subterranean culture persisted, evidenced by surveys, but resoundingly present in the popular media.

Testing Claims about Religion, the Media and Society

At the end of Chapter 1, we set out a series of paired propositions which brought together the various theses that were current in debates about religion, media and society. With the benefit of evidence from our research data and analysis, we return to them here in order to test those claims and make our final intervention into these debates.

Religion in the Media: Secularization or Return?

1. As society has become more secularized, the media coverage of religion has declined and been marginalized.
2. 'Religion never really went away, so that talk of its "re-emergence" or "return" … is misleading', and the same is true of religion in the media.[9]

---

[9]   Woodhead 2012a, p. 7.

With strong public and scholarly discourse about decreasing identification with Christianity, declining levels of participation through the generations, and the secularization of society, it is not unreasonable to expect all this to be reflected in the media coverage. Yet, as we saw in Chapter 3, in terms of the raw figures, the number of mainstream media references to Christianity had not declined since the early 1980s. Furthermore, as later chapters showed, there was a conservative media backlash against secularization and what was perceived to be a process of Christian marginalization, or even persecution, with one BBC commentator warning against complacency and reminding viewers that more might be lost than gained by sidelining Christianity in society or erasing it from the nation's culture.[10]

Although there had been no decline in the number of references to Christianity, their nature had changed. A larger number were general in type, and fewer referred to different Christian denominations. There had been a substantial decrease in the number of hours afforded to religious broadcasting since the early 1980s – though references to religion on television had not declined overall – and there was less reporting of theological issues in *The Times*. But the discussion of religious issues in general was still very much in evidence, particularly in the press but also on TV, and the number of references to nearly all religions as well as to atheism and secularism were up.

Was this a 're-emergence' or had religion never disappeared from the media in the first place? As our research involved only two points in time, it did not provide sufficient evidence for us to answer this. Robin Gill, who analysed the religious content of British newspapers at three points – in 1969, 1990 and 2011 – found that 'the relative proportion of space given to religious items had declined overall … between 1960 and 1990', but between 1990 and 2011, a different pattern was observed.[11] Overall religious content had increased slightly rather than declined, with an increase also in the amount of material 'deemed hostile' to religion. Gill concluded that 'the perception of journalists is that religion is somewhat more newsworthy than it was 21 years ago (although not quite as newsworthy as it was 42 years ago) but that, in some of its manifestations at least, religion is to be regarded with considerable suspicion'.[12] Whilst religion had by no means disappeared from society, by 2011 it had become a little more visible in the media than it had been several decades before.

We will return to the issue of bad news and hostility below, but nevertheless take Gill's point, that an increase in media coverage of religion should not be assumed to signal its positive affirmation. It might just as well be read as an intensive critical turn masking *either* a secularist urge to dismiss all religion irrevocably *or* a deep-seated fear and antagonism towards Islam and its place in British society. Although over-stated as media strategies, we have discerned both of these at work at times in the media reporting of religion.

---

[10] Nicky Campbell in *Are Christian being Persecuted?*, BBC1, 4 April 2010.

[11] Gill 2012, p. 47.

[12] Ibid., p. 49.

*The Secularity or Religiosity of Media Professionals and
the Reporting of Religion*

1. The media's reporting of religion is unfair and inaccurate because of the secularity of media professionals who have no interest in religion or are biased against it.
2. The media and media professionals are animated by the religious values that are embedded in the national culture.

Taken together these propositions raise questions about the identity and beliefs of those who work in the media, their ability to be neutral, and how they see their role in respect of their audiences and the wider society.

Claims that people in the media are less religious and more secularist than the general population have been made repeatedly by both scholars and religious representatives, with the attendant case made for their failure to 'get' religion or to do it justice. Berger, Davie and Fokas have discussed this in relation to Eurosecularity; Silk has considered but refuted it in his work on religion and secularity in the American press.[13] It has been used to explain the media 'blind spot' about religion, and to account for the decline in religious broadcasting on British television.[14] According to Holmes, a YouGov poll showed that, whilst 71 per cent of people in the general population said they considered themselves to be religious, only 21 per cent of those who worked in television did.[15]

A rather different picture emerged in interviews with those responsible for covering religion in the British broadsheet newspapers.[16] Editors-in-Chief, religious correspondents and journalists with a brief to report on religion claimed not only a strong interest in religion, but – in many cases – a religious background and/or active faith commitment and participation. The editor-in-chief of *The Times* refuted the claim that the media is full of atheists, noting rather that it contains many people of faith.[17] Those responsible for reporting on religion rather than commenting on it – an important distinction in the British press – were keen to point out that it was not their place to voice their own religious or non-religious beliefs: 'I don't think at all you have to be what you cover. Therefore, you don't need to be religious. It possibly helps but what you need is a sympathetic understanding.'[18] It is not what media professionals believe but how they approach the subject of religion that is important. Non-religious reporters, commentators and producers are not necessarily biased against it.

---

[13]   Berger, Davie and Fokas 2008; Davie 2000; Silk 1998.

[14]   Marshall, Gilbert and Ahmanson (eds) 2009; Holmes 2010.

[15]   Holmes 2010, p. 1. Holmes refers to the results of an earlier YouGov poll, we have not been able to identify the poll or substantiate the findings.

[16]   Mutanen 2009.

[17]   James Harding in Mutanen 2009, p. 44.

[18]   John Lloyd, *Financial Times*, in Mutanen 2009, pp. 43–4.

The other proposition in this pairing – that the media is animated by the religious values of the national culture – derives from a more overtly religious context than Britain: America. In *Unsecular Media*, Silk concluded that, despite common perceptions that the media must be promoting its own secularist agenda, it was in fact telling a very different story – 'that people of faith are leading a counterrevolution against a morally impaired, if not bankrupt, secular society' – and telling it largely from 'the standpoint of the religious themselves'.[19] Our research showed that, although this discourse is clearly not universally articulated in the British mainstream media, there are nevertheless some significant examples of it, particularly in the conservative press, including coverage of the Declaration of Christian Conscience in March 2010 and of the Papal visit later that year. There is also evidence of a liberal counter-discourse, of criticism of religious institutions for being morally impaired, out of touch and intolerant. Other important discourses stress the importance of Christianity for national identity and cultural heritage, and the emergence of a multi-faith Britain in which all religions, though cast as minorities, underpin the 'Big Society'. These discourses – as well as those which focus more explicitly on Islam and extremism, and New Atheism – are mixed and cannot easily be reduced to a single conclusion about the overall stance of British media reporting and the values that underpin it.

On those few occasions when a good story – like the Papal visit, the 2012 Olympics or Remembrance Sunday – can be told to support a case for national solidarity, there is some discursive convergence. In general, however, tension and conflict between discourses is more the order of the day. What is clear, though, is that the media account is not unfailingly secular or driven by an ideologically secularist media.

Religion in the Media: Minority or Majority Interest?

1. Religion is 'positioned, represented and constructed as a minority interest' by the media.[20]
2. Religion is treated as a major public concern as people rely on the media for information and education about religion.

These propositions need not be read as opposing one another, and indeed there is some truth in both. We need only think of the coverage of Islam to understand this. Even though Islam is the second largest religion in Britain after Christianity, Muslims constitute only 4.8 per cent of the population.[21] Yet Islam is represented as a major concern in the media. In the newspapers, it accounted for more than 9 per cent of all references to religion and the secular sacred.

---

[19]   Silk 1998, p. 141.

[20]   Woodhead 2012a, p. 25.

[21]   Office of National Statistics.

In public policy and human rights law, religion – along with other aspects of identity – is recognized and religious people are protected from discrimination. In part, this contributes to a sense of religion as a minority issue, as do the surveys on religious attendance which show the small numbers who participate actively on a regular basis. In the local media, we observe religious events and services listed along with those of other cultural interest groups; and in the travel and culture pages, religion comes across as a feature of leisure activity. No longer protected to the same degree as it was in the 1980s, religion is cast as a minority interest placed outside peak viewing times. But it is also ever-present on television and in the papers, in all genres, embedded in language and gesture, in the landscape and the news. The Church of England, the Catholic Church and increasingly other religious organizations, interfaith bodies, and atheist and humanist groups are drawn on by the media for comment; they provide leadership and volunteers, places of worship, and moral, pastoral and spiritual resources at times of crisis, celebration, commemoration and annual festivals. And, as we saw in earlier discussions of Christianity, the state and remembrance, religion – particularly the Church of England – is represented as integral to the nation, its identity and well-being.

Religion – like other aspects of society, culture, politics and the economy – has the potential to be the big story, the issue of major public concern, as it was at the time of the Catholic sex abuse scandal, for example, or in debates about faith schools, gay marriage or women bishops. It can become the news. But more important, it would seem, is the fact that it endures irrespective of the transient and ephemeral nature of much that is reported in the media, and can be drawn on when needed for different purposes.

This function – 'religion as resource' – must be distinguished from the issue of religious literacy. More and more, people depend on the media – newspapers, radio, television, and increasingly the internet – for education, information and news about religion. Arguably then, of greater importance than their religious or secular identity is what media professionals know about religion, and how much knowledge they have: not enough, according to the contributors to *Religion and the News*.[22] Woolley, for example, calls for those responsible for reporting on religion to be as well versed in their subject as those reporting on business or politics: such positions should be filled by experts who should be required to have taken a course on religion and to understand their religiously diverse audiences.[23] What is also clear, though, is that many media professionals are themselves over-stretched in a context where funding has been reduced and time for research squeezed; they are expected to cover areas in which they have little expertise, and they do not have ready or easy access to convenient, accessible sources of information about religion.[24] First and foremost, the media role is to tell a compelling story, to do

---

[22]   Mitchell and Gower (eds) 2012.

[23]   Woolley 2012, p. 75.

[24]   Brown 2012, p. 125.

what is necessary to attract an audience with the resources that are available. As the evidence has shown, this often involves religion.

The Status of Religion in the Shaping of Media Narratives

1. Because of their commercial interests and priorities, the media are only interested in bad news and controversy about religion.
2. Religion is important to the media because it provides language and subject matter that are essential for the construction of media narratives.

Our research has shown that references to religion turn up in every kind of newspaper article, programme or advert; religion is an essential media resource. It is fundamental in representations of the landscape, of small English villages, historic capitals, or new multicultural urban habitats. It enables the expression of hopes and fears, luck, fate and destiny, us and them, mystery and magic, morality, depravity and the sacred, personal, social and national identity, the most intimate and the transcendent. Religious language, along with religious subject matter, haunts sports reporting, adds colour to advertising, and offers an opportunity for humour and entertainment. Because of its historical position, it is primarily Christianity – both elite and popular – that provides these resources, but increasingly other religions and belief systems are adding to the cultural stock on which the media draw: images of yoga, calligraphy, Rastas, Muslim girls in hijab and Sikhs in turbans, and references to Shabbat, Eid and Diwali.

But the presence of religion as wallpaper for drama, comedy, news and sport is not what comes to mind when people think about religion in the media. When religious representatives criticize newspapers or the BBC for their coverage of religion, they often forget this other side to media religion, one that is important for keeping religion in the public eye, for maintaining its cultural presence. Their criticisms are generally focused on the bad news stories about religion and what Gill refers to as media hostility to it.[25] The prevalence of 'bad news' has been discussed for decades, with religion by no means the only target. Islamophobia and the misrepresentation of Islam have provided a focus for recent critical research and analysis of negative news reporting, and in our research too they have been no less an issue. Muslims, and to a lesser extent Indian Hindus and Israeli Jews, were commonly associated with extremism and violence, and the target of bad news. Catholics too – in the run up to the Papal visit – were associated with sexual abuse; and Anglican clerics were frequently represented as anti-egalitarian and intolerant, schismatic and out of touch.

Media portrayals of religion, like those of other issues, continue to be shaped by the rhetoric of the media, particularly its fascination for controversy, conflict and celebrity.[26] As Landau notes, there will always be a mismatch between the

---

[25]   Gill 2012.

[26]   Hart, Turner and Knupp 1980, pp. 256–75.

good news that religious organizations would like to see in print and on television, and what is actually covered.[27] But, as our research has shown, the latter is not all bad. Broadly speaking, religion came out quite positively in the struggle with New Atheism, particularly in the conservative media. Even in BBC programmes and the liberal press, the middle ground was favoured over either of the extremes, whether atheist or evangelical. And the Papal visit was narrated as a tale of the triumph of success and solidarity over doubt and the protests of a minority.

Religions and the Media: Disempowerment or Agency?

1. 'Contemporary religion is increasingly mediated through secular, autonomous media institutions, and is shaped according to the logics of those media'.[28]
2. Religious individuals and organizations are active agents in the use and appropriation of the media, and are influential in setting media agendas.

The persistence of religion across mainstream media sources and in all genres is probably the most significant finding of this study, but there will be some readers who will argue that this is not real religion but only banal religion.[29] It is not *religious*, but a secular distortion of religion, and emptied of its intended meaning. Arguably, however, real religion is the business of religious individuals and organizations and not the responsibility of the media. But religion and media are not discontinuous. They have in common their participation in the symbolic order, as agents of communication, representation and meaning-making. That is why, as we will discuss below, it makes sense to debate religion as media and media as religion. Here though, the issues are mediation, mediatization and agency.

It has not been the task of this book to research how religious bodies and individuals use the media in their religious lives. This has been widely examined elsewhere in a scholarly literature that shows how they have often been at the technological cutting edge in mediating religion, in adopting and adapting the latest media as agents of religious innovation. Simultaneously, religious institutions have been seen to be responsive and dynamic. What is important in our study, though, is who gets to determine the agenda and content of British mainstream media religion? Are religious people and ardent non-believers active users and shapers? Are they instrumental in changing media discourses of religion and the secular sacred, or do media professionals have it all their own way in constructing religion according to the logic of the media?

One important change between the 1980s and late 2000s was the loss of a formal religious voice in decision-making about religious broadcasting on television. Early in 2008, the Central Religious Advisory Council (CRAC), which since the

27 Landau 2012.
28 Lövheim and Lynch 2011, p. 111; Hjarvard 2011, pp. 119–35.
29 Hjarvard 2011.

1920s had advised the BBC and independent television on matters of religion, was dropped as it was no longer deemed to fit new governance arrangements.[30] The BBC argued there were adequate opportunities for all stakeholders within its new consultative model, but it was nevertheless evidence of the ousting of religion from its formerly privileged position in the structures of power. We may hypothesize – in the absence of current evidence – that the loss of CRAC has had a direct bearing on the reduction in hours for religious broadcasting, in oversight of the religion and ethics brief in general, and coverage of Christianity and other organized religions in particular. Nevertheless, the General Synod of the Church of England had sufficient power to get the question of the demise of religious broadcasting into the broadsheet newspapers and the BBC in 2010.[31] Periodically, too, we have seen campaigns effectively organized either to criticize the media treatment of religion (for example in advertising), or to use the media to get a particular message across. A good example of the latter was the 2009 atheist bus campaign.

Moreover, we witnessed repeatedly the presence of religious and atheist representatives in the papers and on television. They were there, of course, at the behest of the media, in accordance with programming or editorial decisions, to illustrate a particular viewpoint, to argue in a debate, to provide information or fill in a context, or to provide a critical, moral, spiritual or pastoral standpoint. The extent to which such representatives can be autonomous agents is therefore questionable, given that they are always there to fulfil a higher media purpose. They are given a voice, but one that is editorially constrained both by the limits of the initial invitation to participate and later by being cut down to fit the format, agenda, time and space available. Such voices are some of the many resources the media creatively draw on to produce narratives and craft discourses. But it is this process of editorial attenuation that often brings charges of misrepresentation and distortion from religious bodies; though the absence of a voice is deemed to be equally problematic.

In religious environments, religious actors are active agents who choose to develop and use available media technologies for their own purposes, including the transformation of religion. Those religious practices, ideas, experiences and innovations which occur in media saturated environments take place alongside and in engagement with other cultural and social expressions and as a result of the conditions, purposes and values of that environment: they are mediatized.[32] We have seen this repeatedly in terms of the choice and types of content, use of particular frames, and selection of discourses in reporting and commenting on religion and the secular sacred. Furthermore, we saw it in the construction of events by which various media sources generated competing narrative and visual accounts in accordance with their own political agenda, style and rhetoric.

---

[30]   Noonan 2008, p. 161.

[31]   Holmes 2010; BBC News 2010a; BBC News 2010b; Beckford 2010a.

[32]   Lundby 2013a.

The coverage of the 2010 Papal visit, above all, illuminated the capacity of the media to create a shared socio-religious event that revolved around the tale of a 'conservative', 'rottweiler' Pope who was won over by the warmth of an 'open', 'tolerant', 'multi-faith' but nevertheless secular Britain, a media transformation of doubt to success.

Religion as Media; Media as Religion

1. Religions 'can only be manifested through some process of mediation' and are themselves media.[33]
2. The media have become 'a form of religion in themselves' (media as religion).[34]

In the 1980s, television was both feared and celebrated for its power not only to construct media events like the Papal visit, but to eclipse religion in its ability to reach and captivate a mass audience, to communicate the myths of the age and to generate shared values.[35] Television was variously associated with Mammon, consumption and capitalism, and seen as a medium for popularizing and dumbing-down culture in general and religion in particular, as an agent of the permissive society, as unfitting for the communication of the Gospel and incapable of communicating it without distortion. Portrayed as shallow, strong, commercial and secular, and amoral if not immoral, it was seen by its religious critics as the antithesis of religion. But the power of television was not underestimated. Representing television - through a Durkheimian lens - as a functional equivalent to religion, meant understanding it as having the ability to generate myths, produce and perform ritual, and create a moral community with solidarity around sacred values.[36] More recently, in a postmodern move, television has been understood as the medium which best illustrates the sacred imaginary of the media, and its capacity and power to manage the visual illusion and manifest things as if truly real and present.[37]

As Stolow notes, both 'religion' and 'communication' refer to 'the work of *binding together*'.[38] But, as we noted above, the symbolic continuity between religion and the media means that the simile works the other way too. Religions are understood as media, not only because of their ability to appropriate new technologies for their own ends, but because of the centrality to religion of communication, transmission and transformation. And, of course, through a complex process of mediation which draws not only on communications

---

[33] Stolow 2005, p. 125.
[34] Davie 2000, p. 114.
[35] Arthur (ed.) 1993; Silverstone 1981.
[36] Silverstone 1981; Couldry 2003.
[37] Stolow 2005 (writing on the views of Derrida).
[38] Stolow 2005, p. 125.

technologies but on oral, textual, ritual, material and sensory media, religions seek to generate new communities of belief and practice.

That the media too are in the business of communication and seek to generate audiences and represent communities is not in question, but are the latter comparable to those collectivities generated in religious contexts? In our analysis, there was evidence of the reproduction by different newspapers of leading discourses that would both appeal to target publics but also contribute to the construction of their social worlds. We witnessed the way in which the media construct different religious groups, either as 'us' or 'them', of Christianity as fundamental to national identity and heritage, of Islam as an extremist and intolerant 'other', a challenge to integration. And we saw instances of the making of popular ritual moments (weddings and funerals, and the Papal visit), in which social and moral solidarity and emotional intensity were generated through accomplished story-telling and camera work, appropriate framing, and a focus on audiences as well as central characters.

However, despite all this creative social and ritual work, no single authoritative sacred canopy was discernible, no one – secularist or religious – world-view. Rather, what emerged were the competing standpoints of various media sources in which different discourses struggled for supremacy, some more dominant than others. And – in the newspapers at least, in letters and in online posts – media users were increasingly present, generally voicing support for particular standpoints, but sometimes there as evidence of a paper's balance and its toleration of alternative views. Furthermore, if we extend our gaze and take in the wider media landscape – incorporating print, radio, web and social media – a range of secular sacred and religious interlocutors can be found putting forward their arguments and expressing their concerns. The contemporary media landscape as a whole is permissive, although – as we have seen – some voices can nevertheless be heard more loudly than others.

But our focus was much narrower: newspapers and television – and just a selection from two periods separated by nearly thirty years. As a result, our account of media, religion and society – refracted as it is through two empirical studies of religion – is one that is necessarily mainstream and British, even predominantly English. Conducting a similar study using this approach in Norway, the Netherlands, Australia, Ghana or Brazil would produce other religious and secular sacred categories, and differing representations, discourses and interpretations. We think it is important to defend this strategy at a time when much research on communications technology, new media, news and films focuses on the impact of globalization. Understanding the contextual nature and local forms of media content, representation and their production is essential if we are to interpret them reliably. This does not mean that what we have identified and discussed for religion in the British media is irrelevant for other cases or for theorizing about religion in the media more generally. Rather, our approach provides a methodology for the conduct of other national studies, a foil for their interpretation, and possibilities for cross-national comparisons. Furthermore, the propositions we have identified and discussed summarize general theories and current anxieties about the religion/ media/society nexus and are open to consideration in other contexts, times and places.

Appendix 1:
Main Categories and Subcategories used in Coding References to Religion and the Secular Sacred in 2008–2009

A coding list of main categories and sub-categories was established for the content analysis in 1982. Although this formed the basis of the list used in 2008–2009, it was developed still further with the separation of some main categories and addition of new subcategories (whilst being attentive to the need for comparison between the two data-sets).

A] Main Categories

CONVENTIONAL RELIGION: Roman Catholicism; Protestantism; Church Foreign; Councils of Churches; Religious Cosmology; Religious Practice; Religious Concepts; Doctrines; Religious Texts; Modern Religious Issues; Religion General; Other Christian Churches and Groups; Church History; Religious Television; Academic Study of Religion; New Religious Movements; Islam; Hinduism; Buddhism; Sikhism; Judaism; Other World Religions.

COMMON RELIGION: Magic; Witchcraft; Chance; Signs; Ghosts; Spiritualism and Spirit Possession; Psychic Powers; Luck; Superstitions; Gambling; Fortune Telling Techniques; Fate and Destiny; Other Supernatural Beings; The Unexplained; Folk Religion; Folk Practices; Mythology; Gypsies.

SECULAR SACRED: Secularism, Religion and Secular; Atheism; Humanism; Religion and Science; Sacred; Liberalism; Spirituality; Religion-like.

B] Subcategories

Conventional Religion

ROMAN CATHOLICISM: Pope; Vatican; Papal visit; Catholicism; Roman Catholic Hierarchy; Roman Catholic Church; Roman Catholic Church in England; Roman Catholic Church in Ireland; Catholics in England/Britain; Cardinals; Latin

Mass Movement; Polish Catholics in England; Saints, including beatification; Jesuits and other orders; Second Vatican Council; Leeds Roman Catholic Churches and Clergymen; Opus Dei; Catholicism and Catholic Priests Outside Britain; Order of St Gregory.

PROTESTANTISM: Protestantism; Church of England; Methodists; Baptists; Evangelicals; Non-Conformism and the Free Churches; Church of England Hierarchy; Parishes; Protestantism in Ireland; Archbishop of Canterbury; Leeds Church of England Churches and Clergy; Leeds (and Yorkshire) Methodist Churches; Prayer Book Society; Leeds Baptist Churches; Anti-Roman Feeling; Protestant Reformation Society; Mission; Bishops; Leeds Evangelicals; Trinity United Church of Christ.

CHURCH FOREIGN: Poland; Africa; Russia; India; South America; Greek Orthodox Church; Russian Orthodox Church; China; Bulgaria; Serbian Orthodox Church.

COUNCILS OF CHURCHES: World Council of Churches; British Council of Churches; Other; Parish Councils (local).

RELIGIOUS COSMOLOGY: God; Jesus Christ; Virgin Mary; Angels; Devil, Satan; Hell and Damnation; Heaven and Salvation; Oaths and Petitions; Holy Trinity; Goddess.

RELIGIOUS PRACTICE: Sunday; Pilgrimage; Sacraments; Life cycle rites; Congregation; Sermon; Worship; Prayer, Praising; Exorcism; Fasting; Conversion; Social and Pastoral Work; Evangelism, Preaching; Missionary Work, Religious Aid; Blessing; Sunday Services; Religious Music; Special Religious Services; Religious Trances; Rituals, Ceremonies, Festivals; Food Preparation; Easter; Christmas; Meditation; Faith Healing; Visions; Remembrance; Ordination; Mass; Confession; Vows; Sacrifice; Sign of the Cross; Vestments; Lent; Baptism.

RELIGIOUS CONCEPTS AND DOCTRINES: Prophets and Prophecy; Martyrs; Miracles; Mercy and Forgiveness; Faith (and Belief); Reincarnation and the Afterlife; Morality; Doctrine; Grace; Revelation; Charisma; Holy Spirit; Ecstacy; Mysticism; Guru, Guruism; Messiah; Church and State; Crucifixion; Apocalypse; Repentance; Suffering; Resurrection; Jihad; Redemption; Sin; Exodus; Demonology; Judas; Creation; Karma; Canon.

RELIGIOUS TEXTS: Bible; Gospel; Other Christian Texts; Biblical Stories; Book of Common Prayer; Qur'an and other Islamic texts; Ramayana; Texts of Judaism.

MODERN RELIGIOUS ISSUES: Moral Majority and Religious Right; Clergy and Women; Ecumenism; Women in World Religions; Non-Religious; Creationism and Intelligent Design; Homosexuality; Dialogue, Diversity, Interfaith, Multi-faith; Contraception, Abortion etc.; Euthanasia, Assisted Suicide; Vaccination in Schools Controversy; Cultural Products (television, film, theatre, art etc.); Adoption; Sex Education; Embryo Experimentation; Christian Nymphos.

RELIGION GENERAL: Religion; Religious; Priests and Clergy; Religion and Education; Church (general and buildings); Altars and Shrines; Hallowed, Sacred, Consecrated, Blessed; Divine and Holy; World Religions; Christianity; Monks, Nuns and Monasteries; Politics and Political Parties; Religious Communities; Religion and Violence (without specification); Cross, Crucifix, Necklace, Grail (material item).

OTHER CHRISTIAN CHURCHES AND GROUPS: Salvation Army; Pentecostalism; Rastafarianism general; Rastafarianism in Leeds; Mormonism; Society of Friends (Quakers); Jehovah Witnesses; Christian Science; Church of Christ.

CHURCH HISTORY: Reformation; Religious Art and Architecture; Religious Orders and Institutions; Church Archaeology; Crusade and Other Battles; Greek And Roman Religious History; American Religious History.

RELIGIOUS TELEVISION: Sunday Best; Credo; Father Charlie; Bless Me Father; Religious TV general; Choices.

ACADEMIC STUDY OF RELIGION: Religious Language; Religion and Science; Paranormal and Science; Theology; Academic Study of Religion General; Religious Studies.

NEW RELIGIOUS MOVEMENTS: Cults and Sects; Unification Church; Yoga; Krishna Consciousness; Swami Muktananda; Humanism; Vedanta; Scientology; New Age; Freemasonry.

ISLAM: General; Muslims in Britain; Muslims in Leeds; Muslims Outside Britain; Militant Action; Satanic Verses Affair; Extremism (attitudes and individual action); Adjustment to Culture; Gender and Sexuality; Art; Mecca; Sufism; Mosques (buildings).

HINDUISM: General; Hindus in Britain; Hindus in India; Tantrism.

BUDDHISM: General; Buddhists in Britain; Buddhists in the US; Festivals; Persons (celebrities); Tibetan Buddhism (including Dalai Lama); Zen.

SIKHISM: General; Sikhs in Britain; Sikhs Outside Britain.

JUDAISM: General; Anti-Semitism; Zionism; Kabbalah.

OTHER WORLD RELIGIONS: Shinto; Baha'i; Confucianism; Taoism; Jainism.

Common Religion

MAGIC: Magic; Magical; Magician; Spell; Black Magic; Conjuring.

WITCHCRAFT: Witches; Witchcraft; Voodoo; Curse; Bewitched; Sorcery; Witch Doctors; Satanism; Witch Hunts; Wizards; Evil-eye.

CHANCE: Chance; Odds; Throwing the Dice.

SIGNS: Omen; Hunch; Jinx; Signs.

GHOSTS: Ghosts; Spectres and Poltergeists; Haunted; Phantoms; Spooks.

SPIRITUALISM AND SPIRIT POSSESSION: Spiritualism; Spirit Possession, Spirits; Occult; Séance and Oiuja Board; Spirit World.

PSYCHIC POWERS: Telepathy and ESP; Psychic; Paranormal; Telekinesis, Psychokinesis; Regression; Premonition; The Third Eye; Sixth Sense; Precognition; Magnetism; Channelling; Déjà Vu; Hypnotism.

LUCK: Luck; Lucky; Bad Luck; Unlucky; Good Luck; Lucky Colour; Lucky Number; Lucky Letter; Mascots and Charms; Lady Luck; Lucky Streak.

SUPERSTITIONS: Throwing Salt; Keeping Fingers Crossed; Superstitions; Touch Wood; Saluting Magpies; Avoiding Colour Green.

GAMBLING: Gambling; Bingo; Betting and Race Tote; Lottery and Other Money Games.

FORTUNE-TELLING TECHNIQUES: Astrology; Fortune Telling; Clairvoyance; Prediction; Crystal Ball; Palmistry; Tea Leaves; Oracles; Intuition; Graphology; Tarot; Horoscope.

FATE AND DESTINY: Fate; Fatalism; Destiny; Predestined; Fortune.

OTHER SUPERNATURAL BEINGS: Fairies; Vampires (Dracula) and Werewolves; Zombies; General; Headless Horseman.

THE UNEXPLAINED: UFOs; Alien Intelligence, Aliens; The Unexplained; Mystery; Extraterrestrial.

FOLK RELIGION: Stone Circles; Druids; Pantheism; Pagans, Paganism; Folk Religion; Folklore; Wicca; Stonehenge; Native American Religion (North and South); African Indigenous Religion; Mandaeans.

FOLK PRACTICES: Folk Festivals and Occasions; May Day; Equinox Festivals; Folk Rites; Halloween.

MYTHOLOGY: Greek and Roman; Arthurian Legends; Dragons; Cannibalism; Myths and Legends General; Unicorns; Egyptian; Snowman; Loch Ness Monster; Neo-Nazism.

GYPSIES: Gypsy curse; Gypsy fortune telling.

Secular Sacred

SECULARISM: General; Secularization; Non-Religion, Non-Religious.

ATHEISM: General.

HUMANISM: General.

RELIGION AND SCIENCE: General.

SACRED: Market; Home Ownership; Music; Public Services (library); Life (assisted suicide without references to religion); Judgment in Court.

SPIRITUALITY: General.

RELIGION-LIKE: Ecology, Environment (Global warming, etc.); Football; Market, Credit Crunch etc.; Elvis; Marxism; Health; Individualism; Humanity.

Appendix 2:
Percentages of Newspaper References to Main Categories of Conventional Religion, Common Religion and the Secular Sacred, 1982 and 2008

In 1982, the total number of references from one month's newspapers was 2,454. In 2008, the total number was 4,370.

A] Percentage of newspaper references: Conventional religion

Conventional religion: main categories	Percentage of total newspaper references 1982	Percentage of total newspaper references 2008
Roman Catholicism	17.8	4.2
Protestantism	10.8	3.2
Church foreign	1.8	0.3
Church Councils	0.5	0
Religious cosmology	5.1	8.4
Religious practice	15.3	9.8
Religious concepts/ doctrines	4.7	4.5
Religious texts	2.4	1.6
Modern religious issues	3.8	2.4
Religion general	7.8	6.9
Other Christian Churches	0.6	0.9
Church history	1.1	0.9
Religious television	0.2	0
Academic study of religion	0.1	0.4
New religious movements	0.5	0.9
World religions other than Christianity (1982 only)	6.6	–
Islam (2008 only)	–	9.5
Hinduism (2008 only)	–	1.1

Conventional religion: main categories	Percentage of total newspaper references 1982	Percentage of total newspaper references 2008
Buddhism (2008 only)	–	1.0
Sikhism (2008 only)	–	0.4
Judaism (2008 only)	–	3.0
Other world religions (2008 only)	–	0.2

B] Percentage of newspaper references: Common religion

Common religion: main categories	Percentage of total newspaper references 1982	Percentage of total newspaper references 2008
Magic	2.5	3.3
Witchcraft	1.3	1.3
Chance	0.5	0.2
Signs	0.5	0.3
Ghosts	1.4	1.7
Spiritualism, spirit possession	0.2	0.2
Psychic powers	0.2	0.5
Luck	5.2	4.8
Superstitions	0.2	0.3
Gambling	3.1	10.4
Fortune-telling techniques	1.4	3.2
Fate and destiny	0.5	1.1
Other supernatural beings	0.2	1.0
The unexplained	0.4	2.4
Folk religion	0.1	0.6
Folk practices	0.9	2.7
Mythology	0.4	2.2
Gypsies	0.2	0

C] Percentage of newspaper references: Secular Sacred

Secular sacred: main categories	Percentage of total newspaper references 1982	Percentage of total newspaper references 2008
Secularism (2008 only)	–	0.4
Atheism	0.2	0.7
Humanism	0.1	0
Religion and Science	0.2	0.1
Sacred	0.3	0.7
Spirituality	0.1	1.0
Religion-like	0.4	1.5

Appendix 3:
Percentages of Television References to Main Categories of Conventional Religion, Common Religion and the Secular Sacred, 1982 and 2009

In 1982, the total number of television references collected from one week's viewing was 1,630. In 2009, it was 1,672.

A] Percentage of television references: Conventional religion

Conventional religion: main categories	Percentage of total television references 1982	Percentage of total television references 2008
Roman Catholicism	6.0	1.1
Protestantism	1.8	0.5
Church foreign	0.1	0.1
Church Councils	0.1	0
Religious cosmology	12.6	10.1
Religious practice	22	11.4
Religious concepts/ doctrines	6.9	2.5
Religious texts	2.8	1.4
Modern religious issues	0.9	0.4
Religion general	7.8	15.7
Other Christian Churches	0.4	0.2
Church history	0.8	0.7
Religious television	0.2	0
Academic study of religion	0.1	0.2
New religious movements	0.2	0.5
World religions other than Christianity (1982 only)	5.5	–
Islam (2008 only)	–	3.1
Hinduism (2008 only)	–	0.4
Buddhism (2008 only)	–	0.9
Sikhism (2008 only)	–	0.2

Conventional religion: main categories	Percentage of total television references 1982	Percentage of total television references 2008
Judaism (2008 only)	–	0.6
Other world religions (2008 only)	–	0.8

B] Percentage of television references: Common religion

Common religion: main categories	Percentage of total television references 1982	Percentage of total television references 2008
Magic	1.8	3.5
Witchcraft	1.6	1.6
Chance	1.5	0.5
Signs	0.1	0.1
Ghosts	2.2	0.5
Spiritualism, spirit possession	0.6	1.1
Psychic powers	1.4	1.1
Luck	6.7	12.1
Superstitions	0.4	1.1
Gambling	6.2	10.9
Fortune-telling techniques	1.2	0.8
Fate and destiny	0.8	1.9
Other supernatural beings	0.4	1.3
The unexplained	1.2	5.7
Folk religion	0.4	0.5
Folk practices	1.9	0.5
Mythology	2.0	3.9
Alchemy	0	0.1

C] Percentage of television references: Secular Sacred

Secular sacred: main categories	Percentage of total television references 1982	Percentage of total television references 2008
Secularism (2008 only)	0.1	0.4
Atheism	0.1	0.7
Humanism	0.1	0
Religion and Science	0.7	0.4
Sacred	0.4	0.3
Spirituality	0.1	0.1
Religion-like	0.1	0.2

Bibliography

Ahmed, Murad, 'Video game doll that must go from rags to riches for Sony', *The Times*, 20 October 2008.

Ahmed, Nazir, 'Wilders' ban is in Britain's best interests', *The Guardian*, 13 February 2009.

Allan, Stuart, *News Culture*, 2nd edn, Maidenhead: Open University Press, 2004.

Altholz, Josef L., *The Religious Press in Britain 1760–1900*, New York, Westport and London: Greenwood, 1989.

Antinoff, Steve, *Spiritual Atheism*, Berkeley: Counterpoint, 2009.

Arthur, Chris (ed.), *Religion and the Media: An Introductory Reader*, Cardiff: University of Wales Press, 1993.

Asad, Talal, *Formations of the Secular: Christianity, Islam, Modernity*, Stanford: Stanford University Press, 2003.

Ash, Timothy Garton, 'Liberty in Britain is facing death by a thousand cuts. We can fight back', *The Guardian*, 19 February 2009.

Awad, Ammar, 'Two wings and some prayers', *The Times*, 28 October 2008.

Ayres, Chris, 'This was it... Gold bands, red carpets, VIP guests and a made-for-TV event', *The Times*, 8 July 2009.

Baggini, Julian, 'Divided we stand', *The Guardian*, 17 September 2010.

Baig, Anita, 'Attacks on Muslims are poison', *The Sun*, 13 February 2009.

Baker, John Austin, 'The Papal Visit to Britain', *The Furrow*, 33/8, 1982, pp. 475–81.

Baker, Paul, Gabrielatos, Costas and McEnery, Anthony, *Discourse Analysis and Media Bias: The Representation of Islam in the British Press*, Cambridge: Cambridge University Press, 2012.

Bakewell, Joan, 'No-God squad climb aboard the atheist bus', *The Times* (Times2), 24 October 2008.

Baldwin, Katie, 'Bishop's "save your cash" plea', *Yorkshire Evening Post*, 22 October 2008.

BARB, May 2010. http://www.barb.co.uk/. Accessed 10/7/12.

Barrett, Justin, 'Theological Correctness: Cognitive Constraint and the Study of Religion', *Method and Theory in the Study of Religion*, 11/4, 1999, pp. 325–39.

Barnes, Simon, 'Confidence can make all the difference', *The Times*, 7 October 2008a.

Barnes, Simon, 'Sin when you are winning in the fight against racism', *The Times*, 24 October 2008b.

Barnes, Simon, 'Darwin at the National History Museum: The original of the species', *The Times*, 12 November 2008c.

BBC, Look North, 15 September 2010.

BBC News, 'Pope's Westminster Hall speech in full', *BBC News Online*. http://www.bbc.co.uk/news/uk-11352704. Accessed 18/12/12.

BBC News, 'Pro-God buses for London streets', *BBC News Online*, 6 February 2009a.

BBC News, 'Should thought stay sacred?', *BBC News Online*, 15 July 2009b.

BBC News, 'Church of England concerned by "religious TV cuts"', *BBC News Online*, 10 February 2010a.

BBC News, 'TV programming "concerns" Church', *BBC News Online*, 10 March 2010b.

BBC News, 'Pope Equality Comments Condemned', *BBC News Online*, 12 March 2010c.

BBC News, *News at Ten*, 16 September 2010d.

BBC Religion, http://www.bbc.co.uk/religion/. Accessed 20/8/12.

BBC Wiltshire, 'Wootton Bassett's "media circus"', 28 July 2009.

Beckett, Charlie, 'Networked Religion', in Jolyon Mitchell and Owen Gower (eds), *Religion and the News*, Farnham: Ashgate, 2012, pp. 99–106.

Beckford, Martin, 'ITV will broadcast just one hour of religious programming this year', *The Telegraph*, 23 June 2010a.

Beckford, Martin, 'Pope Visit: David Cameron welcomes Benedict XVI on 'incredibly important' trip', *The Telegraph*, 15 September 2010b.

Bell, Daniel, 'The Return of the Sacred: The Argument About the Future of Religion', *Zygon: Journal of Religion and Science*, 13/3, 1978, pp. 187–208.

Berger, Peter L., *The Desecularization of the World: Resurgent Religion and World Politics*, Grand Rapids: Eerdmans, 1999.

Berger, Peter, Davie, Grace and Fokas, Effie, *Religious America, Secular Europe: A Theme and Variations*, Aldershot: Ashgate, 2008.

Bhargava, Rajeev, 'The Ethical Desirability of Political Secularism', Paper presented at conference on 'Secularism and Beyond', Copenhagen, May 2007.

Binyon, Michael, 'A God-fearing man with a taste for tradition', *The Times*, 8 November 2008a.

Binyon, Michael, 'From Punjab to Putney: The rise of British Sikhism', *The Times*, 22 November 2008b.

Bird, Steve, 'Doctor on fire seen punching and kicking police', *The Times*, 11 October 2008.

Blair, Tony, 'Pope visit: Six street cleaners arrested as cops foil plot to kill the Pope', *Daily Mirror*, 18 September 2010.

Blakely, Rhys, '10,000 flock to sit at the feet of teenage "Buddha Boy" after he leaves the jungle', *The Times*, 13 November 2008.

Bowman, Marion, 'Learning from Experience: The Value of Analysing Avalon', *Religion*, 39, 2009, pp. 161–8.

Boyce, George, Curran, James and Wingate, Pauline, *Newspaper History from the Seventeenth Century to the Present Day*, London: Constable, 1978.

Brasher, Brenda, *Give Me That On-Line Religion*, Piscataway, NJ: Rutgers University Press, 2004.

Brennan, Zoe, 'Camp faithless: Is Britain's first atheist summer camp harmless fun or should we be worried?', *Daily Mail*, 29 July 2009.

British Religion in Numbers, 'Religious Affiliation and Monthly Church Attendance, 1983–2008', http://www.brin.ac.uk/. Accessed 5/7/12.

British Religion in Numbers, 'Churches and Churchgoers: Patterns of Church Growth in Britain 1700–1970', http://www.brin.ac.uk/. Accessed 5/7/12.

British Religion in Numbers, 'Estimates of the Hindu, Muslim and Sikh Populations of England and Wales 1961-2001', http://www.brin.ac.uk/. Accessed 5/7/12.

Brown, Andrew, 'Cumberland Blues', in Jolyon Mitchell and Owen Gower (eds), *Religion and the News*, Farnham: Ashgate, 2012, pp. 117–25.

Brown, Callum G., *The Death of Christian Britain: Understanding Secularisation 1800–2000*, 2nd edn, London and New York: Routledge, 2009.

Brown, David and Gledhill, Ruth, 'Rowan Williams haunted by suicide of troubled student "who fell for him"', *The Times*, 10 November 2008.

Brown, Derek, 'Video games axed over Koran ditty', *The Sun*, 18 October 2008.

Bruce, Steve, *Religion in the Modern World: From Cathedrals to Cults*, Oxford: Oxford University Press, 1996.

Bruce, Steve, *God is Dead: Secularization in the West*, Oxford: Blackwell, 2002.

Bruce, Steve, *Secularization: In Defence of an Unfashionable Theory*, Oxford and New York: Oxford University Press, 2011.

Bunglawala, Inayat, 'A timely reminder', *The Guardian*, 13 February 2009.

Bunt, Gary, *iMuslims: Rewiring the House of Islam*, London: Hurst and Co., 2009.

Bunting, Madeleine, 'Faith. Belief. Trust. This economic orthodoxy was built on superstition', *The Guardian*, 6 October 2008.

Burchill, Julie, 'As Page 3 girls come under fire, Julie Burchill says … I'd rather see Keeley like this … than like this', *The Sun*, 10 October 2008.

Butt, Riazat, 'Archbishop backs disestablishment (and the Muppets)', *The Guardian*, 18 December 2008.

Butt, Riazat, 'Your equality laws are unjust, Pope tells UK before visit', *The Guardian*, 2 February 2010.

Campbell, Heidi A., *When Religion Meets New Media*, London and New York: Routledge, 2010.

Carey, George and Carey, Andrew, *We Don't Do God: The Marginalisation of Public Faith*, Oxford: Monarch Books, 2012.

Carey, Most Rev. Lord George, and other signatories, 'The religious rights of Christians are treated with disrespect', *The Daily Telegraph*, 28 March 2010.

Carrette, Jeremy and King, Richard, *Selling Spirituality: The Silent Takeover of Religion*, London: Routledge, 2005.

Casanova, José, *Public Religions in the Modern World*, Chicago: Chicago University Press, 1994.

Casanova, José, 'Public Religions Revisited', in Hent de Vries (ed.), *Religion: Beyond a Concept*, New York: Fordham University Press, 2008, pp. 101–19.

Casanova, José, 'Immigration and the New Religious Pluralism: European Union-United States Comparison', in Geoffrey Brahm Levey and Tariq Modood (eds), *Secularism, Religion and Multicultural Citizenship*, Cambridge: Cambridge University Press, 2009, pp. 139–63.

Charter, David, 'Banned MP hits out at "cowards" after being sent back', *The Times*, 13 February 2009a.

Charter, David, 'Geert Wilders allowed to escape scrutiny', *The Times*, 13 February 2009b.

Christians in Parliament, *Clearing the Ground Inquiry: Preliminary Report into the Freedom of Christians in the UK*, Evangelical Alliance, 2012.

Clark, David, *Between Pulpit and Pew: Folk Religion in a North Yorkshire Fishing Village*, Cambridge: Cambridge University Press, 1982.

Clark, Lynn S., *From Angels to Aliens: Teens, the Media, and Beliefs in the Supernatural*, New York: Columbia University Press, 2001.

Clench, James and Phillips, Martin, 'Her Maj has tea as Pope sticks to pop', *The Sun*, 17 September 2010.

Cockshut, A.O.J., *The Unbelievers: English Agnostic Thought 1840–1890*, London: Collins, 1964.

Coghlan, Tom, 'Taleban shoot aid worker for "preaching"', *The Times*, 21 October 2008.

Cohen, Yoel, *God, Jews and the Media: Religion and Israel's Media*, London and New York: Routledge, 2012.

Coles, John, 'Top Gun vs. Alien', *The Sun*, 20 October 2008.

ComRes, 'BBC Catholic Survey on Papal Visit 12 September 2010', http://www.comres.co.uk/poll/849/bbc-catholic-survey-on-papal-visit-12-september-2010.htm. Accessed 14/6/13.

Comte-Sponville, André, *The Little Book of Atheist Spirituality*, trans. Nancy Huston, London: Viking, 2007.

Conlan, Tara, 'TV turns to religion', *The Guardian*, 17 June 2005.

Cornwell, John, *Darwin's Angel*, London: Profile Books, 2007.

Cottle, Simon, 'Race', Racialization and the Media: A Review and Update of Research', *Sage Race Relations Abstracts*, 17/2, 1992, pp. 3–57.

Cottle, Simon, 'Mediatized Rituals: Beyond Manufacturing Consent', *Media, Culture and Society*, 28/3, 2006, pp. 411–32.

Couldry, Nick, *Media Rituals: A Critical Approach*, London: Routledge, 2003.

Couldry, Nick, *Media, Society, World: Social Theory and Digital Media Practice*, Cambridge: Polity, 2012.

Couldry, Nick and Rothenbuhler, Eric, 'Review Essay: Simon Cottle on "Mediatized Rituals": a Response', *Media, Culture and Society*, 29, 2007, pp. 691–5.

Craft, Stephanie and Waisbord, Silvio, 'When Foreign News Remains Foreign: Cartoon Controversies in the US and Argentine Press', in Elisabeth Eide, Risto Kunelius, and Angela Philips (eds), *Transnational Media Events: The*

Mohammed Cartoons and the Imagined Clash of Civilizations, University of Gothenburg: Nordicom, 2008.

Crisell, Andrew, 'Broadcasting: Television and Radio', in Jane Stokes and Anna Reading (eds), *The Media in Britain: Current Debates and Developments*, New York: Palgrave, 1999, pp. 61–73.

Crisell, Andrew, *An Introductory History of British Broadcasting*, 2nd edn, London: Routledge, 2002.

Cupitt, Don, *Taking Leave of God*, London: SCM, 1980.

Cupitt, Don, *New Religion of Life in Everyday Speech*, London: SCM, 1999.

Curran, James (ed.), *The British Press: A Manifesto*, London and Basingstoke: Macmillan, 1978.

Daily Express, 'Pope's plea to help save Christmas from the PC brigade', 18 September 2010.

Daily Mail, 'Affront to freedom', 12 February 2009a.

Daily Mail, 'Jacqui Smith bars extremist preacher aiming to protest over pro-gay play', 20 February 2009b.

Daily Mail, 'Editorial', 16 September 2010a.

Daily Mail, 'Editorial', 17 September 2010b.

Daily Mail, 'Editorial', 18 September 2010c.

Daily Mail, 'Editorial', 20 September 2010d.

Daily Mirror, 'Pope's aide to miss visit after blast at UK', 16 September 2010a.

Daily Mirror, 'Pope visits Britain – Brian Reade: The warmth of his flock's welcome melted away any fears the Pontiff had', 17 September 2010b.

Daily Star, 'Sixth arrest in Pope plot probe', 17 September 2010a.

Daily Star, 'Editorial', 17 September 2010b.

Darwin, Charles, *Evolutionary Writings, Including the Autobiographies*, Oxford: Oxford University Press, 2010.

Davie, Grace, *Religion in Modern Europe: A Memory Mutates*, Oxford: Oxford University Press, 2000.

Davie, Grace, *Europe: The Exceptional Case: Parameters of Faith in the Modern World*, London: Darton, Longman and Todd, 2002.

Davie, Grace, 'Vicarious Religion: A Methodological Challenge', in Nancy T. Ammerman (ed.), *Everyday Religion: Observing Modern Religious Lives*, Oxford: Oxford University Press, 2007, pp. 21–37.

Davies, Nick, *Flat Earth News*, London: Vintage, 2009 [2008].

Davies, Owen, *The Haunted: A Social History of Ghosts*, London: Palgrave Macmillan, 2007.

Dawson, Lorne L. and Cowan, Douglas E. (eds), *Religion Online: Finding Faith on the Internet*, New York and London: Routledge, 2004.

Day, Abby, *Believing in Belonging: Belief and Social Identity in the Modern World*, Oxford: Oxford University Press, 2011.

Day, Abby, Cotter, Christopher and Vincett, Giselle (eds), *Social Identities between the Sacred and the Secular*, Farnham: Ashgate, 2013.

Dayan, Daniel and Katz, Elihu, *Media Events: The Live Broadcasting of History*, Cambridge, MA: Harvard University Press, 1992.

De Botton, Alain, *Religion for Atheists: A Non-Believer's Guide to the Uses of Religion*, London: Hamish Hamilton, 2012.

Deacon, David, Pickering, Michael, Golding, Peter and Murdock, Graham, *Researching Communications: A Practical Guide to Methods in Media and Cultural Analysis*, 2nd edn, London: Hodder, 2007.

Deller, Ruth, 'The Representation of Religion and Spirituality in *The Archers* and *EastEnders*', MA dissertation, Sheffield: Sheffield Hallam University, 2007.

Derrida, Jacques, 'Faith and Knowledge: Two Sources of "Religion" at the Limits of Reason Alone', in Jacques Derrida and Gianni Vattimo (eds), *Religion*, Stanford: Stanford University Press, 1998, pp. 1–78.

Derrida, Jacques, 'Above All, No Journalists!', in Hent de Vries and Samuel Weber (eds), *Religion and Media*, Stanford: Stanford University Press, 2001, pp. 56–93.

Desmond, Adrian and Moore, James, *Darwin*, London: Michael Joseph, 1991.

Dixon, Rachel, 'How Britain became a nation of ghost hunters', *The Guardian*, 30 October 2009.

Dobbs, Joy, Green, Hazel and Zealey, Linda (eds), *Focus on Ethnicity and Religion: National Statistics*, Houndsmill and New York: Palgrave Macmillan, 2006.

Doughty, Steve, 'Now fewer than 6 in 10 say they are Christians as religion goes into decline', *Mail Online*, 12 December 2012.

Edwards, Richard, 'United for the Cup!', *Yorkshire Evening Post*, 14 October 2008.

Ekklesia, 'Mixed Picture Emerges on British Attitudes to Religion in Public Life', 24/2/09. http://www.ekklesia.co.uk/node/8761. Accessed 5/7/12.

Elgamri, Elzain, *Islam in the British Broadsheet Press: The Impact of Orientalism on Representations of Islam in the British Press*, Reading: Ithaca Press, 2011.

Engage, http://www.iengage.org.uk/. Accessed 13/07/12.

Erdem, Suna, 'Turkey puts 86 on trial over planned coup', *The Times*, 20 October 2008a.

Erdem, Suna, 'Lonely drinker with a weakness for women: It's Atatürk on film', *The Times*, 8 November 2008b.

Evans, Michael, 'Taleban on the rise, says US agencies', *The Times*, 10 October 2008a.

Evans, Michael, 'Close encounter: The airman who tried to shoot down a UFO', *The Times*, 20 October 2008b.

Everett, Flic, 'Are you ruled by superstition?', *Daily Mail*, 24 May 2010.

Featherstone, Mark, Holohan, Siobhan and Poole, Elizabeth, 'Discourses of the War on Terror: Constructions of the Islamic Other in the Wake of 7/7', *Journal of Media and Cultural Politics*, 6/2, 2010, pp. 169–86.

Ferrari, Nick, 'You've got to have faith', *Sunday Express*, 19 September 2010.

Field, Clive D., 'Religious Statistics in Great Britain: An Historical Introduction', *British Religion in Numbers*. http://www.brin.ac.uk/wp-content/uploads/2011/12/development-of-religious-statistics.pdf. Accessed 5/7/12. 2009a.

Field, Clive D., '7. Changing Belief in Britain', *British Religion in Numbers*. http://www.brin.ac.uk/figures/#BSA2008. Accessed 26/8/12. 2009b.

Field, Clive D., 'Who Believes in Horoscopes', *British Religion in Numbers*. http://www.brin.ac.uk/news/2010/who-believes-in-horoscopes/. Accessed 26/8/12. 2010.

Field, Clive D., 'Hereafter Report', *British Religion in Numbers*, 28/1/11. http://www.brin.ac.uk/news/2011/hereafter-report/. Accessed 26/8/12. 2011a.

Field, Clive D., 'Feeling Lucky', *British Religion in Numbers*, 25/2/11. http://www.brin.ac.uk/news/2011/feeling-lucky/. Accessed 26/8/12. 2011b.

Field, Clive D., 'Census Christians', *British Religion in Numbers* (2012). http://www.brin.ac.uk/news/2012/census-christians/. Accessed 2/8/12. 2012.

Finkelstein, Norman G., *Beyond Chutzpah: On the Misuse of Anti-Semitism and the Abuse of History*, Berkeley and Los Angeles: University of California Press, 2008.

Fiske, John and Hartley, John, *Reading Television*, London and New York: Methuen, 1978.

Flood, Christopher, Hutchings, Stephen, Miazhevich, Galina and Nickels, Henri C., *Islam, Security and Television News*, Basingstoke and New York: Palgrave Macmillan, 2012.

Ford, Richard and Gledhill, Ruth, 'Church will be stripped of its special status within 50 years', *The Times*, 22 October 2008.

Fox, Kate, *Watching the English: The Hidden Rules of English Behaviour*, London: Hodder, 2004.

Fox, Robert, 'Geert Wilders? He's not worth it', *The Guardian*, 11 February 2009.

France, Anthony and Coles, John, 'Muslim gang brainwashed my son', *The Sun*, 16 October 2008.

Franklin, Jonathan, 'Hallowed be the left foot of Maradona', *The Guardian Weekly*, 19 December 2008, pp. 62–3.

Fraser, Giles, 'Reading between Rowan's lines', *The Guardian*, 18 December 2008.

Fresco, Adam, 'Bomber brainwashed over the Internet', *The Times*, 16 October 2008.

Garnett, Jane, Grimley, Matthew, Harris, Alana, Whyte, William and Williams, Sarah, *Redefining Christian Britain: Post 1945 Perspectives*, London: SCM, 2006.

Gaunt, Jon, 'Tolerance? That's just double dutch', *The Sun*, 13 February 2009.

Geddes, Diana, 'Runcie Attacks Change in School Religion', *The Times*, 18 March 1982.

Gertel, Elliot B., *Over the Top Judaism: Precedents and Trends in the Depiction of Jewish Beliefs and Observances in Film and Television*, Lanham and Oxford: University of America Press, 2003.

Gibb, Frances, 'Extradition bid raises fears of 'thought crime', *The Times*, 20 October 2008.

Gibb, Sean and Herbert, Christopher, 'Should the Church be disestablished?, *The Times*, 24 October 2008.

Giddens, Anthony, 'Living in a Post-Traditional Society', in Ulrich Beck, Anthony Giddens and Scott Lash (eds), *Reflexive Modernization: Politics and Tradition in the Modern Social Order*, Cambridge: Polity Press, 1994, pp. 56–109.

Gill, Robin, 'Religion, News and Social Context: Evidence from Newspapers', in Jolyon Mitchell and Owen Gower (eds), *Religion and the News*, Farnham: Ashgate, 2012, pp. 45–60.

Glasgow University Media Group, *Bad News*, London: Routledge and Kegan Paul, 1976.

Glasgow University Media Group, *More Bad News*, London: Routledge and Kegan Paul, 1980.

Gledhill, Ruth, 'Mirrors to the World', in Jolyon Mitchell and Owen Gower (eds), *Religion and the News*, Farnham: Ashgate, 2012, pp. 89–98.

Glover, Stephen, 'If only the Archbishop of Canterbury dared to speak with a fraction of Benedict's authority', *Daily Mail*, 20 September 2010.

Godson, Suzi and Stuttaford, Thomas, 'Sex advice', *The Times*, 11 October 2008.

Goethals, Gregor T., *The TV Ritual: Worship at the Video Altar*, Boston: Beacon Press, 1982.

Goodhew, David (ed.), *Church Growth in Britain, 1980 to the Present*, Farnham: Ashgate, 2012.

Gower, Owen, *Religion and the News: A Summary Report of a Conference*, Windsor: Cumberland Lodge, 2009.

Graham, Elaine, 'Religious Literacy and Public Service Broadcasting: Introducing a Research Agenda', in Gordon Lynch, Jolyon Mitchell and Anna Strhan (eds), *Religion, Media and Culture: A Reader*, London and New York: Routledge, 2012, pp. 228–35.

Grayling, A.C., 'Silencing free speech', *The Guardian*, 13 February 2009.

Green, Jonathon, *A Dictionary of Contemporary Quotations*, New York: W. Morrow, 1982.

Grimley, Matthew, 'Public Intellectuals and the Media', in Jane Garnett, Matthew Grimley, Alana Harris, William Whyte and Sarah Williams, *Redefining Christian Britain: Post 1945 Perspectives*, London: SCM, 2006, pp. 267–77.

Guest, Mathew, Olson, Elizabeth and Wolffe, John, 'Christianity: Loss of Monopoly', in Linda Woodhead and Rebecca Catto (eds), *Religion and Change in Modern Britain*, London and New York: Routledge, 2012, pp. 61–5.

Guardian, The, 'Poll: Should Geert Wilders be allowed to enter Britain?', 12/2/09. http://www.guardian.co.uk/commentisfree/poll/2009/feb/12/netherlands-islam?INTCMP=SRCH. Accessed 10/1/12. 2009.

Guardian, The, 'Harsh judgements on the Pope and religion', 15 September 2010a.

Guardian, The, 'Pope Benedict XVI flies in amid row', 15 September 2010b.

Guardian, The, 'Editorial', 18 September 2010c.

Guardian, The, 'Editorial', 20 September 2010d.

Gunter, Barrie and Viney, Rachel, *Seeing is Believing: Religion and Television in the 1990s*, London: John Libbey, 1994.

Hagan, Lucy, 'Buses to have "No God" Ads', *The Sun*, 22 October 2008.

Hall, Stuart (ed.), *Representation: Cultural Representations and Signifying Practices*, Milton Keynes: Open University Press, 1997.

Hari, Johann, 'Despite these riots, I stand by what I wrote', *The Independent*, 13 February 2009.

Harrison, Bernard, *The Resurgence of Anti-Semitism: Jews, Israel and Liberal Opinion*, Lanham and Plymouth: Rowman and Littlefield, 2006.

Hart, R.P., Turner, K.J. and Knupp, R.E., 'Religion and the rhetoric of the mass media', *Review of Religious Research*, 21/3, 1980, pp. 256–75.

Hartley-Brewer, Julia, 'Wilders ban is a liberty', *Daily Express*, 15 February 2009.

Hartley, Clodagh, 'Geert lost', *The Sun*, 13 February 2009.

Heelas, Paul and Woodhead, Linda with Benjamin Seel, Bronislaw Szerszynski and Karin Tusting, *The Spiritual Revolution: Why Religion is Giving Way to Spirituality*, Oxford: Blackwell, 2005.

Herbert, David, *Religion and Civil Society: Rethinking Public Religion in the Contemporary World*, Aldershot: Ashgate, 2003.

Herbert, David, 'Theorizing Religion and Media in Contemporary Societies: An Account of Religious "Publicization"', *European Journal of Cultural Studies*, 14/6, 2011, pp. 626–48.

Hider, James, 'Secular businessman Nir Barkat is Jerusalem's new mayor', *The Times*, 13 November 2008.

Hilder, Jennifer, 'The wanted oligarch, software tycoon and zealous rabbi vying to become mayor', *The Times*, 12 November 2008.

Hill, Annette, *Paranormal Media: Audiences, Spirits and Magic in Popular Culture*, London and New York: Routledge, 2011.

Hill, Mark, 'Law, Religion and the Media: More Spinned Against than Spinning?', in Jolyon Mitchell and Owen Gower (eds), *Religion and the News*, Farnham: Ashgate, 2012, pp. 193–202.

Hirst, Michael, 'The UK visits of Benedict XVI and John Paul II compared', *BBC News online*, 8/9/10. http://www.bbc.co.uk/news/uk-11186463. Accessed 15/1/11. 2010.

Hjarvard, Stig, 'The Mediatization of Religion: A Theory of the Media as Agents of Religious Change', *Northern Lights*, 6, 2008, pp. 9–26.

Hjarvard, Stig, 'The Mediatisation of Religion: Theorising Religion, Media and Social Change', *Culture and Religion*, 12/2, 2011, pp. 119–35.

Hjarvard, Stig and Lövheim, Mia (eds), *Mediatization and Religion: Nordic Perspectives*, Gothenburg: Nordicom, 2012.

Holmes, Nigel, *Losing Faith in the BBC*, Cumbria: Paternoster Press, 2000.

Holmes, Nigel, 'Religious Television: A Background Paper', *Church of England General Synod: Private Member's Motion*, GS 1762a. http://www.churchofengland.org/media/39102/gs1762a.pdf. Accessed 20/6/12. 2010.

Horne, Marc, 'Richard Dawkins calls for Pope's arrest', *The Times*, 11 April 2010.

Hoover, Stewart M., *Religion in the News: Faith and Journalism in American Public Discourse*, Thousand Oaks, CA: Sage, 1998.

Hoover, Stewart M., *Religion in the Media Age*, London and New York: Routledge, 2006.

Horsnell, Mike, 'Loyalists issue battle threat on Papal visit', *The Times*, 27 April 1982.

Nicholas Howe, 'Secular Iconoclasm: Purifying, Privatizing, and Profaning Public Faith', *Social and Cultural Geography*, 10/6, 2009, pp. 639–56.

Howse, Christopher, 'What the Pope's visit changed', *The Telegraph*, 23 October 2010.

Hughes, Simon, 'Doctors in "wholesale murder bid"', *The Sun*, 10 October 2008.

Huhne, Chris, 'Geert Wilders: Good riddance', *The Independent*, 13 February 2009.

Hussain, Monawar, 'Islam and the News', in Jolyon Mitchell and Owen Gower (eds), *Religion and the News*, Farnham: Ashgate, 2012, pp. 129–38.

Hutchinson, Peter, '"Persecuted Christians" join forces', *The Telegraph*, 15 April 2010.

Hutchison, Tom, 'Double Dutch: Fury as Euro MP is barred', *The Daily Star*, 13 February 2009.

Independent, The, 'A ban that only helps the extremists on both sides', 13 February 2009.

Independent, The, 'Editorial', 15 September 2010a.

Independent, The, 'Editorial', 19 September 2010b.

Independent, The, 'Editorial', 20 September 2010c.

Independent Broadcasting Authority, *The End of a Road? Report of the Seventh IBA Religious Consultation*, London: Independent Broadcasting Authority, 1983.

Independent Broadcasting Authority, *Religion in Britain and Northern Ireland*, London: Independent Television Authority, 1970.

Ingrams, Richard, 'Atheism could do without Dawkins as its advocate', *The Independent*, 18 September 2010.

Ipsos MediaCT, *Tomorrow's Readers: How Print Will Survive the Digital Age*. http://www.ipsos-mori.com/DownloadPublication/1445_IpsosMediaCT_TomorrowsReaders_Oct2011.pdf. Accessed 20/6/12. 2011.

Jackson, Kate, 'Charles meets kindertransport refugees 70 years on', *The Sun*, 24 November 2008.

Jackson, Kate, 'Seen a ghost? It's para-normal', *The Sun*, 28 January 2011.

Jacoby, Susan, 'Religion remains fundamental to US politics', *The Times*, 31 October 2008.

Jamieson, Alastair, 'Christians launch pre-election "declaration of conscience" on values', *The Telegraph*, 4 April 2010.

Jardine, Cassandra and Savill, Richard, 'Wootton Bassett: A very British way of mourning', *The Telegraph*, 7 July 2009.

Jenkins, Philip, *God's Continent: Christianity, Islam and Europe's Religious Crisis*, Oxford: Oxford University Press, 2007.

Johnston, Philip, 'Whatever happened to free speech?', *The Telegraph*, 13 February 2009.

Johnston Press, www.johnstonspress.co.uk. Accessed 6/12/10.

Kaletsky, Anatole, 'Act of faith is needed to stop the flight of cash', *The Times*, 7 October 2008.

Kamm, Oliver, 'Should we hate bankers?', *The Times*, 14 October 2008.

Kavanagh, Trevor, 'Fanatics are on the rise and Labour has let it happen', *The Sun*, 23 February 2009.

Kepel, Gilles, *The Revenge of God: The Resurgence of Christianity, Islam and Judaism in the Modern World*, Cambridge: Polity Press, 1994.

Kerbaj, Richard, Denmark 'has failed friends too', *The Times*, 10 October 2008.

Kerbaj, Richard and Gledhill, Ruth, 'Police are warned of Ramadan tensions during (Olympic) games', *The Times*, 27 October 2008.

Klaushofer, Alex, 'The rise of religion', *Catalyst: Debating Race, Identity, Citizenship and Culture*, 22 September 2006.

Klein, Emma, 'Picking up the pieces of Kristallnacht', *The Times*, 15 November 2008.

Knott, Kim, 'Media portrayals of religion: A quantitative analysis of religious references in selected media outputs', unpublished data-set, Leeds: University of Leeds, 1982.

Knott, Kim, 'Through a Glass Darkly: Media Perceptions of Religion', *The End of a Road? Report of the Seventh IBA Religious Consultation*, London: Independent Broadcasting Authority, 1983, pp. 61–8.

Knott, Kim, *Media Portrayals of Religion and their Reception: Final Report*, Leeds: University of Leeds, 1984a.

Knott, Kim, 'Conventional Religion and Common Religion in the Media: Transcript of a talk given at the IBA Religious Broadcasting Consultation, April 1983', *Religious Research Paper* 9, Leeds: University of Leeds, 1984b.

Knott, Kim, 'Other Major Religious Traditions', in Terence Thomas (ed.), *The British: Their Religious Beliefs and Practices 1800–1986*, London and New York: Routledge, 1988, pp. 133–57.

Knott, Kim, *The Location of Religion: A Spatial Analysis*, London and Oakville: Equinox, 2005.

Knott, Kim, 'Theoretical and Methodological Resources for Breaking Open the Secular and Exploring the Boundary between Religion and non-Religion', *Historia Religionum*, 2, 2010, pp. 115–33.

Knott, Kim, 'The Secular Sacred: In-between or both/and?', in Abby Day, Christopher Cotter and Giselle Vincett (eds), *Social Identities between the Sacred and the Secular*, Aldershot: Ashgate, 2013a.

Knott, Kim, 'Religion, Space and Contemporary Media', in K. Lundby (ed.), *Religion Across Media*, New York: Peter Lang Publishing, 2013b.

Knott, Kim and Mitchell, Jolyon, 'The Changing Faces of Media and Religion', in Linda Woodhead and Rebecca Catto (eds), *Religion and Change in Modern Britain*, London and New York: Routledge, 2012, pp. 243–64.

Kuhn, Raymond, *Politics and the Media in Britain*, Basingstoke: Palgrave, 2007.

Kundnani, Arun, *The End of Tolerance: Racism in 21st Century Britain*, London: Pluto Press, 2007.

Kunelius, Risto and Alhassan, Amin, 'Complexities of an Ideology in Action: Liberalism and the Cartoon Affair', in Elisabeth Eide, Risto Kunelius, and Angela Philips (eds), *Transnational Media Events: The Mohammed Cartoons and the Imagined Clash of Civilizations*, University of Gothenburg: Nordicom, 2008, pp. 91–8.

Landau, Christopher, 'What the Media Thinks about Religion: A Broadcast Perspective', in Jolyon Mitchell and Owen Gower (eds), *Religion and the News*, Farnham: Ashgate, 2012, pp. 79–88.

Larcombe, Duncan and Spratt, Charlotte, 'Poppies banned in palace', *The Sun*, 8 November 2008.

Laughland, John, 'Why Liberals don't believe in tolerance', *Daily Mail*, 15 February 2009.

Lawson, Dominic, 'My home remedy for religious squabbles', *The Sunday Times*, 19 September 2010.

Lawson, Mark, 'Holy smoke: Religion and television's uneasy pact', *The Guardian*, 8 November 2011.

Lee, Lois, *Being Secular: Towards Separate Sociologies of Secularity, NonReligion and Epistemological Culture*, unpublished PhD thesis, Cambridge: University of Cambridge, 2011.

Lord Justice Leveson, *An Inquiry into the Culture, Practice and Ethics of the Press*, London: The Stationery Office, 2012.

Levey, Geoffrey Brahm and Modood, Tariq (eds), *Secularism, Religion and Multicultural Citizenship*, Cambridge: Cambridge University Press, 2009.

Lewis, Aidan, 'Looking behind the Catholic sex abuse scandal', *BBC News Online*, 4 May 2010.

Lievrouw, Leah A. and Livingstone, Sonia (eds), *The Handbook of New Media*, London: Sage, 2002.

Linklater, Magnus, 'Rescuing Afghanistan remains a noble ambition', *The Times*, 22 October, 2008.

Lister, Martin, Dovey, Jon, Giddings, Seth, Grant, Iain and Kelly, Kieran, *New Media: A Critical Introduction*, London: Routledge, 2003.

Longley, Clifford, 'Church said to be acting too much like a Sect', *The Times*, 12 February 1982.

Longley, Clifford, 'The End of a Road?', *The End of a Road? Report of the Seventh IBA Religious Consultation*, London: Independent Broadcasting Authority, 1983, pp. 33–60.

Lövheim, Mia and Lynch, Gordon, 'The Mediatisation of Religion Debate: An Introduction', *Culture and Religion*, 12/2, 2011, pp. 111–17.

Luft, Oliver, 'Yorkshire Evening Post down 12%', *The Guardian*, 26 February 2009.

Lundby, Knut (ed.), *Mediatization: Concept, Changes, Consequences*, New York: Peter Lang, 2009.

Lundby, Knut (ed.), *Religion Across Media*, New York: Peter Lang, 2013a.

Lundby, Knut, 'Media and Transformations of Religion', in Knut Lundby (ed.), *Religion Across Media*, New York: Peter Lang, 2013b.

Lyle, Eddie, 'Changing the way we deliver aid', *The Times*, 23 October 2008.

Lynch, Gordon, *The New Spirituality: An Introduction to Progressive Belief in the Twenty-First Century*, London: I.B. Tauris, 2007.

Lynch, Gordon, 'What can we Learn from the Mediatisation of Religion Debate?', *Culture and Religion*, 12/2, 2011, pp. 203–10.

Lynch, Gordon, Mitchell, Jolyon and Strhan, Anna, *Religion, Media and Culture: A Reader*, London and New York: Routledge, 2012.

McCloskey, Carol, *Media Portrayals of Religion: Focus Groups*, The Focus Group, 2010.

McGarry, Ian, 'City fans think I'm a God', *The Sun*, 4 October 2008.

McLuhan, Marshall, *Understanding Media*, New York: Mentor Books, 1964.

McKinstry, Leo, 'Why Christianity is on the ropes in Labour's Britain', *Daily Express*, 16 February 2009.

McLuhan, Marshall, *Understanding Media*, London: Routledge and Kegan Paul, 1964.

McNair, Brian, *News and Journalism in the UK*, 4th edn, London: Routledge, 2005.

McPhee, Rod, 'Fuss on the bus', *Yorkshire Evening Post*, 27 October 2008.

Maddox, Bronwen, 'Retreat to the past would condemn millions to poverty', *The Times*, 16 October 2008.

Mail Online, 'Recession could help heal "me, me" society of selfish Britain, says Catholic leader', 14 February 2009.

Maisel, Eric, *Atheist's Way: Living Well without Gods*, Novato: New World Library, 2009.

Marrin, Minette, 'Labour bares its appeaser's teeth to unbending Muslims', *The Times*, 15 February 2009.

Marshall, John, 'The Papal Visit to Britain', *The Furrow*, 33/8, 1982, pp. 481–85.

Marshall, Paul, Gilbert, Lela and Ahmanson, Roberta G. (eds), *Blind Spot: When Journalists Don't Get Religion*, Oxford and New York: Oxford University Press, 2009.

Martin, David, *The Religious and the Secular*, London: Routledge and Kegan Paul, 1969.

Martin, David, *A General Theory of Secularization*, Oxford: Blackwell, 1978.

Media Matters for America, 'Left Behind: The Skewed Representation of Religion in Major News Media'. http://mediamatters.org/research/leftbehind/. Accessed 13/7/12. 2007.

Media Trust in association with the Inter Faith Network for the UK and Respect, *National Conference on the Media and a Multi-Faith Society: Report*, London, 2004.

Meyer, Birgit and Moors, Annelies (eds), *Religion, Media and the Public Sphere*, Bloomington and Indianapolis: Indiana University Press, 2006.

Micklethwait, John and Wooldridge, Adrian, *God is Back: How Global Rise of Faith is Changing the World*, London: Allen Lane, 2009.

Mitchell, Jolyon, *Visually Speaking: Radio and the Renaissance of Preaching*, Edinburgh: T&T Clark, 1999.

Mitchell, Jolyon and Marriage, Sophie (eds), *Mediating Religion: Conversations in Media, Religion and Culture*, Edinburgh: T&T Clark/Continuum, 2003.

Mitchell, Jolyon, 'Religion and the News: Stories, Contexts, Journalists and Audiences', in Jolyon Mitchell and Owen Gower (eds), *Religion and the News*, Farnham: Ashgate, 2012, pp. 7–30.

Mitchell, Jolyon and Gower, Owen (eds), *Religion and the News*, Farnham: Ashgate, 2012.

Modood, Tariq, 'Muslims, Religious Equality and Secularism', in Geoffrey Brahm Levey and Tariq Modood (eds), *Secularism, Religion and Multicultural Citizenship*, Cambridge: Cambridge University Press, 2009, pp. 164–85.

Modood, Tariq, 'Moderate Secularism, Religion as Identity and Respect for Religion', *Political Quarterly*, 81, 2010, pp. 4–14.

Moore, Charles, 'Banning Wilders plays into the hands of our Islamist enemies', *The Telegraph*, 13 February 2009.

Moore, Kerry, Mason, Paul and Lewis, Justin, *Images of Islam in the UK: The Representation of British Muslims in the National Print News Media 2000-08*, University of Cardiff: Cardiff School of Journalism, Media and Cultural Studies, 2008.

Moore, Matthew, 'Religious leaders blame bankers' greed for financial crisis', *The Telegraph*, 25 December 2008.

Moore, Matthew, 'Westboro Baptist Church announces first anti-homosexuality picket in Britain', *The Telegraph*, 16 February 2009.

Morey, Peter and Yaqin, Amina, *Framing Muslims: Stereotyping and Representation After 9/11*, Cambridge, MA: Harvard University Press, 2011.

Morgan, Sally (adapted by John Perry), 'I told Diana's aide, I can see them pulling a body out of the car', *The Sun*, 13 October 2008a.

Morgan, Sally (adapted by John Perry), 'I told Zeebrugge orphan of his parents' last moments', *The Sun*, 14 October 2008b.

Moreton, Cole, 'A Church of everywhere', *The Guardian*, 2 April 2010.

Morrison, Geoffry, 'Pope pleads for Muslim links', *The Times*, 14 February 1982.

Morrison, Richard, 'When life tends to be a hit and myth affair', *The Times*, 8 October 2008.

Muir, Hugh, Petley, Julian, and Smith, Laura, 'Political Correctness Gone Mad', in Julian Petley and Robin Richardson (eds), *Pointing the Finger: Islam and Muslims in the British Media*, Oxford: Oneworld, 2011, pp. 66–99.

Mukarji, Daleep, 'Christian in name?', *The Times*, 24 October 2008.

Mutanen, Annikka, *To Do or Not to Do God: Faith in British and Finnish Journalism*, Reuters Institute Fellowship Paper, Oxford: Oxford University. http://reutersinstitute.politics.ox.ac.uk/fileadmin/documents/Publications/ fellows__papers/2008-2009/Mutanen_-_To_do__or_not_do_God.pdf. Accessed 27/12/12. 2009.

Nazir-Ali, Michael, Bishop of Rochester, 'Extremism has flourished as Britain has lost its faith in a Christian vision', *The Telegraph*, 6 January 2008a.

Nazir-Ali, Michael, Bishop of Rochester, 'India must protect its Christians', *The Times*, 18 October 2008b.

Newsworks, 'Facts and Figures'. http://www.newsworks.org.uk/Facts-Figures. Accessed 2/12/12.

Noonan, Catriona, 'The Production of Religious Broadcasting: The Case of the BBC', PhD thesis, Glasgow: University of Glasgow, 2008.

Noonan, Catriona, 'Big Stuff in a Beautiful Way with Interesting People: Spiritual Discourse in UK Religious Television', *European Journal of Cultural Studies*, 14/6, 2011, pp. 727–46.

NOREL, 'The Role of Religion in the Public Sphere. A Comparative Study of the Five Nordic Countries'. http://www.kifo.no/index.cfm?id=266149. Accessed 13/7/12.

Nossek, Hillel and Philips, Angela, 'Ourselves and Our Others: Minority Protest and National Frames in Press Coverage', in Elisabeth Eide, Risto Kunelius, and Angela Philips (eds), *Transnational Media Events: The Mohammed Cartoons and the Imagined Clash of Civilizations*, University of Gothenburg: Nordicom, 2008.

Obelkevich, J., *Religion and Rural Society in South Lindsey, 1825–1875*, Oxford: Oxford University Press, 1976.

Observer, The, 'Ban on Wilders was folly', 15 February 2009.

Office of National Statistics 2010, *Marriages in England and Wales*. http:// www.ons.gov.uk/ons/rel/vsob1/marriages-in-england-and-wales-- provisional-/2010/marriages-in-england-and-wales--2010.html#tab-Number- of-marriages. Accessed 11/12/12.

Office of National Statistics 2011, 'Religion in England and Wales. http://www. ons.gov.uk/ons/rel/census/2011-census/key-statistics-for-local-authorities-in- england-and-wales/rpt-religion.html. Accessed 27/12/12.

Okri, Ben, 'Our false oracles have failed. We need a new vision to live by', *The Times*, 30 October 2008.

O'Neill, Sean, 'Deadly loners who don't show on the radar', *The Times*, 16 October 2008.

O'Neill, Sean and Bird, Steve, 'Doctors planned campaign of indiscriminate, wholesale death', *The Times*, 10 October 2008.

O'Shea, Gary, 'Taliban hit squad kill Christian Brit', *The Sun*, 21 October 2008.

O'Sullivan, Timothy, *The Papal Visit: Official Souvenir*, London: Sphere Books, 1982.

Page, Jeremy, 'Trucks bear the fruits of peace as trade route reopens after 61 years', *The Times*, 22 October 2008.

Page, Jeremy and Blakely, Rhys, 'Gods, drums and weapons: The creed that drives the Hindu "storm troopers"', *The Times*, 11 October 2008.

Papal Visit, http://www.thepapalvisit.org.uk/. Accessed 16/12/12.

Parry, Richard L., 'Emperor should atone personally for war atrocities', *The Times*, 11 November 2008.

Partridge, Christopher, *The Re-Enchantment of the West: Alternative Spiritualities, Sacralization, Popular Culture, and Occulture*, 2 vols, London: T&T Clark, 2004–2005.

Patrick, Guy, '172 grandkids at supernan funeral', *The Sun*, 14 November 2008.

Pearce, Augur, Letter, *The Times*, 25 October 2008.

Perry, Michael, 'The psychic and the spiritual', *The Times*, 20 February 1982.

Petley, Julian and Richardson, Robin (eds), *Pointing the Finger: Islam and Muslims in the British Media*, Oxford: Oneworld, 2011.

Pettifor, Ann, 'Face to Faith', *The Guardian*, 11 October 2008.

Pew Forum on Religion and Public Life, 'Islam and Politics Dominate Religion Coverage in 2011'. http://www.pewforum.org/Government/Religion-in-the-News--Islam-and-Politics-Dominate-Religion-Coverage-in-2011.aspx. Accessed 13/7/12. 2012.

Phillips, Melanie, 'We must not let the Weaknesses of our Bishops destroy this Nation's Soul', *Daily Mail*, 22 December 2008.

Phillips, Melanie, 'How Britain, the cradle of liberty, is sleepwalking towards cultural suicide', *Daily Mail*, 12 February 2009.

Pitcher, George, 'Advent chimes with our economic times', *The Telegraph*, 25 November 2008.

Plunkett, John, 'BBC defends coverage of Pope's visit', *The Guardian*, 22 September 2010.

Poole, Elizabeth, *Reporting Islam: Media Representations of British Muslims*, London: I.B. Tauris, 2002.

Poole, Elizabeth, 'The Effects of September 11 and the War in Iraq on British Newspaper Coverage', in Elizabeth Poole and John Richardson (eds), *Muslims in the News Media*, London: I.B. Tauris, 2006, pp. 89–102.

Poole, Elizabeth, 'Immigration, Islam, and Identity in the UK and the Netherlands', in Diane Winston (ed.), *The Oxford Handbook of Religion and the American News Media*, Oxford: Oxford University Press, 2012a, pp. 453–68.

Poole, Elizabeth, 'The Case of Geert Wilders: Multiculturalism, Islam, and Identity in the UK', *Journal of Religion in Europe*, 5/2, 2012b, pp. 1–30.

Poole, Elizabeth and Richardson, John E. (eds), *Muslims and the News Media*, London: I.B. Tauris, 2006.

Poole, Elizabeth and Taira, Teemu, 'Researching Religion in British Newspapers and Television', in Linda Woodhead (ed.), *How to Research Religion: A Study of Methods in Practice*, Oxford: Oxford University Press, 2013.

Power, Carla, 'Liberal dares to challenge prohibitionist Islam', *The Times*, 11 October 2008.

Purves, Libby, 'Please – enough of this ghoulish sideshow', *The Times*, 6 October 2008a.

Purves, Libby, 'Children need to be sprinkled with fairy dust', *The Times*, 27 October 2008b.

Pyatt, Jamie, 'My little angels', *The Sun*, 11 October 2008.

Pyatt, Jamie, 'Evil thief steals poppy proceeds', *The Sun*, 12 January 2011.

Rees, Martin, 'ET may be out there, but would he talk to us?', *The Times*, 21 October 2008.

Reidy, Padriag, 'Geert Wilders should not be banned from Britain', *The Guardian*, 12 February 2009.

Richards, Jonathan, 'Crunch time: A story in data. The appearance of religious festivals in *Times* stories since 1985', *The Times Magazine*, 5 December 2009.

Richardson, John E., *(Mis)Representing Islam: The Racism and Rhetoric of British Broadsheet Newspapers*, Amsterdam: John Benjamins, 2004.

Robinson, John A.T., *Honest to God*, London: SCM, 1963.

Rosser, Ian, 'Police are given six of the best', *Yorkshire Evening Post*, 21 October 2008.

Rothenbuhler, Eric, *Ritual Communication: From Everyday Conversation to Mediated Ceremony*, London: Sage, 1998.

Rowland, Tracey, *Benedict XVI: A Guide for the Perplexed*, London: T&T Clark, 2010.

Royal Wedding, http://www.officialroyalwedding2011.org/. Accessed 1/9/12. 2011.

Rusbridger, Alan, 'The Cudlipp Lecture: Does journalism exist?', *The Guardian*, 25 January 2010.

Runnymede Trust, *Islamophobia: A Challenge for Us All*, London, 1997.

Saeed, Abdullah, 'Muslims in the West and their Attitudes to Full Participation in Western Societies: Some Reflections', in Geoffrey Brahm Levey and Tariq Modood (eds), *Secularism, Religion and Multicultural Citizenship*, Cambridge: Cambridge University Press, 2009, pp. 200–215.

Said, Edward, *Covering Islam: How the Media and Experts Determine How We See the Rest of the World*, London: Routledge, 1981.

Salter, Martin, 'The Pope's misleading comments about the Equality Bill only highlight his hypocrisy', *The Telegraph Blogs*, 12 March 2010.

Sanderson, Terry, 'The Archbishop's gamble', *The Guardian*, 18 December 2008.

Savill, Richard, 'Credit crunch "will return traditional Christmas values", Bishop says', *The Telegraph*, 23 December 2008.

Seymour-Ure, Colin, *The British Press and Broadcasting since 1945*, 2nd edn, Oxford: Blackwell, 1996.

Shepard, Matthew, 'Coming to Britain: Church with a mission to demonise homosexuals', *The Independent*, 18 February 2009.

Sherine, Ariane, 'Hey Preacher – leave those kids alone', *The Guardian*, 18 November 2009.

Shils, Edward and Young, Michael, 'The Meaning of the Coronation', *Sociological Review*, 1/2, 1956, pp. 63–82.

Shortt, Rupert, *Benedict XVI: Commander of the Faith*, updated edn, London: Hodder & Stoughton, 2006.

Shortt, Rupert, 'September 11: Where the hell was God?', *The Times* (Times2), 10 November 2008.

Siedentop, Larry, 'The Dutch MP and the retreat of British liberalism', *The Financial Times*, 16 February 2009.

Silk, Mark, *Unsecular Media: Making News of Religion in America*, Urbana and Chicago: University of Illinois Press, 1998.

Silverstone, Roger, *The Message of Television: Myth and Narrative in Contemporary Culture*, London: Heinemann Educational Books, 1981.

Singh, Indarjit, 'Respect, Religion and the News', in Jolyon Mitchell and Owen Gower (eds), *Religion and the News*, Farnham: Ashgate, 2012, pp. 147–52.

Skidelsky, Robert, 'The moral dimension of boom and bust', *The Guardian*, 23 November 2008.

Smoker, Barbara, 'Pope and population', *The Times*, 23 March 1982.

Social Surveys (Gallup Poll), on behalf of ABC Television, *Television and Religion*, London: University of London Press, 1964.

Spencer, Nick, *Darwin and God*, London: SPCK, 2009.

Stolow, Jeremy, 'Religion and/as Media', *Theory Culture Society*, 22/4, 2005, pp. 119–45.

Stout, Daniel A. and Buddenham, Judith M., 'Approaches to the Study of Media and Religion', *Religion*, 38, 2008, pp. 226–32.

Strange, Roderick, 'We have been beguiled and betrayed by Mammon', *The Times*, 18 October 2008.

Stringer, M.D., *Contemporary Western Ethnography and the Definition of Religion*, London and New York: Continuum, 2008.

Sun, The, 'Living under the Clough curse', 6 February 1982.

Sun, The, 'Labour blasted over religion', 7 June 2008a.

Sun, The, 'Depravity of the prim Vicar's wife', 1 October 2008b.

Sun, The, 'Threat to kill Vicar Yvonne: Death note hidden in Bible', 3 October 2008c.

Sun, The, '£3m bill as Evil Hook stays put for 5 years', 6 October 2008d.

Sun, The, 'Suicide bid by perv trial choir teacher', 7 October 2008e.

Sun, The, 'Army parade through town', 12 October 2008f.

Sun, The, 'Cardinal sin', 21 October 2008g.

Sun, The, 'Charities warn on Afghanistan', 22 October 2008h.

Sun, The, 'Jacksie potato', 31 October 2008i.

Sun, The, 'More he, Vicar?', 12 November 2008j.

Sun, The, 'Naughty Vicar gets a 7yr ban', 19 November 2008k.

Sun, The, 'Faces behind names on Party's leaked list', 20 November 2008l.

Sun, The, 'Cardinal: Crunch broke trust, Cardinal Cormac Murphy O'Connor', 25 December 2008.

Sun, The, Front page and 'Editorial', 18 October 2010a.

Sun, The, 'Editorial', 19 October 2010b.

Sun, The, 'Editorial', 20 October 2010c.

Sunday Express, 'Editorial, 19 September 2010.

Sunday Times, The, 'Richard Dawkins: I will arrest Pope', 11 April 2010.

Svennevig, Michael, *Godwatching: Viewers, Religion, and Television*, London: John Libbey, 1988.

Sylvester, Rachel, 'There's a God-shaped hole in Westminster', *The Times*, 21 October 2008.

Taira, Teemu, 'New Atheism as Identity Politics', in Mathew Guest and Elisabeth Arweck (eds), *Religion and Knowledge: Sociological Perspectives*, Farnham: Ashgate, 2012a , pp. 97–113.

Taira, Teemu, 'Atheist Spirituality: A Follow-on from New Atheism?', in Tore Ahlbäck (ed.) *Post-Secular Religious Practices*, Turku: Donner Institute for Religious and Cultural History, 2012b, pp. 388–404.

Telegraph, The, 'Faith Must Have a Voice in the Citadels of Power', 20 December 2008a.

Telegraph, The, 'The religious rights of Christians are treated with disrespect', 28 March 2008b.

Telegraph, The, 'The priorities of a Christian country', 14 February 2009.

Telegraph, The, 'Editorial', 16 September 2010a.

Telegraph, The, 'Editorial', 18 September 2010b.

Telegraph, The, 'Editorial', 19 September 2010c.

Telegraph, The (front page), 20 September 2010d.

Temple, Mick, *The British Press*, Maidenhead: Open University, 2008.

Theos, 'UK: Christian or Secular'. http://www.theosthinktank.co.uk/. Accessed 15/7/12. 2008.

Thomson, Alice and Sylvester, Rachel, 'How banana insult inspired fight for immigration', *The Times*, 18 October 2008.

Thompson, Hannah, 'Stars in their Eyes', *YouGov: What the World Thinks*, 14/10/10. http://yougov.co.uk/news/2010/10/14/stars-their-eyes/. Accessed 27/8/12. 2010.

Thompson, Hannah, 'Trust in the Media', *YouGov: What the World Thinks*, 14/11/11. http://yougov.co.uk/news/2011/11/14/trust-media/. Accessed 20/6/12. 2011.

Thompson, Mark, *Faith and the Media*, Faith and Life in Britain Today: Cardinal Cormac Murphy O'Connor Lecture Series, London: Westminster. http://www.bbc.co.uk/print/pressoffice/speeches/stories/thompson_faith.shtml. Accessed 29/6/12. 2008.

Tibi, Bassam, *The Challenge of Fundamentalism: Political Islam and the New World Disorder*, Berkeley: University of California Press, 1998.

Times, The, 'Taking manhood into God', 16 January 1982a.

Times, The, 'Carol ban head to retire', 11 February 1982b.

Times, The, 'Tide of the Faith', 20 March 1982c.

Times, The, 'The Times Portrait: King Fahd of Saudi Arabia', 2 July 1982d.

Times, The, 'Prince praises religion', 11 February 1982e.

Times, The (Times2), 'Is the truth out there?', 21 October 2008.

Times, The, 'A relationship of service to the nation', 22 October 2008a.

Times, The, 'Church and Nation', 22 October 2008b.

Times, The, 'Ferguson exclusive', 28 October 2008c.

Times, The, 'The very Rev John Hughes', 'The right Rev "Bill" Flagg' and 'Canon John Bown', 30 October 2008d.

Times, The, 'Jewish school ruling', 1 November 2008e.

Times, The, 'Pope has four names on his list as Cardinal decides to step down', 22 November 2008f.

Times, The, 'Leading light', 18 September 2010.

Toon, Richard, 'Methodological Problems in the Study of Implicit Religion', *Religious Research Paper* 3, Leeds: Department of Sociology, University of Leeds, 1981.

Towler, Robert, *Homo Religiosus: Sociological Problems in the Study of Religion*, London: Constable, 1974.

Towler, Robert, 'Conventional Religion and Common Religion in Great Britain', *Religious Research Paper* 11, Leeds: Department of Sociology, University of Leeds, 1983.

Traynor, Ian, 'Profile: Geert Wilders', *The Guardian*, 12 February 2009a.

Traynor, Ian, 'Maverick who loves the limelight', *The Guardian*, 13 February 2009b.

Trzebiatowska, Marta and Bruce, Steve, *Why are Women More Religious Than Men?* Oxford: Oxford University Press, 2012.

Tunstall, Jeremy, *The Media in Britain*, London: Constable, 1983.

Turner, Janice, 'I have no faith in these unholy warlords', *The Times*, 18 September 2010.

Twomey, John and Pilditch, David, 'Muslim plot to kill Pope', 18 September 2010.

Van Zoonen, Liesbet, Mihelj, Sabina and Vis, Farida, 'YouTube Interactions between Agonism, Antagonism and Dialogue: Video Responses to the Anti-Islam Film Fitna', *New Media and Society*, 13/8, 2011, pp. 1283–300.

Viney, Rachel, 'Religious Broadcasting on UK Television: Policy, public perception and programmes', *Cultural Trends*, 36, 1999, pp. 4–28.

Vleigenthart, Rens and Van Zoonen, Liesbet, 'Power to the Frame: Bringing Sociology Back to Frame Analysis', *European Journal of Communication*, 26/2, 2011, pp. 101–15.

Voas, David and Crockett, Alasdair, 'Religion in Britain: Neither Believing Nor Belonging', *Sociology*, 39/1, 2005, pp. 11–28.

Voas, David and Bruce, Steve, 'The Spiritual Revolution: Another False Dawn for the Sacred', in Kieran Flanagan and Peter C. Jupp (eds), *Sociology of Spirituality*, Aldershot: Ashgate, 2007, pp. 43–61.

Von Hügel Institute, *Moral, But No Compass: A Report to the Church of England*, Cambridge, 2008.

de Vries, Hent, 'In Media Res: Global Religion, Public Spheres, and the Task of Contemporary Comparative Religious Studies', in Hent de Vries and Samuel Weber (eds), *Religion and Media*, Stanford: Stanford University Press, 2001, pp. 3–42.

Wade, Mike, 'Discord as Pope begins his historic visit in Scotland', *The Times*, 15 September 2010.

Wagner, Rachel, *Godwired: Religion, Ritual and Virtual Reality*, London and New York: Routledge, 2012.

Wakelin, Michael, *Still Small Voice*, Like for Like Productions, 2011.

Ward, Graham and Hoelzl, Michael (eds), *The New Visibility of Religion*, London: Continuum, 2008.

Warner, Rob, *Secularization and its Discontents*, London and New York: Continuum, 2010.

Welborn, Amy, 'The Popes', in Paul Marshall, Lela Gilbert and Roberta Green Ahmanson (eds), *Blind Spot: When Journalists Don't Get Religion*, Oxford: Oxford University Press, 2009, pp. 107–28.

Weller, Paul, *Time for a Change: Reconfiguring Religion, State and Society*, London: T&T Clark, 2005.

Weller, Paul, *Religious Diversity in the UK: Contours and Issues*, London: Continuum, 2008.

Wells, Tom, 'The X Fatwa', *The Sun*, 21 October 2008.

Westminster Declaration of Christian Conscience. http://www.westminster2010. org.uk/declaration. Accessed 20/4/10. 2010.

Wheeler, Virginia, 'Nice day for a wide wedding', *The Sun*, 28 October 2008.

White, Michael, '2011 Census: Good news, bad news or both?', *The Guardian*, 12 December 2012.

Willey, David, 'Pope's visit is deemed to challenge stereotypes', *BBC News*, 20 September 2010.

Williams, Raymond, *Problems in Materialism and Culture*, London: Verso, 1980.

Williams, Sarah, *Religious Belief and Popular Culture in Southwark, c1880–1939*, Oxford: Oxford University Press, 1999.

Williamson, Howard, 'Close-up on stylist "Talking to the dead"', *Yorkshire Evening Post*, 7 October 2008.

Wilson, Alan, 'Comment is free: The media's trouble with religion', *The Guardian*, 19 January 2010.

Wilson, Bryan, *Religion in Secular Society*, London: Watts, 1966.

Wilson, Bryan, *Religion in Sociological Perspective*, Oxford: Oxford University Press, 1982.

Wilson, Graeme, 'Pope's dope brands UK as Third World', *The Sun*, 16 September 2010.

Winston, Diane and Green, John, *Most Americans Say Religion Coverage Too Sensationalized: Report*. http://annenberg.usc.edu/~/media/PDFs/winston-bliss.ashx. Accessed 6/8/12. 2012.

Winston, Robert, *The Story of God*, London: Bantam Press, 2005.

Wolfe, Kenneth M., *The Churches and the British Broadcasting Corporation 1922–1956*, London: SCM Press, 1984.

Woodhead, Linda, 'Why So Many Women in Holistic Spirituality: A Puzzle Revisited', in Kieran Flanaghan and Peter C. Jupp (eds), *A Sociology of Spirituality*, Farnham: Ashgate, 2009, pp. 115–26.

Woodhead, Linda, 'Introduction', in Linda Woodhead and Rebecca Catto (eds), *Religion and Change in Modern Britain*, London and New York: Routledge, 2012a, pp. 1–33.

Woodhead, Linda, 'Richard Dawkins has uncovered a very British form of Christianity', *The Guardian*, 14 February 2012b.

Woodhead, Linda and Catto, Rebecca (eds), *Religion and Change in Modern Britain*, London and New York: Routledge, 2012.

Woodward, Grant, 'The truth is out there', *Yorkshire Evening Post*, 24 October 2008.

Woolley, Paul, 'A Relationship Worth Getting Right', in Jolyon Mitchell and Owen Gower (eds), *Religion and the News*, Farnham: Ashgate, 2012, pp. 61–75.

Wyen, Charlie, 'Scolari Prayer Works Miracles', *The Sun Supplement*, 4 October 2008.

Yinger, John Milton, *The Scientific Study of Religion*, London: Macmillan, 1970.

Yorkshire Post, 'Remembrance service at Military cemetery', 5 November 2008a.

Yorkshire Post, 'Malcolm Barker: The shadow of sacrifice and the power of remembrance', 10 November 2008b.

Yorkshire Post, 'Nation remember war dead on poignant 90th anniversary', 10 November 2008c.

Yorkshire Post, 'Pakistan's ban on You Tube', 25 February 2009.

Yorkshire Evening Post, 'Unholy thieves take tree after it was blessed by Priest', 3 October 2008a.

Yorkshire Evening Post, 'Home truths over financial downturn', 22 October 2008b.

Yorkshire Evening Post, 'Lights have kept the Faith', 7 November 2008c.

Yorkshire Evening Post, '25,000 at hero's funeral', 8 November 2008d.

Yorkshire Evening Post, 'Reflecting on remembrance', 14 November 2008e.

Yorkshire Evening Post, Marriage notices, 15 October 2008f.

Yorkshire Evening Post, 'Papal visit: School choir to perform for Pope', 15 September 2010.

YouGov, 'Press Gazette poll: The most trusted news brands', January 2005.

YouGov, 'Channel 4 survey results on media and society', November 2007.

YouGov, 'UFOs: The Sun Survey Results'. http://d25d2506sfb94s.cloudfront.net/today_uk_import/YG-Archives-lif-sun-UFO-080728.pdf. Accessed 26/8/12. 2008.

Index

advertisements
    religion in 42, 46–7, 50–52, 54, 104–7
Afghanistan 39, 48, 80, 83, 85–6, 94
Ahmed, Aaqil 53–4, 71
Ahmed, Nasir 146–9
AKP (Turkish Justice and Development
    Party) 116
Alam, Fareena 110
al-Muhajaroun 146; *see also* Muhammad,
    Omar Bakri
Alpha course 106–7
al-Qaeda 48, 84, 166
anti-Semitism 90–91; *see also* Auschwitz;
    Holocaust
Arab Spring 85
Archbishop of Canterbury 63, 70–73,
    77–8, 109, 131, 167
Are Christians Being Persecuted? (BBC1)
    77–8
*Are We Too Embarrassed to Talk about
    God?* (BBC1) 57, 102; *see also The
    One Show*
Around the World in 80 Faiths (BBC2) 48,
    51, 53, 93, 96
assisted suicide 45, 773
astrology 10, 123, 131; *see also* horoscopes
Atatürk, Kemal 115–16
atheism 1, 12, 20, 27, 44, 49–51, 101–20,
    158, 162, 164–5, 168–85
atheist bus campaign 101, 105–7, 114, 186
Atkins, Peter 109–10
Attenborough, David 108
Auschwitz 91; *see also* anti-Semitism;
    Holocaust
Aveling, Edvard 109

Baggini, Julian 169
Barrow, Simon 31
Benedict XVI, Pope 8–11, 73, 155–71, 187

BBC1 9–10, 23, 39, 40, 49–52, 57–8, 62,
    77, 78, 93–4, 104, 108
BBC2 9–10, 23, 39–40, 49–52, 55, 61–2,
    72, 75, 81, 93–5, 104, 107–8, 115–16,
    128, 130, 132, 156
Bible, The 61, 70, 97, 108–9
Bidisha 110
Big Questions, The (BBC1) 53, 70,
    108–10, 132
Blackmore, Susan 168
Boyle, Susan 158
Britain
    armed forces 8, 67–8
    colonialism 58, 85
    heritage 20, 35, 56, 58, 65–7, 70–71,
        76–8, 151, 177, 188
    identity 77, 79, 92, 149–51; *see also*
        Christian, identity
    nation 7, 58, 62–4, 68, 70, 76, 79, 87,
        126, 140, 149–56, 167, 177–8; *see
        also* Christianity, and the state
    population census 17–19, 102, 173–4;
        see also religious statistics
British Broadcasting Corporation (BBC)
    10, 15, 20–26, 28, 32, 50–57, 62,
    70–76, 81, 93–5, 106, 123, 156–8,
    162–4, 171, 175, 178, 180, 184–6;
    see also BBC1; BBC2
    Charter 70
    Trust 174
British Government 4, 21, 24, 31, 62,
    64–7, 77, 143–53, 165, 177
    Home Secretary 139, 152
    House of Lords 62, 65, 112, 139, 148
British Humanist Association (BHA) 156
Brown, Callum 35
Brown, Gordon 84
Buddhism 43, 46, 80–81, 90–94, 98,
    103–4, 178

Buddhists 17–19
Burchill, Julie 88
burqa 88, 173

Cameron, David 165
Camp Quest UK 106
Campbell, Nicky 78, 109, 180
Carey, George 70, 77, 109–10
Casanova, José 34
Channel 4 9, 20, 23, 28, 50, 51, 62, 71, 95,
    156, 174
Charles Darwin and the Tree of Life
    (BBC2) 70, 107–9
child abuse 159–63, 168–9
Christian 57–78, 155–71
    heritage 65–7
    Identity 35, 76–7
    language 3–6, 38, 55–6, 69–70, 76–8,
        177, 183–4
    music 21, 29, 53, 62, 69–72, 125, 159
Christian Science 42, 60
Christianity 19–20, 35, 42–3, 53–4, 56,
    47–8, 57–78, 79, 96–8, 104, 108,
    111–12, 114–17, 149–50, 155–71,
    177–80, 186
    Anglicanism 17, 42, 53, 58, 63–4,
        71–7, 93, 120, 129, 131, 155,
        163–4, 168, 177, 184
    Evangelicalism 61, 70–72, 75, 77, 109,
        117, 129, 160, 185
    marginalization; *see* marginalization
        of Christianity; persecution of
        Christianity
    Methodism 17, 42, 105, 120
    Protestantism 42–3, 48, 51, 60, 64, 69,
        79, 109, 163–6, 169, 179
    and public life 8, 12, 42, 57–79; *see
        also* religion, and public life
    Roman Catholicism 8, 10, 15–17, 19,
        42, 45, 47–8, 54, 60–61, 71–5,
        79, 106, 112–13, 120, 128, 144,
        156–71, 179, 183–4
    and the state 35, 58, 62–8, 70, 78–9,
        162, 180, 183; *see also* Britain,
        nation
Christianity: A History (Channel 4) 71
Christian Party, The 107
Christmas 3, 104, 128–9, 162, 166, 177

Church of England 8, 42, 48, 64–6, 77,
    109, 111, 129, 177, 183
    disestablishment 62–4
    General Synod 53, 186
    women 74–5, 183
civil religion 65, 67, 69
clergy 6, 60, 68, 105, 127–30, 137, 171
    abuse by 58, 72–4, 158–63, 168–9,
        183–4
    media representation of 72–7
    women 74–5, 178, 183
comedy
    religion in 55, 75, 95, 117, 126, 130–32,
        184
common religion 13, 41–52, 56, 59, 121,
    124–6, 160, 175–6, 179
    definition 10–11, 13
communism 150
conflict 82–7, 91–3, 177; *see also*
    Afghanistan; Falklands War; Iraq
Conservative Party 24, 77, 143, 162–5; *see
    also* Cameron, David
conventional religion 41–2, 45, 48, 50–53,
    69, 120, 124, 175, 179
    definition 10–11, 13
Cornwell, John 106
Couldry, Nick 126, 140
Central Religious Advisory Council
    (CRAC) 185–6
creationism 39, 109–10, 117
Credo (ITV) 53, 96
cultural differences 43, 89; *see also*
    diversity

Daily Express 142–3, 147–8, 150, 157, 166
Daily Mail 64, 106, 112, 134–5, 141–52,
    157, 160, 162, 167–8
Daily Mirror 141, 142, 149, 157–8, 162,
    164, 166
Daily Telegraph 15, 23, 64, 77–8, 111–12,
    142–3, 147, 149, 151, 156–60, 162
Daily Star 142, 153, 157, 166–7
Dalai Lama 91
Danish cartoons 145, 151
Darwin, Charles 39, 70–71, 107–10
Darwin, Emma 108
*Darwin's Struggle: The Evolution of The
    Origin of Species* (BBC4) 70

Davie, Grace 30
Dawkins, Richard 101, 105–7, 111, 114, 117, 158, 161, 168–9, 178
Demons (ITV1) 66, 130
Derrida, Jacques 34
Diwali 167, 184
discourse 5, 11–13, 22, 28, 31–6, 44, 58–9, 68–71, 76–8, 82–9, 94–9, 102–4, 110–12, 116, 132, 140–56, 163–70, 173–82, 185–8
discrimination 82, 88–91, 148–50, 183
Dispatches (Channel 4) 96
diversity 5, 16, 19, 20, 26, 35, 43, 48, 53–6, 60–62, 72, 78–9, 89–90, 93–5, 128, 137, 140, 155–8, 164–76; *see also* cultural differences
double standards 11, 77, 112, 142, 144–8, 152, 154, 162
Dutch Freedom Party (PW) 144; *see also* Wilders, Geert

ecumenism 61, 95, 164, 170, 179
Eid 135, 167, 184
Elizabeth II, Queen 126, 160
Ellis, Jenny 105
entertainment
    religion in 1, 6, 9–10, 49, 51, 55, 81, 126, 130, 184
Everyman (BBC) 15, 53, 72, 95
evolution 39, 70, 107–10, 176, 178
Explore: From Istanbul to Anatolia (BBC2) 94, 115–16
extremism 28, 43, 47, 56, 77, 79–82, 86, 88, 97–8, 139, 145, 148, 165, 168, 177–9, 182, 184

faith schools 183
Falklands War 8, 64, 159
Field, Clive 57, 122
financial crisis 1–4, 39, 45, 65, 73
Financial Times 142–3, 149–50
Fitna 11, 112, 139, 143–7, 154
focus groups 12, 21, 96, 99, 113, 119, 151–2; *see also* research methods
Fordyce, John 109
freedom of speech 87–8, 113, 139–54, 178
Fry, Stephen 132, 162, 168–9
Fuller, Steve 109

fundamentalism 28, 33, 54, 83, 116, 166
funerals 42, 67, 122, 126–9, 137, 188

Garnett, Jane 69, 70
Ghost Hunters (Sci Fi Channel) 124, 132
Giddens, Anthony 35
Gill, Robin 27, 39, 45, 112, 180, 184
Glasgow Airport terrorist attack 83–3
Gledhill, Ruth 21, 23, 77, 99, 129
globalization 2, 7, 26, 36, 188
God Delusion, The 101, 106–7
'God-slot' 26
Gokturk, Mete 115
Goody, Jade 129
Gower, Owen 26, 43
Gray, Asa 109
Grayling, A.C. 113, 168
Grimley, Matthew 71
Guardian, The 63, 77, 103, 112–13, 129, 136, 141–52, 157, 160–61, 163, 168, 170, 174, 178
Guest, Mathew 19, 59, 61–2

Halloween 39, 44–5, 129, 132–3
Hamza, Abu 86, 143
Hanukkah 167
Hari, Johann 113
'hate preachers' 28, 86, 112
Hawking, Stephen 169
Heelas, Paul 33, 131
Hereafter (Warner Brothers) 122
hijab 89, 184; *see also* burqa
Hill, Annette 129
Hinduism 11, 43, 49, 56, 80–81, 90–94, 98, 178; *see also* Hindus
Hindus 17, 19, 20, 153, 184; *see also* *Hinduism*
Hitchens, Christopher 169
Hjavard, Stig 36
Hoelzl, Michael 34
Holocaust 43, 90–91; *see also* anti-Semitism; Auschwitz
Holtam, Nicholas 72
homosexuality 86, 105, 158, 162
horoscopes 44–6, 122–3
Huhne, Chris 149
Hume, Basil (former Roman Catholic Cardinal) 72

Hussein, Saddam 95

Immigration 89–90, 139–40, 150
Independent, The 112–13, 141–5, 148–9, 152, 157–63, 178
India 18, 76, 92, 94, 114–15
Ingrams, Richard 169
Inness, J.B. 109
interfaith relations 7, 11, 61, 155, 164–6, 170, 177–9, 183
Iran 39, 48, 80, 94–6
    Islamic Revolution 39, 94–5; *see also* Khomeini, Ayatollah
Iran and the West (BBC2) 39, 94–5
Iraq 8, 48, 83, 85, 89, 91, 95, 178
Islam 5, 7, 11–12, 26–33, 39, 42–8, 54–6, 60, 79–81, 85, 88, 91–9, 103–4, 113, 116, 121, 128, 136–9, 147, 173–7, 182
Islamification of Britain 33, 77, 82–4, 87, 115, 150–51, 154, 178, 180, 182
Islamists 28, 83–5, 112, 115, 142–3, 146–8, 177–9
Islamophobia 1, 11–12, 28, 30, 33, 77, 82–9, 95–8, 112, 139, 142–8, 154, 165–6, 178–84, 188
Israel 40, 48, 90–91, 96, 114–15, 184
ITV 9–10, 20, 22–3, 39, 49–50, 62, 81, 130–31; *see also* ITV1
ITV1 10, 23, 39–40, 49, 50–55, 66, 93–4, 104, 107, 126, 130–32, 156; *see also* ITV

Jews 17, 19, 91, 184
John Paul II, Pope 8, 11, 40, 60, 72, 104–5, 155, 158–60, 163–5, 167, 169
journalists 2, 6, 25, 30, 60, 65, 73, 83, 99, 111, 129, 151, 167, 174, 178, 180–81; *see also* media professionals
Judaism 43–9, 56, 80–81, 90, 98, 104, 178; *see also* Jews

Kashmir 92
Kasper, Walter 158, 168
Khomeini, Ayatollah 95
Klaushofer, Alex 31
Knott, Kim 5, 6, 9, 19, 26, 29, 40, 71, 75, 96, 144, 150, 155, 160–61, 164
Kundnani, Arun 83–4, 89

Labour Party 77, 143, 147–8, 150, 162, 165, 174, 177; *see also* New Labour
Lawson, Dominic 169
Lawson, Mark 71, 75
Lebanon 146
Lennon, John 106
Leveson Report 99
liberalism 7, 140–41, 150–54, 158, 168, 170, 176–8
Liberal Democrats 112
life-cycle rites 46, 49, 52, 126, 127; *see also* funerals; rites of passage; weddings
Little Big Planet (Sony) 88
Look North (BBC1) 164
luck 8, 10, 12, 42, 44, 46, 49–52, 69, 120–24, 134–5, 184
Lynch, Gordon 26, 33, 36–8, 185

McKinstry, Leo 150
marginalization of Christianity 26, 35, 76, 97, 112, 154, 163–8, 178; *see also* persecution of Christianity
Marrin, Minette 147
media and religion
    history 1, 6–7, 12, 20–21, 25–8, 40–41, 69, 71, 76, 104
    propositions 7, 32, 37–8, 179–86
    research 7–11, 25–31, 35–7
media *as* religion 27, 30, 36, 38, 185–7
media diversification 9–12, 20–21, 24, 54–6, 61, 79–82, 93–4, 117, 124–6, 130–33, 151, 154, 161–79, 184–88
media events 2, 5, 12, 40, 72–4, 126–9, 133, 139–44, 154–60, 166, 170–71, 174, 179, 183, 186
media professionals
    religiosity/secularity of 1, 5, 13–16, 20–26, 37, 58–9, 98–117, 129, 134, 169–70, 175–7, 180–86
media reception 2, 7–8, 22, 25, 38, 67, 96–9, 105, 119–21, 127–35, 152–3, 158–61, 184–5
media technologies 1–2, 6, 9, 20–21, 26, 35, 39, 72, 186, 188
mediation 12, 26, 35–8, 55, 77–8, 109, 126–8, 185–7

mediatization 12, 22, 35–7, 59, 66–70, 83–90, 140–41, 185–6
meditation 49, 52, 68, 165
metaphorical references 5–6, 40, 44–9, 54–5, 60, 69, 72, 94, 125–6, 135–7, 179
Micklethwait, John 16, 34
Midsomer Murders (ITV1) 66, 128, 130–32
Mitchell, Jolyon 26
morality 3, 39, 45, 101, 115, 167, 177, 184
Morgan, Sally 131
Mormons 42, 60
Morning Star 170
Most Haunted (Living TV) 132
Muhammad, Omar Bakri 86, 146; *see also* al-Muhajaroun
multiculturalism 5, 7, 12, 78, 89, 92–3, 129, 139–54, 162–3, 165, 178
Murdoch, Rupert 9, 21, 23–4
Muslims 5, 11, 17–20, 27–8, 43, 56, 76–84, 87–98, 102, 116, 121, 144–54, 166, 173, 177, 182, 184; *see also* Islam
Mutanen, Annikka 62, 111
mysticism 165

national identity 17, 64–5, 98, 114, 139, 148, 178, 182, 184, 188; *see also* Britain, nation
National Secular Society 63, 101, 104–5, 109, 156, 161, 169
Nazism 162; *see also* Holocaust; Auschwitz
Netherlands 144, 148, 188
New Age 7, 15, 131
New Labour 23–4, 31, 178; *see also* Labour Party
New Religious Movements (NRMs) 10, 43, 48, 51, 56, 103, 175
Newman, John Henry 73, 156
News International 21, 24
newspapers 4–6, 9, 20–24, 39, 45, 129, 161
    and religion 1, 11, 25–7, 35, 40–43, 47–51, 55, 60, 68, 76–82, 90, 105–7, 112, 124, 130–43, 150–67, 175–88
    editorials 22, 44–6, 62–3, 91, 104, 142, 145, 149, 155–63, 167, 174
'nones' 19, 102; *see also* non-religious

non-religious 12, 18, 20–21, 29, 31, 96, 102, 104–19, 153–6, 163–5, 173, 176–7, 181
    beliefs 11, 45, 54–7, 97–8, 120–23, 181
Noonan, Catriona 22, 33

Olson, Elizabeth 19, 59–62
Olympics (2012) 90, 135, 182
On the Origin of Species 70; *see also* Darwin, Charles
One Show, The (BBC1) 57–9, 76, 79, 93–4, 101–2, 108, 119–20, 173
Owen-Jones, Peter 93–4

Paganism 44
Paisley, Ian 161, 169
Pakistan 18, 77, 84, 146
Papal visits 12, 48, 60, 105, 139, 155–71, 173, 179, 182, 184–5, 187–8
paranormal 10, 12, 121–2, 129–37, 179
Pearson, Malcolm 139
persecution of Christianity 60, 76–7, 85, 92, 180; *see also* marginalization of Christianity
Phillips, Melanie 64, 148
Pitcher, George 111
places of worship
    attendance 36, 17–18, 33, 59, 60, 70, 76, 102, 175, 183
    numbers 19–20
Poole, Elizabeth 5, 28, 40, 144
popular beliefs 119–37, 179
Pratchett, Terry 168
prayer 49, 52, 55, 68, 70, 75–7, 87, 122, 125–6, 135–6
Protestant Loyalists 163, 166
psychics 121–3
Pullman, Philip 168

QI (BBC2) 132
Quakers 42, 60
Qur'an 87, 139, 143, 147–8, 152

racism 28, 82–3, 88–90, 103, 149, 153
Rani, Anita 57–8, 79, 119
Rashtriya Swayamsevak Sangh (RSS) 92
Rees, Martin 133
Reilly, Nick 83–4

relativism 78, 104, 165
religion
    privatization 34
    and public life 5–7, 16, 20, 27,
        31–2, 102, 117, 150–71; *see also*
        Christianity, and public life
religion in Britain 5–6, 18, 29, 67, 182
religious literacy 22, 26, 36, 183
religious minorities 58, 76, 116, 177
religious statistics 17–19, 33, 57–9, 70,
    76, 102, 119–23, 174, 182; *see also*
    Britain, population census
remembrance 49, 66–7
    Remembrance Day 68–9, 177, 182
representation 2, 5, 28, 43, 59, 74–5,
    86–90, 95–6, 117, 127, 141, 146–9,
    155, 175, 176–9, 184–6
research methods 8–12, 39–40, 59, 142;
    see also focus groups
research questions 8; *see also* media and
    religion, propositions
rites of passage *see* life-cycle rites
ritual practice 36, 61, 66–8, 119–39, 176,
    179, 187–8
royal weddings 67, 126
Runcie, Robert 72, 78, 167
Rushdie Affair 144

Sacks, Jonathan 91
sacred, return of the 32, 36
Salvation Army 42, 60
Satanic Verses, The 51, 144
science and religion 107–111
secular sacred 5, 7, 12–13, 39–56, 59, 71,
    110, 144, 175–8, 182, 185–8
    definition 5–6, 11
secularism
    in Britain 11–12, 20, 27, 35, 44, 49, 57,
        78, 101–4, 109–17, 139, 150–55,
        162–9, 173–8, 180
    in India 114–15
    in Israel 114–15
    in Turkey 114–16
secularization 1, 7, 12–17, 20, 27, 31–7,
    57–9, 65, 72, 75, 78, 101–2, 112, 124,
    179–80
Sedgewick, Alan 70
Sentamu, John 75

September 11 (9/11) 73, 82, 87, 131–2,
    152, 161
Serve Afghanistan 85
sexual abuse 21, 73–4, 158–9, 184–5; *see
    also* child abuse; clergy, abuse by
Shamanism 49
Sherine, Ariane 101, 105, 117
Shinto 80, 93
Shortt, Rupert 73
Sikhs 17, 19, 92, 184
Sikhism 43, 46, 49, 56, 80–81, 90, 92, 94,
    98
Silk, Mark 25, 181–2
Smith, Jacqui 152
Smoker, Barbara 104–5, 169
social media 6, 21, 30, 188
Society for Psychical Research 40, 130
Songs of Praise (BBC1) 53, 62, 71–2, 76,
    125
Sony 87–8
South Bank Show (ITV1) 49, 132
South Korea 93
spiritualism 10, 49, 51, 121, 131
spirituality 1, 7, 15, 33, 45, 48, 56, 79, 94,
    98, 101, 110, 119–20, 131, 175–6
sport
    religion in 1, 5, 10, 46–7, 51, 55, 69,
        81, 89, 90, 126, 135–6, 184
Stringer, Martin 122, 131
Sun, The 9, 20, 23–4, 39–42, 44–7, 50, 55,
    61, 67–8, 74, 77, 81–8, 91, 93, 104–5,
    112, 122, 126–7, 131–6, 142–3, 146–8,
    153, 160, 162, 166, 175
Sunday People 170
superstition 3, 10, 12, 69, 120–24, 134–5
Sylvester, Rachel 64–5

Taira, Teemu 5, 40
Taleban 39, 48, 85–6
Taoism 43, 80, 93
televangelism 29, 40
television 5–6, 9–10, 20–23, 25
    and religion 8, 11–12, 15, 28–31,
        39–42, 48–56, 59–62, 66, 72–6,
        79–81, 87, 93–9, 101–7, 115, 120,
        124–32, 135, 137, 155–60, 164,
        170–76, 180–88

television genres 10, 26, 66, 72, 93–5, 104, 128–31; *see also* comedy; entertainment; sport

terrorism 1, 28, 43, 47, 56, 80, 82–6, 98, 140, 161, 165–6, 177–8

Thatcher, Margaret 156

Theos 32, 105–6

This Morning (ITV1) 49, 108–9, 120

Thompson, Mark 15–16, 31

Thought for the Day (BBC Radio 4) 106

Tibet 91, 94

Times, The 3, 9, 20–24, 30, 39, 40–51, 55, 60–65, 73, 75, 77–8, 80–93, 104, 107, 114–15, 127–33, 136, 142–3, 147–50, 157–64, 168–9, 175, 178, 180–81

Toben, Fredrick 90

Towler, Robert 6, 10

tradition 4–6, 20, 25, 35–6, 42–3, 51, 58, 63, 65–70, 72, 78, 94, 119–21, 127–9, 134, 137, 167, 177

trust 64
    in Government 4
    in the media 6, 20–21, 24, 45

Turner, Janice 169

Turkey 48, 80, 94, 114–16, 133, 139

UFOs 44, 122–4, 130–34, 179

UK Independence Party (UKIP) 139

unexplained, The 1, 42, 44, 49, 51–2, 55, 124, 129–30, 131, 133; *see also* paranormal; UFOs

United States 6, 27, 130
    Government 2, 39, 64, 94–5

Van Zoonen, Liesbet 139, 142

Vicar of Dibley, The (BBC1) 75

Vine, Jeremy 102

Viney, Rachel 29, 62

Ward, Graham 34

Weakest Link, The (BBC1) 49, 70

weddings 42, 52, 67, 122, 126–8, 137, 188

Weller, Paul 114

Westboro Baptist Church 86, 146; *see also* 'hate preachers'

Westminster Declaration of Christian Conscience 60, 77

Wilders, Geert 11–12, 86–7, 90, 112–13, 139–54, 162, 173, 178

Williams, Gayle 85

Williams, Rowan 73, 91

Williams, Sarah 121, 124

Winston, Robert 79, 101, 108

Wolffe, John 19, 59, 61–2

Woodhead, Linda 18, 32, 33, 37, 76, 131

Wooldridge, Adrian 16, 34

Wootton Bassett 67

X Factor (ITV1) 87

yoga 43, 48, 125, 165, 184

Yoido Full Gospel Church 60

Yorkshire Evening Post 9, 24, 39, 40–45, 55, 61, 68, 74, 81–2, 87–91, 93, 104, 133, 142, 157, 163

You Tube 84

Zen 43

Zoroastrianism 80, 94